SMART AND HUMAN

G.R.K. Reddy is the Chairman and Managing Director of MARG Group, a leading infrastructure development company with diverse projects such as ports, IT parks, malls, commercial and residential real estate, and an integrated city. An alumnus of the Kellogg School of Management in the United States, he recognized early on in his career that infrastructure development would drive the second generation reforms in India and understood the importance of 'space creation' in the economy. He is today seen as a thought leader and the new face of India's sustainable and inclusive infrastructure.

Srijan Pal Singh is a gold medallist MBA holder from the Indian Institute of Management, Ahmedabad, and has worked with the Boston Consulting Group. He is a social entrepreneur who has been involved in studying and evolving sustainable development systems with a thrust on rural areas. He also works as an advisor to former President of India Dr A.P.J. Abdul Kalam on promoting the concepts of energy independence and Providing Urban Amenities in Rural Areas (PURA) and has co-authored with him *Target 3 Billion* (2011). He was named as one of the Global Leaders of Tomorrow by the St Gallen Leadership Symposium in Switzerland in 2014.

SMART AND HUMAN

Building Cities of Wisdom

G.R.K. Reddy
and
Srijan Pal Singh

HarperCollins *Publishers* India

First published in India in 2015 by
HarperCollins *Publishers* India

Building 10, Tower A, 4th Floor, DLF Cyber City, Phase II,
Gurugram Haryana – 122002, India
www.harpercollins.co.in

P-ISBN: 978-93-5177-380-1
E-ISBN: 978-93-5177-381-8

2 4 6 8 10 9 7 5 3 1

Typeset in 11.5/14.5 Dante MT by
R. Ajith Kumar

Printed and bound at
MicroPrints India, New Delhi

To my parents, Shri Raghav Reddy and Smt. Pushpalata
G.R.K. Reddy

To my parents, Rachna and R.D., who through their untiring struggles in life taught me to believe that impossible dreams are likely to come true
Srijan Pal Singh

Contents

Preface

We are the modern homo sapiens, or the 'wise men'. Our history is unique, as we were hunters and foragers for the first 58,000 years of the total 70,000 years—more than 80 per cent—of our existence. Agriculture began 12,000 years ago, and the industrial era only 150 years ago. Since 1900, representing about 0.1 per cent of our total time on the planet, we have outdone all other species, conquered all land available, explored outer space, set foot on Mars, destroyed the environment more harshly than ever before and killed many of our own kind in two major world wars and a string of conflicts. But also since 1900, medicine has saved millions of humans from premature death. The last century has been a period of constant quarrel between greed and conscience, with mankind striving to develop and destroy itself with the same tools.

All other animals have gone down the road of genetic evolution, with the offspring being born slightly better adapted to the environment than its parents. But within a single lifetime, all members of any species were more or less similar—the swimming pattern of a particular fish or the flight of a bird did not change much in its own lifetime. Humans, on the other hand, learnt a new technique of evolution called cognitive (mental) evolution. A single member of a species, within his lifetime, could be taught and equipped with a number of tools and lessons to enable leapfrogging genetic evolution and acquire abilities he wasn't born with!

For instance, it took hundreds of thousands of years for a whale to develop the ability to dive for food and rise to the surface for air and thereby live in water and swim across seas. Humans, on the other hand, never had to develop this ability genetically—we never grew fins or larger lungs. We just went through a revolution in our minds—a cognitive evolution—and invented the boat and crossed the oceans. When other species spent millions of years growing claws, we invented the knife and leapfrogged them. This cognitive evolution gave us the ability to dominate the land, sea and air. It also led to the development of technology, whose benefits we all reap today, or suffer from the problems caused by it.

One distinctive feature of the human cognitive evolution is the ability of humans to live in large groups—much larger than any other species. The first tribes, the first religion, the first God, the first social norm and the first set of laws and government were thus evolved—perhaps about 15,000 to 20,000 years ago—when humans started living together in numbers of more than 500 individuals. Soon these tribes and little settlements united as grand civilizations across the globe—in Egypt, Mesopotamia, Europe and India, spreading across the Americas. This was the start of the first form of habitation planning: common spaces to move, trade, specialization of labour, rules and regulations, social hierarchies, festivals, religion and documentation of knowledge.

But even with the security of large-scale living, the human population remained more or less constant throughout the period from the Roman civilization, around 1 AD, to the Industrial Revolution around 1900 AD. Whenever the population rose rapidly and started getting concentrated, it would be struck by widespread deadly diseases. Nearly half of Europe's population was wiped off by the black plague, which reduced the world's population from an estimated 450 million to 350 million in the 14th century. Then there were natural calamities and human conflicts. For instance, Christopher Columbus's landing in America in the 15th century marked the beginning of the manslaughter of a hundred million native Americans over the next hundred years, wiping out about 90 per cent of their population.

The net effect of such a three-pronged challenge to the growth of human population was that the average age of a human being rose from around 28 in 1 AD to about 35 at the start of 1900. Then the true miracle of science happened. Germ theory and anti-bacterial drugs gave us almost a total victory over diseases and pathogens. Modern construction became resilient to natural disasters, though little could be done about world peace. Nevertheless, since 1900, humans have seen an unimaginable growth in population—from less than 1.5 billion in 1900 to 7 billion in 2010. Average life expectancy has gone up to over 70, with some nations like Monaco having a life expectancy of almost 90 years.

The rising population has come with one additional effect: most of the new growth is coming into the urban areas. Driven by the hope of better income, better life and better amenities, more and more people are driven to live in urban areas, with modern construction allowing vertically stacked living and working spaces. Cities and megacities were thus born in the last hundred years—each vying for a higher concentration of population and more economic wealth, yet grappling with the problems of maintaining basic cleanliness, living standards and ensuring happiness.

Asia has been the epicentre of the growth in numbers, and over the last few decades, in wealth as well. From the continent, China, South Korea, Japan and India have been the leaders in this race.

India itself would have her Gross Domestic Product (GDP) multiplied five times by 2030 compared to 2015, with over 70 per cent of new employment generated in cities. It is further estimated that 68 cities will have a population of more than a million, and a total of 590 million people will live in urban areas in the country. Close to 800 million sq m of commercial and residential space needs to be built by 2030, roughly meaning a new Chicago every year. This is over $1.2 trillion worth of total investment.

What will be the next model of urban development in the nation? How to improve the quality of life? How to make cities which promote equity as a way of life and where happiness thrives? How to ensure a worthier life for the citizens of the nation and the world, and a better future for the children? Or is this all utopian and a mere castle of dreams?

Our book attempts to answer these questions and, in the process, realize these new habitations—these dream castles. As a final word, we emphasize,

Conflict will end, pollution will end, anxiety will end,
frontiers and divisions will end.
Then love will rise, confluence will rise and harmony will rise,
a new revolution will rise,
And humans will then begin to thrive.

G.R.K. Reddy
and Srijan Pal Singh
March 2015

1

The Global Demographic Shift: When Did Who Start Living Where?

This chapter covers the evolution of cities from the start of civilization till present times. It takes the example of four cities and the different stages of urbanization they have traversed through history. The case studies also point out the impact that the world wars had on the urbanization of the four cities in question. It deals with the various factors which influenced the growth of the cities, from their historical boundaries to the current geographical limits.

London, 1940. The cloudy autumn skies of the city came with a perilous warning. As the sun set, these clouds could be hiding behind them hundreds, perhaps even a thousand, of the Luftwaffe (German Air Force) fighter jets and bombers, stealthily advancing upon the city with their bombs and ammunitions, determined to destroy its infrastructure and people. As the Second World War raged in Europe, with almost every single nation in the continent fighting on one of the two sides, London, the long-standing financial and cultural capital of the world, ominously became the arena for the world's largest aerial battle—the Battle of Britain. Decimating this city became the sole goal of the Germans led by Adolf Hitler; and defending it was the prime motto of the Royal Air Force under Winston Churchill. For the rest of the world, it was a spectacle to watch with bated breath.

At the end of the Battle of Britain, towards the closing of 1940, more than two-thirds of the German Air Force, about 1,900 aircraft, would be destroyed. The war also cost the British Air Force 1,600 aircraft. One city became the centre where the air forces of both nations almost got eliminated. Winston Churchill would commend his airmen: 'Never was so much owed by so many to so few.'

London was the prize. The British had successfully defended it.

London, the British Capital

London—the capital of the British Empire—was the global cultural, political, financial and trading capital at the end of the 19th century. The city had grown in all respects during the century and its economic holdings were the largest in the world. It also boasted of being the first city to support a population in the excess of a million at the start of the century. The city was already amongst the most developed cities of the world with metropolitan railways, suburbs, museums and landmarks of historical importance like Big Ben, the Houses of Parliament, the Tower Bridge, the Royal Albert Hall and Trafalgar Square.

The city had a well-connected public transport system, with a large tram network to complement it. The motorbus service operated in the city, which was already undergoing improvements in over-the-ground and underground rail networks, as well as large-scale electrification. Despite such well-developed infrastructure, the rapid urbanization that had taken place over the past two centuries had led to many problems of urban agglomeration. The city had a large number of urban poor living in overcrowded and unsanitary slums. The slums were bursting at the seams and had badly planned infrastructure, serving as home to the urban poor and migrants. The rich and the wealthier classes were migrating to the suburbs, leading to a massive outward growth of the city.

This rapid growth also led to a class divide, with the poor getting poorer and the rich getting richer. Contemporary literary works depict a very dismal story of the then developed but unhealthy city of London. The city had already witnessed many epidemics, the last big one being cholera, which wiped out a good portion of the population. This led to the Parliament and the civic authorities coming together to put together the London sewerage system, which curtailed cholera and other diseases to a great extent, resulting in a massive population growth within the city in the next few decades.

Figure 1: Piccadilly Circus, c. 1900, London

New York, the City of Dreams

London's supremacy in the global environment was threatened by the emergence of New York. New York was established around 3000

BC with the arrival of the first Native Americans who were colonized thousands of years later by the French, the Dutch and later by the English. The English named it New York after the Duke of York in 1664.[1] The city, in its slightly consolidated urban modern form, can be traced back to the five boroughs formed in 1898. It was one of the main centres of development during the Industrial Revolution, due to its geographical advantage of being located right across from London on the other side of the Atlantic. It also became the main entry point for European immigrants to the United States. It boomed during the 1910s and the 1920s, with a sustained period of economic prosperity. It was one of the richest and the most populous cities of the time.

The city already boasted of world-class infrastructure and tall buildings—the 'City of Skyscrapers' was the sobriquet it gained at the time. The Woolworth Building was the tallest building in the world at the time of its completion in 1913 as well as for the next 27 years. Many more such skyscrapers were added in the subsequent decades. The city was dominated by the idea of Progressivism or the 'New York Idea'—its main concerns included the righting of social ills, conservation, the discarding of an ineffective and corrupt urban government, and the control of trusts and other industrial combinations. It was also concerned about factory labour and urban problems, and had close ties to immigrants and organized labour.

The city had already seen the first flying machine built by the Wright brothers by the start of the 20th century. The city of dreams and aspirations was home to a large urban population that was being introduced to the latest scientific developments of the era as well as to modern-day gadgets and equipment. The planned nature of the city helped in its rapid urbanization—a growth in excess of 10 per cent was witnessed for four decades till the end of the wars. Much of the population of New York City of 4.7 million in 1910 was housed in Manhattan,[2] which reached its historical high of over 2.3 million people that year.

Electrification took place slowly before the war, but during the 1920s the electricity industry experienced a huge boom. By 1929, the majority of houses in New York had electricity, mainly used for lighting purposes. Its demand went up with the emergence of consumer goods factories, as electrical power was introduced in factories to drive machinery. Thus it became possible to introduce mass production in a number of factories, like those producing refrigerators, washing machines, vacuum cleaners and radio sets.

By the 1930s, the city and the world had already witnessed the Great Depression. The city re-elected the reformer F. La Guardia, whose success in getting New Deal relief funds helped convert the city to a stronghold of the New Deal Coalition. The city recovered economically during the Second World War, gradually lost its industrial base and shifted to service industries. New York, long a great American city with many immigrants, became a culturally international city attracting intellectual, musical and artistic greats from all over the world.

Delhi, the New Capital of the Indian Empire

In the early years of the 20th century, in the largest of the colonies of the British Empire, India, located far east of London and New York, the situation was tense on account of a different reason. The country was going through major changes, with rumours of its capital being shifted from Calcutta to Delhi. Delhi had been an important city in the region for long and was the commercial capital of the Punjab. Electricity and trams had already arrived in the city, with the latter connecting Ajmeri Gate, Paharganj, Sadar Bazaar and Sabzi Mandi to Chandni Chowk and Jama Masjid. Large tracts of land were taken over, trees felled, agricultural land acquired for building roads, railway tracks, railway stations, housing and government offices.

All this was in preparation for the 1911 Delhi Durbar—for the announcement of shifting back the country's capital to Delhi from

Calcutta. The historic location of the ancient cities of Hastinapur and Indraprastha, and the political capital of India since the time of Tughlaq and for the entire period of the Mughals, Delhi was going to return to its former glorious position of being the political and national capital of India. On 12 December 1911 at the Coronation grounds in Delhi, King George V made the announcement. Three days later, the two foundation stones of the new capital were laid at Burari, on the outskirts of modern-day Delhi, by King George V and Queen Mary. These stones were fixed into a pillar—the Coronation Pillar—and stayed there till 1921 when they were shifted to Raisina Hill.

While Delhi has always been an important city, it was never really highly populated till the early 1900s. In fact, around 1820, Delhi had about 100,000 inhabitants, while other important centres like Calcutta (800,000), Lucknow (300,000), Mumbai (150,000), Chennai (140,000) and even Ahmedabad and Hyderabad were much larger cities. Delhi continued to be about the sixth or seventh largest Indian city till early 1900.

The transformation came when the capital of India formally shifted from Calcutta to New Delhi in 1912. The viceroys stayed at the Viceregal Lodge (presently Delhi University's Vice-Chancellor's office). The land where the Durbar was held had to be shifted to Raisina Hill as it had become waterlogged due to heavy rains. Construction of the Viceroy's House began in 1913, and the city's name, thanks to the massive construction and changes taking place, was changed to 'New Delhi'. Delhi's population has grown exponentially since.

Raisina Hill land was cleared of all traces of earlier settlement and the new city was to be unlike any other city in the ancient land. The Palace of the Viceroy was atop the hill and the other officers' residences were around the periphery of the office block. There was a broad avenue with vast emptiness flanked by rows of trees along the line of offices, at the other end of which was the Royal Canopy with a large statue of the king—aloof and dignified. In between lay

Figure 2: Delhi Durbar, 1911

a memorial to those Indian soldiers who had died for the king—India Gate.

The newfound status of the capital did nothing much for the poor agrarian population of the city. Delhi was yet to see the light of the Industrial Revolution, with a majority of its population rural and supported mainly by farming and agricultural activities. By virtue of being located on the fertile Ganga-Yamuna plains, the city suffered very few epidemics or drought situations. India was seeing a rapid growth in industries, but the same was not very evident in Delhi due to its agrarian economy.

Despite the lack of many industries, the political nature of the socio-economic condition of Delhi saw it attracting a horde of landless labourers and tenants who inhabited the outskirts of the city. These people lived in poor conditions and had almost no access to civic amenities. The divide between the British and the Indian was a major constraint in making facilities available to these migrants and landless labourers. They had to live in houses made of rough stones, clay and mortar and were unable to procure daily necessities.

Indian literary authors along with their European counterparts have documented many such stories of people living in extreme poverty. Many of these poor farmers fell into the clutches of the landlords who would usurp their lands in mortgage, which then could never be freed. The dire poverty which existed alongside the ongoing political and social development (mainly of the clerical staff employed with the British government) portrays a very gloomy picture of the Delhi of the time, paving the way for future unrest. The land of political power was going to see the light of urbanization but not much before India gained its Independence.

At the time of Independence, Delhi had a population of about 900,000, still smaller than that of Hyderabad, Chennai, Calcutta and Mumbai. But within the next six decades, Delhi's population grew to over 10 million people—thanks to generous additions of the nearby areas—leading to the formation of the National Capital Region (the combined population of NCR is over 40 million citizens).

Tokyo, the Land of the Rising Sun

Going further east, around 6,000 km away from Delhi, is the city of Tokyo, the three-decade-old capital city of Japan. Despite its location in a region prone to earthquakes and tsunamis, the city was already thriving in the 1900s after recovering from the defeat by the Russians. Under the Imperial Army of the Meiji Dynasty, Japan was already rising as a military power, with the slogan 'Enrich the country, strengthen the military'. The total population of Japan at that time was 50 million—almost the population of modern-day Tokyo. Such was the rise of the military that the samurai numbered more than 2 million around 1910[3]—which was the population of Tokyo in 1905.[4] These samurai were hired Japanese feudal lords called 'daimyo', who were paid in food, shelter and money, which often came from public funds such as taxes. This placed a tremendous financial burden on the state.

The city was still officially based on agriculture, which supported both the farming and the privileged classes. The political leaders were feeling the constraints of limited technological advances, worldwide changes and restricted global trade. As a result, the imperial rule legislated numerous social, political and economic changes in the country. It also opened its borders, sending several high-ranking expeditions abroad and inviting foreign advisors—including educators, engineers, architects, painters, and scientists—to assist them in rapidly absorbing modern technology and Western knowledge. Throughout the century, however, the drive to Westernize was paralleled by continued isolationist tendencies and a desire to resist foreign influences.[5]

The city was already divided into a large and small ward system, which gave central officials control over local decisions. There was a citywide emphasis on beautification and improving infrastructure and services for maintenance and growth. Japan's commitment to modernization transformed the notions of cities and city planning, combining the idea with beauty, relaxation and recreation which were being paid the highest attention by the urban planners. The city's parks, museums, buildings and other infrastructure were modelled after those in Berlin, London and Paris, which in turn became the models for the development of other cities in Japan. Almost all the urban planning and city development were affected by the outbreak of the first Sino-Japanese War and Russo-Japanese War, including the construction of the ultra-modern railway station in Tokyo. The three-storey station building was fashioned after Amsterdam's main station and was designed in restrained celebration of Japan's victory in the Russo-Japanese War.

The advancements by the city in the first two decades were disrupted by the Kanto earthquake of 1923. The strong earthquake resulted in the total destruction of the city of Tokyo. The city suffered an earthquake that measured 8.3 on the Richter scale, followed by a huge tsunami with a height of 12 metres. The entire city was ravaged by fires which destroyed more than 75 per cent of the buildings, causing severe structural damage. About 2-3 per cent of the population lost their lives in the dreaded earthquake, 2 million became homeless and around 5 per cent of Japan's total national wealth was destroyed. Despite the earthquake destroying a significant portion of the national income, the country and city were still in the higher income bracket with respect to the rest of the world.

The city suffered a high rate of typhoid fever, mainly in the densely populated working class areas. This was attributed to the decline in waste disposal. The problem became more serious in light of the collapse of traditional methods of waste disposal due to urbanization. The unsanitary conditions prevailing in the aftermath of the earthquake also resulted in high morbidity rates, which prompted the establishment of anti-typhoid measures implemented by the public authorities, and the building of an urban infrastructure.

Many saw the disaster as an act of divine punishment for the self-centred, immoral and extravagant Japanese lifestyle. The city learnt from the disaster lessons in frugality and resilience, which were evident in the changes in lifestyle and infrastructure. One of the reasons might have been rumours of shifting the capital elsewhere. The city came together for what it thought to be an unparalleled opportunity to rebuild in a way that reflected its Japanese values. A major reconstruction plan was chalked out, with modern networks of roads, trains and public services, parks, public buildings. The city got its first earthquake-resilient building in the Imperial Hotel, which withstood the anticipated earthquake stresses in the coming years and remained in use till 1968.

As we see, all the cities evolved surviving wars, epidemics, invasions and migration to emerge as centres of urban growth—centres for dreams and aspirations of millions and billions. These cities today have crossed the billion mark in terms of population, supporting industries, services, financial and commercial centres, and have gained political prominence—far more than in earlier times.

Tokyo, being the most populous city in the world, has a prominent position in economic, manufacturing and service industries. Delhi is the most powerful city in the South Asian region and is slowly replacing Mumbai as the financial capital and Bangalore as the tech capital of India. New York continues to be the city of dreams, attracting talent from around the world, owing to its economic and technological prominence. London, despite slowing down in terms of population growth, is still considered the cultural capital of Europe. All cities had different paces of urbanization at the start of the 20th century, which played a considerable role in their subsequent growth in the latter part of the century. The increasing urbanization had highlighted the glossy future, but the ugly facets of this very same reality were not largely known and would not become prominent till the end of the century.

History of Urbanization and the Demographic Shift

Urbanization in its modern-day sense is mostly about large metropolises and urban areas with huge populations, industries, high-rise buildings, good transportation, better education and employment opportunities, modern health facilities and civic amenities. In the ancient age when the word 'urban' was not yet coined, the urban areas meant cities or towns—enclosed or fortified places to hold against attackers. These were the most organized forms of habitation in contrast to the rural areas, where houses were built and the population lived around a source of livelihood—farms, rivers or seas.

Ancient towns have their origins in the earliest of civilizations, but the first one to have more than 500 people can be traced back to 8000 BC, the city of Mureybet (Syria) of the Mesopotamian civilization located on the Euphrates River.[6] Then, over the next 3,000 years, other cities emerged in modern-day Jordan, Turkey, Syria, Iraq, namely, Beidha, Basta, Catalhoyuk, Tell Brak, Uruk, Eridu,

Dobrovody, Maydanets, Talianki, which had populations in excess of 1,000 people. None of these cities crossed the 10,000 people mark till 3000 BC—mostly due to fragmented tribes and agrarian economies, and the continuous state of war with the neighbouring cities. Uruk (in modern-day Iraq) remained the largest city with a population of up to 50,000 in 2500 BC.

The ancient city of Uruk, part of the Mesopotamian civilization, was located on the Euphrates River. It was the largest urban centre of the civilization, primarily agricultural in occupation, but having a full-time bureaucracy, military and a stratified society. The fertile lands along with the domestication of native animals and employment of extensive irrigation techniques helped the city support a large population and grow in area with relative ease with respect to other surrounding settlements. The city had a lasting impact on the economies and the social and cultural conditions of the neighbouring cities and people. The period saw the emergence of cities of Memphis (Egypt), Babylon (Iraq), Thebes (Egypt), Tanis (Egypt), Yinxu (China), Haojing (China), Nimrud (Iraq) and Alexandria (Egypt) in the other concurrent civilizations.

Another ancient city which still survives is the Syrian capital of Damascus, where the earliest settlements are believed to have started in 4300 BC. It became an important settlement after the arrival of the Aramaeans, who established a network of canals and waterworks, which still form the basis of its modern water networks. The city fell to the invading armies of Alexander the Great, and has since been in Roman, Arab and Ottoman possession. Its wealth of historical attractions has made it a popular tourist destination.

It is notable here to mention the ancient urban centres of the American civilizations of the Incas, the Aztecs and the Mayans. The Inca economy involved a high degree of central planning, and evidence shows inter-regional trades with their neighbours. There is evidence of the barter system, taxation both in kind and labour or military obligations and axe monies[i] amongst the trading classes. The state was the provider of security, food, emergency resources and occasional feasts. The economy was based on complementary accessing of material resources and reciprocal exchanges. There is no clear evidence of their population sizes (though the estimates range from 4 to 37 million people), due to their records being destroyed during the Spanish conquest. Similar was the fate of the Aztec Empire, which became the foundation of the early Mexico City, in what was the ancient city of Tenochtitlan. It was the centre of political power for the Aztec Empire, and was also a major centre for trade, military operations and culture. Aztec architecture consisted of stepped pyramids from the pre-classic period and cave sites and was related to older Mesoamerican architecture. Similar architecture was found in the Mayan cities. Aztec cities often competed to construct the greatest temples and built over the existing ones in the process of doing so. Aztec houses were large single rooms built with mud bricks. They built pyramids as tall as mountains in the belief that the mountains protected their buildings from getting destroyed by the rains.

The population was less than 1 million for the largest city till around 100 BC. Post 1 AD, Rome (Italy) emerged as the first city to cross the mark. It became an important political centre with the emergence of Christianity and its state-of-the-art urban planning system with advanced sewage disposal and aqueduct systems. The aqueducts were deployed to bring water from distant sources and supply it to public baths, latrines, fountains, private households, and mining industries.[7] The city, owing to its growing political and industrial prominence, was a major attraction for migrants, who added to the population, along with the numerous slaves acquired

---

[i] Axe monies were bronze artifacts which were used in the ancient Mesoamerican and Andean cultural zones as a system of money exchange.

from numerous military conquests. The next 500 years saw the European cities remaining the largest ones in the world, though with fluctuating populations.

Since 500 AD, China with Beijing as its largest city has remained the most populated country despite large cities emerging in Europe. This was the time when the Sui annexed the Southern Dynasty of China and united the region which had been fragmented till then. It introduced the central administrative government structure of the three departments of Chancellery, State Affairs and the Secretariat, standardized coinage, improved defence, expanded the Great Wall, and provided official support for Buddhism. Beijing remained the most populous city from 1600 to 1900, after which London took over, followed by Tokyo, which still remains one of the most populous cities in the world.

The cities on the Indo-Gangetic plains were at the same time showing a very different trend of growth. The largest city was Pataliputra (modern-day Patna in the state of Bihar), having a population of 350,000 at its peak around the 3rd century BC. For most of history, cities in the Indian civilization did not overgrow, unlike their Western or even Eastern counterparts. The reason for the cities to remain stable in terms of population was not the geographical location, as the Indo-Gangetic plains were the most fertile lands in the world since agriculture was invented. These were in fact the 'smart cities' of that era—large-area cities with smaller populations, having sophisticated urban planning, baked brick houses, elaborate drainage systems, water supply systems, and clusters of large non-residential buildings—never growing beyond the physical limits of their geographies. When population grew too high, fresh cities were established rather than burdening the existing ones. Other important settlements in the Indian civilization were the two university towns of Taxila and Nalanda—which, although not highly populated, were highly planned and boasted of the best knowledge centres.

The Industrial Revolution and Rapid Urbanization

The world population stayed in the vicinity of 400-500 million from 1200 AD to 1600 AD.[8] For the first time, it crossed the 500 million mark in 1700 and has since followed an exponential trajectory. Figure 3 shows the increase in population through history. By 1600, there were around 20 cities with populations beyond 500,000.[9]

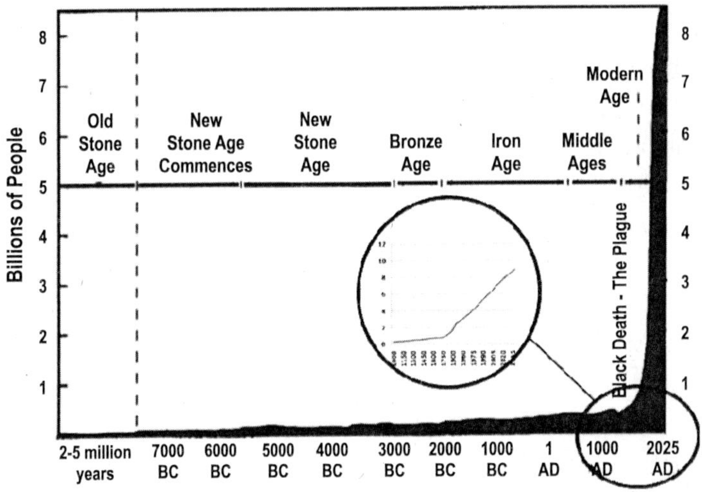

Figure 3: World population growth through history[10]

Till this period, a city grew in a circular manner with its walls marking its growth—the more the city grew the more the diameter increased. This was the basis of a village turning into a city—a definitive feature in the colonial era when the ruling regime erected walls to define the areas under their colonial powers. A visit to any of the historic sites from the colonial era will show remnants of numerous walls built with heavy permanent materials, surrounded by moats—the earliest meaning of 'town' being an enclosed or fortified place which would hold against attackers. These cities or towns with their well-built defences were relatively free from the perils of invading hordes, and hence their population kept increasing,

When the Industrial Revolution set in, the world population started seeing a drastic increase and there was a shift in the urban rural populations. In 1740, the population of England and Wales was steady at 6 million which rose to 8.3 million in 1801[11] and 16.8 million in 1850,[12] and doubled to 30.5 million by 1901.[13] During the same time, Europe's population increased from about 200 million[14] to 400 million.[15] The world population in 1740 was around 600 million[16] which grew to reach 1 billion by 1800[17] and had crossed 1.5 billion by 1900.[18] India and China contributed around 300 million to the world population around 1700[19], which rose to 600 million by 1820[20] and 750 million by 1910.[21]

Such was the effect of the Industrial Revolution, technological prowess and colonization that the Qing Empire—which at its zenith ruled China (and hence had more than one-third of the world's population at the time), and was one of the largest empires ever and had the largest economy in the world in the 18th century—was defeated by a much smaller British Empire in 1840. The First Opium War defeat resulted in the ceding of Hong Kong to the British and the allowing of the import of opium. Subsequent military defeats and unequal treaties with the Western powers saw China getting divided amongst Britain, Germany, Russia, France and Japan in the latter part of the 19th century. Other Asian countries were showing similar trends of colonization, with the exception of Japan, which was a thriving economy, and which was not very involved in the colonization process. The country had already fought a few wars with Russia. It was also one of the only Asian countries to be greatly influenced by the Industrial Revolution and the modernization of military and industries, in contrast to the other countries which still relied on the age-old agricultural economy and older weapons. Irrespective of their being cut off from the modernization of the Western world, these Asian countries had large populations owing to the presence of fertile river plains.

With the increase in population and density came the complexity of the resulting towns and cities. There would be a complex system of social division and social core along with a well-defined political system in place like in the ancient cities. More than the complexity, there was a social organization (or class division) which was seen in the cities developed in the time of the Industrial Revolution. As by then most of the world had already been under European colonial powers, these cities were developed in a manner similar to the European ones, with provisions for infrastructure for the ruling class, and separate areas and infrastructure demarcated for the ruled. The model was seen everywhere—Asia, Africa, Australia, Latin America. North America, or more prominently the United States, with its roots in European colonial powers, was also developing its cities in a similar manner. The steady growth in population since the 17th century had stressed on the limited nature of land and other resources and hence now the focus was on extensive cultivation, massive industrialization and technological change. This was at the core of the colonization process too—one which had the most resources in its control would be the richest and the most powerful, and hence the change from rural agronomy to urban industrialization.

The technological change not just helped the increased production of energy foods and new world food crops like maize and potato to support a large population, but it also turned luxury products like soaps into household utilities. The technological advancements in medicine and commercial goods made a major contribution to hygiene—public and personal. From the beginning of the 19th century, the surplus population made it possible for old cities to expand and new cities to be founded. The population growth was even faster in Germany in the second half of the 19th century than it was in the United States.[22]

The wave of urbanization made a new revelation—the commercial or industrial cities no longer needed the favour of being situated at the merging point of two or more diverse regions with complementary resources and skills. Urbanization's reach was boundless—it could reach any place with coal beds, iron ore, limestone quarries, production units—anything and everything was within reach. Railroads and better transportation made it easier for the industries to group together and take advantage of the surplus labour in the cities.

This growth of industry had marked adverse effect upon the entire environment. The new source of power, namely, coal and the new industrial processes, massed in the new steelworks and coke ovens, released huge amounts of ashes and industrial wastes into the air, water and land. The new chemical plants for manufacturing chlorine, sulfuric acid, etc. released hundreds of other potentially noxious compounds into the air, making the pollutant levels rise drastically. The local environment was no longer able to absorb them as it might have absorbed the effluvia of a village industry or the organic waste of a tannery or a slaughter house.

Demographic Trends from 1900 to 2000

The world population has almost quadrupled, growing from 1,625 million people in 1900[23] to 6.1 billion people in 2000.[24] At the start of the 20th century, the largest country/empire was the Qing Empire of China ruling 415 million people, followed by the Indian Empire (comprising modern-day India, Pakistan and Bangladesh) of 271 million people ruled by the British—this constituted almost 42 per cent of the then world population. The same region in 2000 had 2.55 billion[25] people, with only the People's Republic of China and India contributing 38 per cent or 2.282 billion people—almost nine to ten times the population in 1900.

From the start of the century, Russia occupied the third position in terms of its population until the break-up of the Soviet Union in

1991, and the United States ranked as the fourth most populated country in the world. Since 1991, the United States is the world's third most populated country whereas Russia has fallen to the position of being the sixth.

The staggering feature of the population increase is that there has been a net addition of more than 332 million people to China and India, which was more than the current population of the United States in 2014, at 318 million. Each decade saw a decline in the US share of the world's population, from 4.6 per cent in 1900 to 4.5 per cent in 2000 to 4.35 per cent.[26] Faster growth rates were observed for the Less Developed Countries than for More Developed Countries (MDCs). The combined share of the United States, United Kingdom, Germany, Japan and other MDCs fell from about one-third of the world's population in 1950 to about one-fifth in 2000 and is expected to fall below 15 per cent by 2050.[27] In contrast, the share of world population of the Less Developed Regions is estimated to grow beyond 75 per cent by 2050.[28]

From Table 1, it is evident that over the 100-year period, China, India (both as a part of a British colony and as an independent state), Russia, the United States and Japan stayed among the ten most populated countries. More Developed Countries like Germany, the United Kingdom and France stabilized their populations and thus were replaced by Pakistan, Bangladesh and Nigeria, all Less Developed Countries (LDCs). Furthermore, Russia and Japan (both MDCs) dropped in rank as they developed and enjoyed stable populations, while the ranks of Indonesia and Brazil (both LDCs) increased. Thus the negative correlation between the population increase and the development of the country is evident from the table—the more the country is developed, the more stable its population is.

Figure 5 clearly shows that the population densities of the Less Developed Regions of Africa (all regions), Asia (except Japan), Latin America and the Caribbean have grown at a higher rate than the

Table 1: Top 10 countries (Population in millions)

Region	*1900*[29]	*%**	*Country*	*2000*[30]	*%*	*Country*	*2014*[31]	*%*	*Country*	*2050*[32] *(est)*	*%*
Qing Empire	415	25%	China	1,243	20%	China	1,366	19%	India	1,524	16%
Indian Empire (UK)	271	16%	India	1,040	17%	India	1,248	17%	China	1,393	15%
Russia	132	8%	United States	281	5%	United States	319	4%	United States	361	4%
United States	75	5%	Indonesia	206	3%	Indonesia	252	3%	Indonesia	280	3%
Germany	56	3%	Brazil	170	3%	Brazil	203	3%	Nigeria	258	3%
Austria-Hungary	51	3%	Russia	147	2%	Pakistan	188	3%	Pakistan	234	2%
Dutch East Indies	46	3%	Pakistan	140	2%	Nigeria	178	2%	Brazil	220	2%
Empire of Japan	42	3%	Bangladesh	130	2%	Bangladesh	157	2%	Bangladesh	182	2%
United Kingdom	38	2%	Japan	127	2%	Russia	146	2%	Russia	136	1%
France	38	2%	Nigeria	110	2%	Japan	127	2%	Mexico	135	1%

* Percentage of the global population

average population density growth rate of the world. The More Developed Regions of the Europe, Northern America, Australia/ New Zealand and Japan initially had a higher population density than the least developed countries and have stabilized in the last 60 years. The individual trends for the different countries and regions, though, depict a totally different picture.

Table 2 shows the density figures for the most populous nations of the world. Bangladesh has the highest population density which is almost thrice that of India or Japan. Also Russia and the United States, the eighth and third largest nations in terms of population respectively, don't have a population density in excess of 50 people per sq km. Brazil is the only LDC with a low population density in the table owing to its large area (it is the fifth largest country), Amazonian forests and a mountainous terrain.

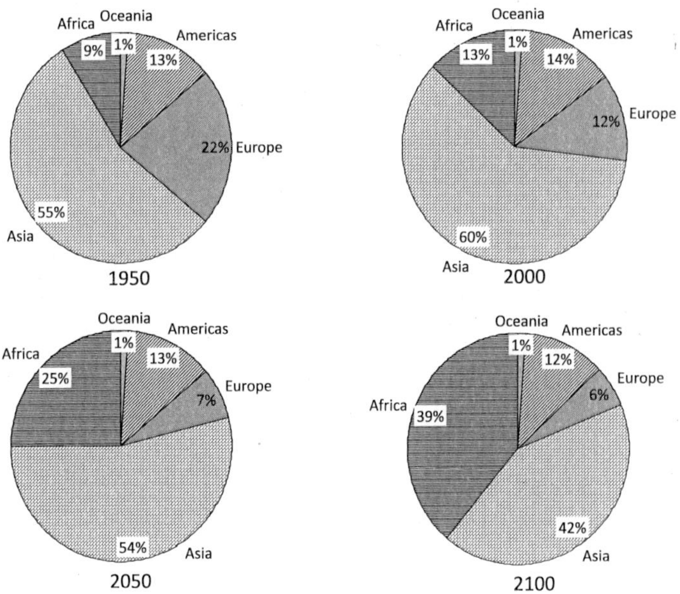

Figure 4: Graphic view of evolution of population by continent[33]

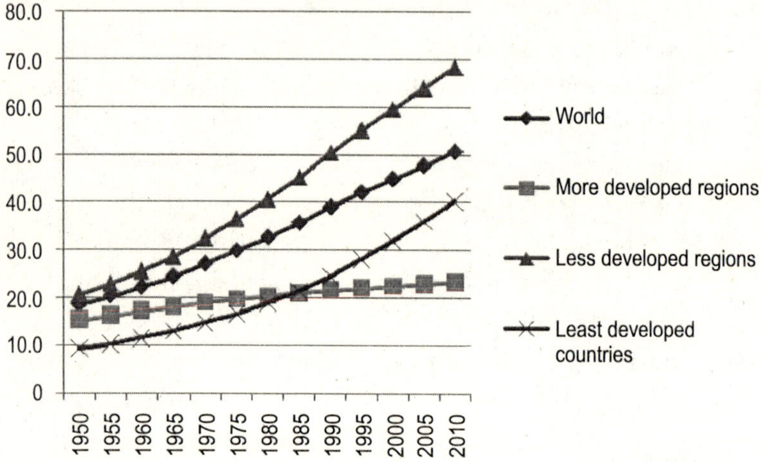

Figure 5: Population density (people per sq km) [Source UN][34]

Table 2: Most populous countries with populations and their densities – 2013

Country	*Population*[35]	*Area (sq km)*	*Density (sq km)*[36]	*Urban Population %*[37]	*GDP per capita (PPP in $)*[38]
China	1,357,380,000	9,640,821	145	53	11,903.6
India	1,252,139,596	3,287,240	421	52	5,410.3
United States	316,128,839	9,826,675	35	81	53,142.9
Indonesia	249,865,631	1,904,569	138	32	9,558.8
Brazil	200,361,925	8,514,877	24	85	15,033.8
Pakistan	182,142,594	803,940	236	38	4,698.9
Nigeria	173,615,345	923,768	191	46	5,601.0
Russia	156,594,962	17,098,242	9	74	24,120.3
Bangladesh	143,499,861	147,570	1,203	33	2,557.4
Japan	127,338,621	377,873	349	92	36,315.5

Source: World Bank

As the instruments of empire and colonization, cities grew to their first urban definition, and with globalization they started taking their modern shapes. The control centres of political, social and cultural dominance, economic prominence and the windows to the future, today's urban centres, metropolises and megalopolises are the drivers for all possible activities.

NOW YOU KNOW:

- Ancient towns originated around 8000 BC in ancient civilizations
- Till 100 BC, a city's population did not cross 1 million
- Rome was the first city to attain a population of over a million
- Post 500 AD, Beijing remained one of the most populated cities of the world
- Industrial Revolution quickened the pace of urbanization
- Urbanization led to increased demands for resources, namely, energy, food and transportation
- Less Developed Regions have 75 per cent of the population
- India and China have more than 35 per cent of the world population
- More Developed Regions have stayed more or less stable in the last 50 years
- There is a negative correlation between a nation's development and its population.

2

Troubles of Agglomeration: Old Order Challenges and Density Pressures on Resources

This chapter will discuss the different problems of urbanization and urban agglomeration. It introduces the growing pressure of urban population increase and the burden of the megacities on resources. The chapter further focuses on the four different types of urban population pressure problems—disparity, overcrowding, scarcity and pressure on environment and resources.

A typical day for Ravi starts at 6 o'clock with the rising sun in Bangalore. Ravi hails from Udaipur, the city of lakes in Rajasthan, and has completed a bachelor's degree in computer science and engineering from a very prestigious college in Bangalore. In the final year of his graduation, Ravi got placed in an MNC as a software developer with a starting salary of Rs 2.5 lakh per annum, after paying off his taxes and Provident Fund, an amount just enough for him to meet his expenses. It was a proud and glorious moment for him when he informed his parents about the future he was going to secure in the big city of Bangalore. He was lucky enough to get employment in a time of job crisis. He could finally see himself fulfilling all his dreams of living in a big city with a high standard of living. The world seemed to be at his feet, but the vision did not last for long.

Figure 1: Heavy traffic on the roads of Bangalore

His morning starts with the daily ablutions and a light breakfast of two idlis and a vada, the typical south Indian breakfast available in Bangalore. Sometimes when he is in a hurry, he skips breakfast and rushes to the Banashankari bus stand to catch the very next bus to reach office on time. His office is in Whitefield, the IT hub of Bangalore. The buses are generally heavily crowded, jam-packed with people, with the conductor manoeuvering himself through that crowd, pushing aside and stepping on his feet, in order to move to the other end of the bus. Despite the cool Bangalore weather, he gets drenched in sweat in no time at all. The bus takes a travel time of two hours to cover a short distance of 15 km due to heavy traffic; ideally it should take him half an hour to cover that distance. Finally

Ravi gets down from the bus, exhausted and sweating because of the tiring journey. He quickly buys a Rs 20 bottle of water, ignoring the municipal water tap. Tap water has been declared unfit for even bathing—and anybody who can afford it spends more than Rs 100 a day on clean water. This is the stark reality of a nation where one-third of the population does not even earn Rs 30 a day.

Ravi has to walk some distance from his bus stand to reach his office premises and stand in a long queue to enter the elevator to reach his office, which is on the 20th floor of a sprawling 25-storey building in the heart of the city. He anxiously rides the elevator to reach his floor, constantly glancing at his watch. As soon as the door opens, he dashes out of the elevator, wiping the sweat on his face with his sleeves to place his finger on the biometric at his office entrance just seconds before it would have marked him late for the day, making him lose half a day's salary. Soon after he gets to his seat, he gulps down two large cups of strong coffee to drive away drowsiness, laziness and despair. The work mainly consists of long hours of coding and staring at the computer screen. He makes it a point to have lunch, which he orders from the office cafeteria, by noon. After lunch he generally has a team meeting at around 3 p.m. to devise strategies for the project and monitor progress. That would be the time when he would again head to the coffee machine for his much-needed dose of caffeine. When he leaves the office at 8 p.m., Ravi has spent ten long hours sitting in his office chair, pulling out Excel sheets sitting in front of the bright computer screens. Occasionally, he heads out for a team lunch which would take another two hours and then instead of a bus, he would have to look for an auto to take him home.

After a hectic schedule of ten hours, Ravi has to again gear up for the strenuous journey back home. He manages to somehow get inside a heavily crowded bus and manages to hang on within—sometimes he gets a seat, often he does not and has to stand for the entire two hours of the journey. After a tiresome journey, cutting through the one-way traffic, but this time on the opposite side of the road, the bus reaches the central bus stand of Banashankari. Ravi rushes to have dinner, which usually is a south Indian meal at some local unhygienic restaurant. He then walks the few yards to his room and falls on the bed to release stress. By the time he can sleep, it would be midnight.

Ravi is having trouble sleeping these days. He keeps on tossing and turning, but sleep is far away. The thought of waking up the next day for office is not the only thought which worries him. He is worried about how to break the news to his family—he has recently been diagnosed with type II diabetes and the doctor has advised him to lead a less stressful life. His family has been asking him to get married. The proposition worries him—it means that he would have to leave his shared apartment and take a separate house, which will further eat away at his meagre salary.

Sometimes he dreams and surprisingly the dreams don't revolve around partying, roaming around the world, starting his own business or having the time of his life. His dreams these days are of the serene lakes of Udaipur, of having a lazy breakfast with his family, open fields—not electronic gadgets or fast cars. It baffles and confuses him. Is this what he wanted?

Increasing Urban Population and Its Challenges

By 2013, more than 50 per cent of the world's population resided in urban areas.[i] Of these urban areas, there are 23 megacities with a population of more than 10 million, accommodating 10 per cent of the world's population in less than 0.01 per cent of the land area. The number of such megacities is expected to increase to 37 in 2030, out of which 22 would be in Asia. The six cities of Delhi,

---

[i] World urban population residing in Asia—53 per cent, in Europe—16 per cent, in Africa—12 per cent, and in the Americas—19 per cent.

Mumbai, Kolkata, Chennai, Bangalore and Hyderabad would together have a population of more than 100 million people in 2030.

According to a McKinsey report,[1] Mumbai has already reached its population tipping point, whereas Delhi and Kolkata have outgrown their natural growth boundaries and need more neighbouring areas to support the ever-increasing population. There are increased health vulnerabilities and many of the urban poor are living a life of poverty and destitution. These urban poor live with little or no access to basic civic amenities, infrastructure, social security and education. More than 12 per cent of the urban population in India lived below the poverty line[ii] in the year 2014, according to the World Bank, and the number is expected to double by 2024.[2]

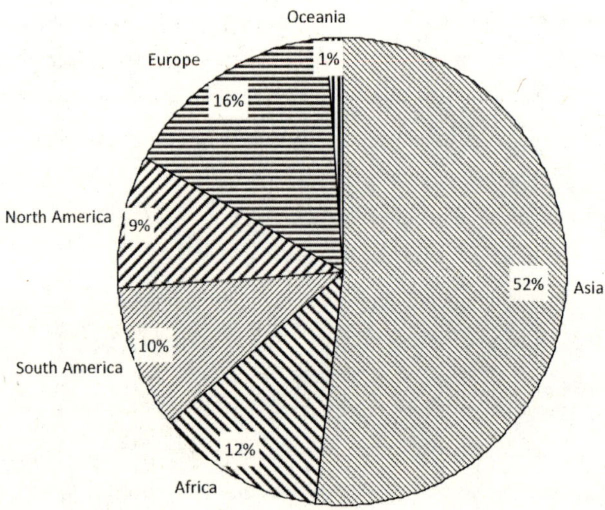

Figure 2: Urban population percentage

[ii] Poverty line in 2014 is defined globally at a minimum income level of $1.78 per day.

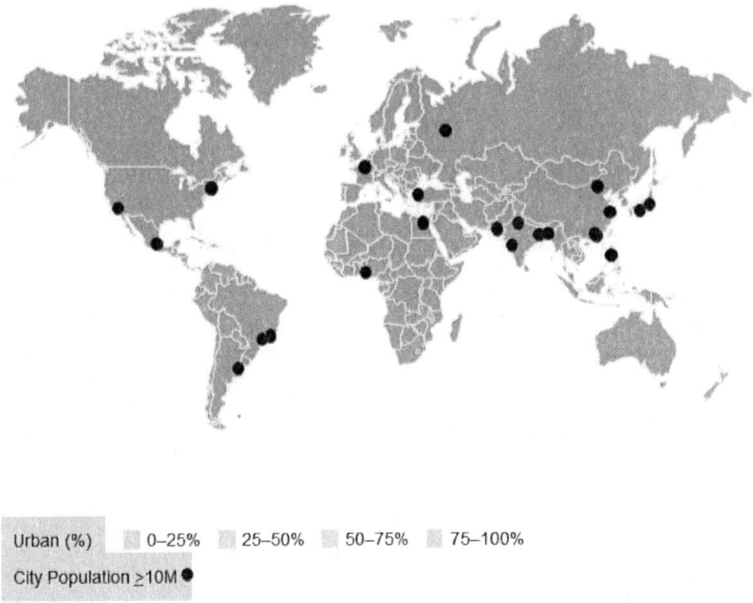

Figure 3: Megacities in 2013

Table 1: World megacities in 2012

Sr. No.	*City*	*Country*	*Habitants (millions)*[3]	*Density (/sq km)*[4]	*Continent*
1	Tokyo	Japan	36.933	4,300	Asia
2	Delhi	India	21.935	11,500	Asia
3	Mexico City	Mexico	20.142	9,500	North America
4	New York	US	20.104	1,800	North America
5	Sao Paulo	Brazil	19.649	6,400	South America
6	Shanghai	China	19.554	6,000	Asia
7	Mumbai	India	19.422	30,900	Asia
8	Beijing	China	15.000	5,000	Asia
9	Dhaka	Bangladesh	14.930	44,400	Asia
10	Calcutta	India	14.283	11,900	Asia
11	Karachi	Pakistan	13.500	18,300	Asia
12	Buenos Aires	Argentina	13.370	5,200	South America

Sr. No.	*City*	*Country*	*Habitants (millions)*[3]	*Density (/sq km)*[4]	*Continent*
13	L.A.	US	13.223	2,400	North America
14	Rio de Janeiro	Brazil	11.867	6,000	South America
15	Manila	Philippines	11.654	15,400	Asia
16	Moscow	Russia	11.472	3,500	Europe
17	Osaka	Japan	11.430	5,300	Asia
18	Cairo	Egypt	11.031	10,400	Africa
19	Istanbul	Turkey	10.953	9,700	Europe
20	Lagos	Nigeria	10.788	12,700	Africa
21	Paris	France	10.516	3,800	Europe
22	Guangzhou	China	10.486	5,300	Asia
23	Shenzhen	China	10.222	6,800	Asia

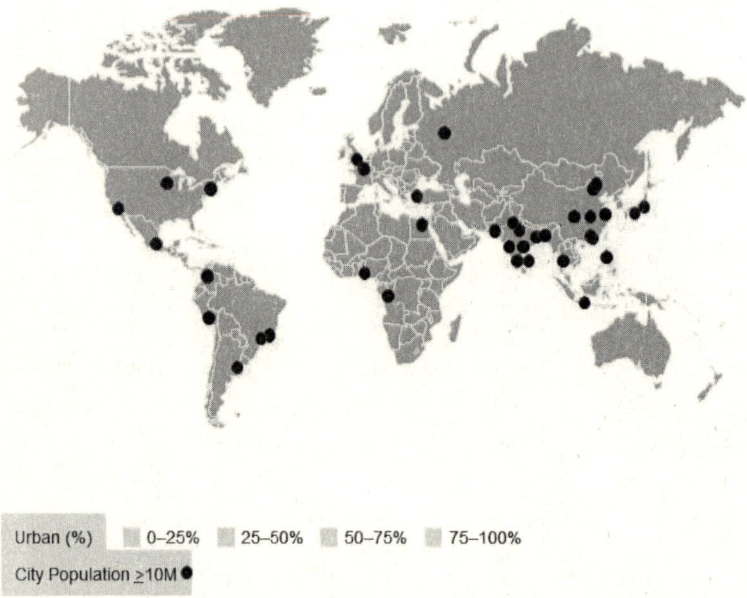

Figure 4: Megacities in 2030

Table 2: Megacities in 2030

Sr. No.	*City*	*Country*	*Habitants*[5]	*Continent*
1	Tokyo	Japan	38.661	Asia
2	Delhi	India	32.935	Asia
3	Shanghai	China	28.404	Asia
4	Mumbai	India	26.557	Asia
5	Mexico City	Mexico	24.581	North America
6	New York	US	23.572	North America
7	Sao Paulo	Brazil	23.175	South America
8	Dhaka	Bangladesh	22.906	Asia
9	Beijing	China	22.633	Asia
10	Karachi	Pakistan	20.190	Asia
11	Lagos	Nigeria	18.857	Africa
12	Calcutta	India	18.711	Asia
13	Manila	Philippines	16.278	Asia
14	L.A.	US	15.687	North America
15	Shenzhen	China	15.545	Asia
16	Buenos Aires	Argentina	15.524	South America
17	Guangzhou	China	15.474	Asia
18	Istanbul	Turkey	14.897	Europe
19	Cairo	Egypt	14.740	Africa
20	Kinshasa	Congo	14.535	Africa
21	Changqing	China	13.627	Asia
22	Rio de Janeiro	Brazil	13.621	South America
23	Bangalore	India	13.193	Asia
24	Jakarta	Indonesia	12.822	Asia
25	Chennai	India	12.814	Asia
26	Wuhan	China	12.727	Asia
27	Moscow	Russia	12.576	Europe
28	Paris	France	12.163	Europe
29	Osaka	Japan	12.031	Asia
30	Tianjin	China	11.934	Asia

Sr. No.	City	Country	Habitants[5]	Continent
31	Hyderabad	India	11.647	Asia
32	Lima	Peru	11.503	South America
33	Chicago	US	11.434	North America
34	Bogotá	Colombia	11.369	South America
35	Bangkok	Thailand	11.369	Asia
36	Lahore	Pakistan	11.190	Asia
37	London	England	10.255	Europe

Urbanization and Key Challenges

The key challenges faced due to urbanization are as follows:

- Disparity and cost inefficiency
- Overcrowding and urban sprawl
- Scarcity of basic utilities
- Pressure on the environment and energy resources, pollution

Disparity and Cost Efficiency

The Forbes list of billionaires featured 54 Indians in 2014 with a combined net worth in excess of $234 billion. The GDP of the country stood at $1.877 trillion in 2013 whereas GNI per capita was $1,570, which is just above the average GNI per capita in South Asia and lower than that of the Lower Middle Income Group countries. According to the HDR report by the UN for 2014, 55.3 per cent of India's population were multi-dimensionally poor,[iii] while an additional 18.2 per cent were near multi-dimensional poverty. It also states that every second malnourished child in the world is Indian whereas with respect to HDR 2013, India's education index lost more than 40 per cent of its value.[6]

[iii] It is the poverty that reflects deprivations in 33.33 per cent of weighted indicators. It was developed by Oxford Poverty & Human Development Initiative and the UNDP to determine poverty beyond income-based lists.

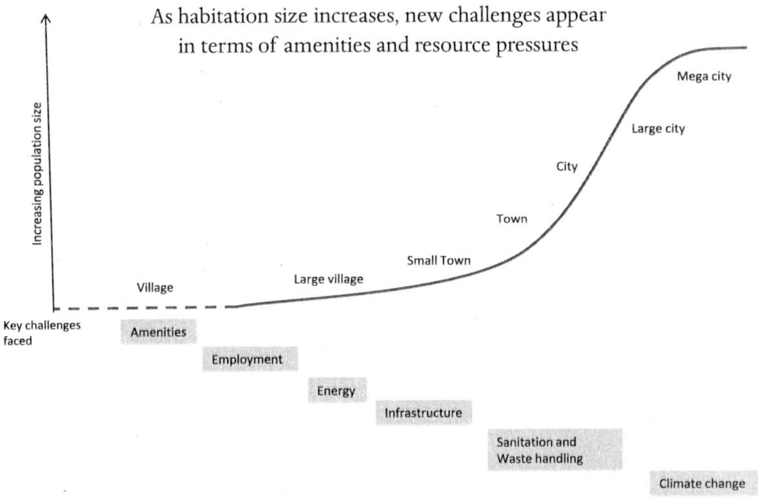

Figure 5: Urbanization and its problems

Inequality in earnings has doubled in India over the last two decades—the top 10 per cent of wage earners now make 12 times more than the bottom 10 per cent, up from a ratio of 6 in the 1990s. In urban areas, the spending of the richest segments increased by 63 per cent while the poorest saw an increase of 33 per cent. In 2000, the average spending of the richest group in urban areas was 12 times that of the poorest group; in 2014, it had increased to fifteen-fold.

Table 3: Odds against poverty

	Urban poor child (%)	*Urban non-poor child (%)*
Being stunted	54.2	33.2
Being underweight	47.1	26.2
Having anaemia	71.4	59.0
Infant Mortality Rate (out of thousand)	54.6	35.5
Child Mortality Rate (out of thousand)	72.7	40.8
Illiteracy (for a boy)	25.1	4.1
Illiteracy (for a girl)	49.8	13.7

The Gini coefficient (or index), published by the World Bank, is a well-accepted measure of income inequality which measures the extent to which the distribution of income or consumption expenditure among individuals or households within an economy deviates from a perfectly equal distribution. A Gini index of 0 represents perfect equality, while an index of 100 implies perfect inequality. India's current Gini coefficient is 33.4.

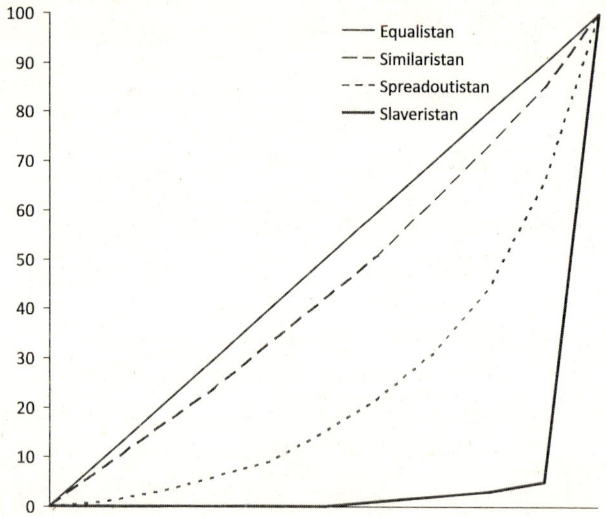

Figure 6: The Gini coefficient

The average per capita monthly expenditure on food in urban areas was less than Rs 1,000 for 50 per cent of the population while it was Rs 2,859 per capita for the people in the richest segment. Food items also show a vast disparity between the rich and the poor. The urban basket contains vegetables, fruits, eggs, fish and meat, and milk products whereas the poor have access only to the basic food items like rice and other coarse grains and potatoes.

These present a very dismal scenario of the urban poor, which make them more likely to say that they are unhappy. As expected, social inequity increases with the rise in population and even with wealth, as most new wealth tends to be oriented towards the already rich. Studies have quantified that inequality in skills can explain about one-third of the variation in income inequality, and skill inequality is itself explained by the educational and vocational training opportunities. There are also substantial differences in the returns to skill, related to local concentrations in different industries, and these too are strongly correlated with inequality.[7]

A society's status of health is a reflection of the status of the development of its individuals. The health status is influenced by different indicators like employment, income, educational attainment, social groups, level of awareness, accessibility to healthcare and availability of health services. Health is unevenly distributed across socio-economic status. Persons of lower income, education or occupational status experience worse health and die earlier. The urban poor have a 5 per cent higher incidence of more than 3 births per female. Less than 50 per cent of these urban poor mothers have access to prenatal or neonatal health facilities and more than 50 per cent suffer from anaemia. More than 50 per cent of the children of the urban poor are either stunted or are underweight and close to 75 per cent suffer from anaemia.[8]

Similar disparities are prevalent in the education, sanitation and drinking water situation amongst the urban poor. The disparities deprive the urban poor from acquiring the skills to enhance their living standards, leading to generations of poverty. Slum vs non-slum differentials in women's educational attainment are large in most of the cities. The education level of poor women is particularly low in these cities. Only 59 per cent of poor females have had some level of education. The number for non-poor urban females stood at 83 per cent, showing the glaring disparity. They also had little access to better private education.

The disparities exist even in the urban non-poor Middle Income Group population and High Income Group. The only difference lies in the fact that all these populations have sustainable incomes and have acquired specific skill sets to enable them to get better employment, health, education opportunities and household and security facilities than the urban poor.

Overcrowding

Divya was in the office, working, when she received an SMS. It was short—'You remember Ajay. He met with an accident this morning while getting down from the local and died on the spot.'

She felt numb. She had always read of people coming in front of Mumbai's local trains, getting down from a local, boarding a local and slipping and getting killed. She never thought it could happen to somebody she knew. The guy, Ajay, had been married recently. He lived in Mumbai and was working as a consultant for a big MNC. To avoid the hassles of traffic he used to take the local trains, which would reduce the commute time by half, when compared to an auto or taxi, to his office located in Bandra-Kurla Complex.

The message reminded her of an incident five years ago. A close friend of hers was engaged to her college sweetheart and they were to tie the knot in two months' time. One day, out of the blue, a friend called and told her that Kailash was killed the previous night in a bike accident. Her friend was devastated—her fiancé was a victim of drunken driving. A group of college brats who were drunk and driving on a Delhi highway had suddenly changed lanes, which had resulted in Sourav swerving to try to avoid an accident—and, in the process, colliding with the divider and being killed instantly.

Images of Ajay and Kailash zoomed past Divya's eyes and her numbness grew. What were these cities growing into? She no longer felt safe getting into a car or a bus—not just due to traffic accidents but also due to the rising crime rates, especially rapes and murders. But was she safe even if she stayed home? She was no longer sure.

In India, 120,000 people die and 1,270,000 sustain serious injuries every year in Road Traffic Accidents (RTA). As per statistics, there is one death on Indian roads every six minutes and this is expected to escalate to one death every three minutes by 2020. The number of accidents per 1,000 vehicles in India is as high as 35, while the figures range from 4 to 10 in the developed countries. World Health Organization's Global Status Report on Road Safety (2009) states that more people die in road accidents in India than anywhere else in the world, including the more populous China. Although India accounts for only 1 per cent of the registered motor vehicles, it accounts for nearly 9 per cent of RTA deaths.

Delhi witnesses on an average five deaths due to road accidents on a daily basis, followed by Chennai at three deaths on the roads, and Mumbai at 10 deaths in the suburban local trains[9] and two in road accidents.[10] On an average, about 600 people died annually on the Mumbai suburban rail network over 10 years (2002–2012), more than 36,152 lives have been lost on tracks and 36,688 people have been injured. This is the result of overcrowding of the roads and the suburban railways despite the number of average vehicles per road being as low as four for India.[11] With the increasing number of motor vehicles on the city roads to support the billion-odd population residing in the urban areas of India, the death toll has increased in the last two decades and will further increase with the increasing population pressure on the urban areas and cities.

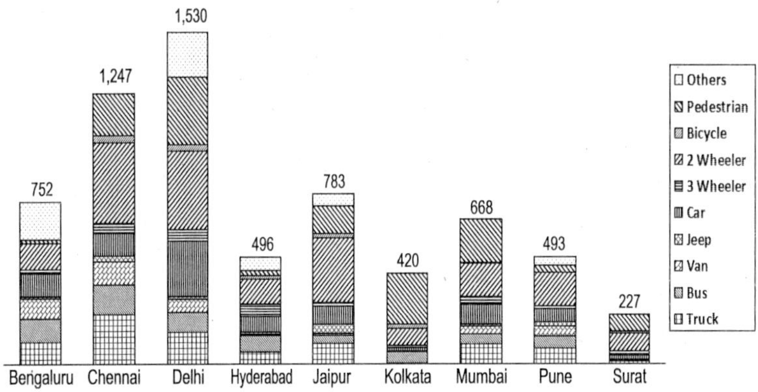

Figure 7: Road accidents and fatalities in select cities of India[12]

Figure 8: A slum in Dharavi, Mumbai[13]

Overcrowding of cities has also resulted in the rise of congested areas in cities and urban areas and the rise of slums. Almost all the cities, despite the limitations of their geographical locations, have witnessed the mushrooming of slums having people—mostly migrants—living in cramped spaces.[14] More than 65 per cent of the people in urban Indian households with more than five members live in just one or two room houses—in spaces less than 800 sq ft in area with no exclusive rooms. Most of these houses are located in urban dwellings where there is a scarcity of land space and hence the buildings and houses have been shrinking in size. Even the Middle Income Group houses have shrunk over the last decade—3 BHK flats earlier had an area of 1,700-1,800 sq ft, which has now shrunk to 1,100-1,200 sq ft.

The census defines slums as 'residential areas where dwellings are unfit for human habitation' because they are dilapidated, cramped, poorly ventilated, unclean, or 'any combination of these factors which are detrimental to safety and health' and covers all 4,041 statutory towns in India. Over 65 million people lived in slums in

India in 2014. However, the figures are not definitive due to high rural migration. The average household living in a slum is no larger than an average urban Indian household, with 4.7 family members. With over 11 million of its residents in slums, Maharashtra has the highest slum population; 4.6 million of them in 'identified' slums. Andhra Pradesh follows with over 10 million in slums, and West Bengal and Uttar Pradesh have over 6 million slum residents each. Over 1 million of Delhi's 1.7 million slum residents live in 'identified' slums.[15]

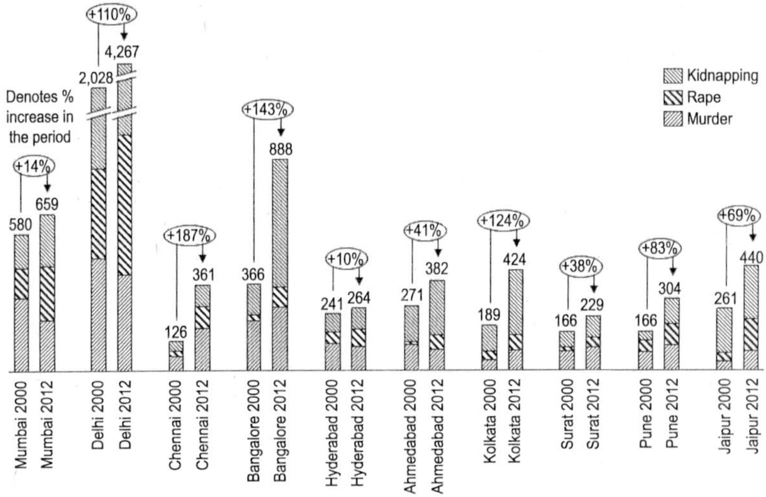

Figure 9: Crime rates in India[16]

Slums and ghettos have very poor living conditions and often add to the criminal activities in the cities. Such is the condition in the ghettos in America that drug abuse, gun firing, murders, trafficking and other anti-social activities are rampant in such areas. Crime trends under major heads from 1953 to 2011 reveal that crimes such as dacoity and burglary/house-breaking have been on the decline over a period of 59 years. However, crimes such as murder, rape, kidnapping and abduction, robbery and riots have been on the rise.

It is evident that heinous and violent crimes are on the rise, which is surely a cause for concern.

A very disturbing fact about the rising criminal acts is the abuse of urban street children. One in every four street children in the metropolitan cities of India is a victim of some form of substance abuse and over half of such children living in difficult conditions are illiterate. These children—mainly boys on the street—are particularly vulnerable to sexual abuse by strangers, adult street dwellers and, at times, by family members. Nearly 86 per cent of boys in the age group of 14-18 years are sexually active; however, a very low number of them know about safe sex and condom usage.

Urban Sprawl

The Indian census defines 'all areas with a municipal corporation, cantonment board or notified town area committee' as an urban area. Alternatively, it includes places with a minimum population of 5,000, with at least 75 per cent of the male working population engaged in non-agricultural pursuits and a minimum density of at least 400 people per sq km. Urban sprawl may be defined as the scattering of new development on isolated tracts, separated from other areas by vacant land.[17] It is also often described as leapfrog development[18] as observed in all the major cities across the world.

Urban sprawl has been criticized for inefficient use of land resources and energy, and large-scale encroachment of the agricultural lands. Due to urban sprawls, cities are expanding in all directions, resulting in drastic changes in urban land use, more prominent on the urban fringes or city peripheral rural areas than in the city centre. Inadvertently, this is causing loss of productive agricultural lands, forest cover, other forms of greenery, loss in surface water bodies, depletion in ground water aquifers and increasing levels of air and water pollution. Fragmented land use is also detrimental to biological conservation as it disturbs the natural environment of the flora and the fauna and involves human intervention.[19]

Massive immigration and urbanization has resulted in expansion of cities beyond their population and geographical areas. A classic example is Mumbai, which is located on a crescent bay area of only 600 sq km, but supported a metropolitan population of close to 20 million in the city in 2014. It also has one of the highest population densities in the world—around 31,000 people living per sq km in Mumbai city and the neighbouring cities or towns of Navi Mumbai, Thane, Bhiwandi and Kalyan. The green forest cover in Mumbai is continuously depleting due to forest land being allotted for development projects and farming land. So far, Mumbai has lost 243,000 acres (93,467 hectares) for farming and 6,627 hectares of forest land for 294 developmental projects till 2013.

The urban expansion of Delhi, the National Capital Territory of India, has grown beyond the NCT to incorporate towns in the neighbouring states (known as NCR—National Capital Region) and at its largest extent can count a population of nearly 27 million residents as of 2014. The NCR includes the neighbouring cities of Gurgaon, Noida, Ghaziabad, Faridabad, Greater Noida, Sonepat, Panipat, Karnal, Rohtak, Rewari, Baghpat, Meerut, Alwar, Bharatpur and other nearby towns. Delhi has a geographical area of 1,483 sq km. Total forest and tree cover in Delhi is 19.97 per cent of the geographical area. Forest cover constitutes 11.88 per cent and tree cover constitutes 8.09 per cent of its geographical area. The area of forest and tree cover per dweller is 17.680 sq m. The forest cover in Delhi, despite a very high rate of increase of population and associated developmental activity, has increased from 1.48 per cent in 1993 to 19.97 per cent in 2011 due to the changing strategies of the Delhi government.

> Cities in developed countries have more trees compared to cities in developing countries, which often fall below the WHO-set minimum standards of 9 sq m of green open space per city dweller.

Table 4: Forest cover in Indian and global cities[20]

City	%	*City*	%
Kolkata	0	Tokyo	14
Mumbai	20	Melbourne	22
Ahmedabad	2	Mexico	33
Delhi	12	London	25
Hyderabad	5	Sao Paulo	21
Bangalore	12		
Surat	31	India	24
Pune	19	World	31

The city of Kolkata had 4.5 million residents and the urban agglomeration, which comprises the city and its suburbs, was home to approximately 14.1 million in 2014. The city and its suburbs occupy an area of around 1,900 sq km and the population density is 24,000 people per sq km. The urban agglomeration of Coimbatore expanded from 38 sq km in 1973 to 79 sq km in 1989, and further to 274 sq km in 2010, registering over a five-fold growth in less than four decades. In terms of spatial pattern, the city developed concentrically during the initial years and later experienced linear radial development along the major roads. The review of the 2002 land use plan for the city indicated that nearly 75 per cent of land within the corporation limits had been taken up for urban land use, while the rest was classified as agricultural land, water bodies, vacant areas and heritage sites.

Urban sprawl has two contradictory facets. On the one hand, the urban areas and the megacities are the growth centres of the nation; on the other, urbanization is accompanied by both poverty and environmental degradation, e.g. encroachment of valuable agricultural land, increasing use of private cars and energy consumption, inner city decline, premature write-down and under-utilization of the existing built environment. Change in land use will have profound impact on environmental sustainability and will become a globally significant issue.

Human settlements represent the most profound alterations to the natural environment. In particular, urbanization which involves a wide spectrum of land-based activities and natural resource extraction leads to loss of habitat and destruction of biodiversity. Therefore, geographical understanding of land use change is critical to assess the impact of urban growth on the local environment.

Scarcity of Basic Utilities

For proper living conditions, civic amenities are essential in the urban areas and are mostly managed by the city municipal bodies. In the rural context, except for roads, other infrastructural amenities which involve high investments are mostly managed by the people themselves in India. Services such as water supply and sanitation, roads and drains, street lights, collection and disposal of solid waste, maintenance of public places, burial grounds and crematoria, cattle pounds, registration of births and deaths, maintenance of markets have long been seen as the functions of municipal bodies. In addition, they perform certain regulatory functions relating to the construction of buildings, public health areas such as eating places, slaughter houses and tanneries, etc. The efficient performance of these responsibilities requires proper institutional structures, unambiguous decentralization of powers, adequacy of

> The study 'Economic Impact of Inadequate Sanitation in India', conducted by the World Bank's South Asia Water and Sanitation Unit, says that lack of toilets and decent sanitation costs India nearly $54 billion (Rs 24,000 crore), or 6.4 per cent of its GDP a year, mainly through premature deaths, especially of children, treatment for hygiene-related illnesses and lost productivity.

resources, support of the state governments and their entities, and a concerted effort to build up capabilities in the various sections of the urban machinery.

India has a high rate of mobile penetration—71 per cent of the population of 1.3 billion are mobile subscribers while only 47 per cent of the 250 million households have latrines within their premises and only 43.5 per cent have access to tap water. The situation is more dismal in the urban areas where around 50 million urban poor defecate in the open and are vulnerable to water pollution. As many as 4,861 out of 5,161 cities across the country do not have even a partial sewerage network.[21]

Lack of proper sanitation and sewage disposal machinery creates major health risks and causes life-threatening illnesses like cholera, typhoid and malaria. Treating diseases such as diarrhoea, malaria and intestinal worms, and early deaths and other health-related impacts, costs India $38.5 billion annually.[22]

Sanitation facilities like sewerage systems, storm water drains, latrines (public or private), and other community sanitation services are important in maintaining good hygiene and a clean environment. Factors such as population pressure, discharge of effluents, addition of agricultural chemicals in water bodies and inappropriate water pricing mechanisms have contributed to the deterioration of water quality, depletion of water and unhygienic sanitation.[23]

Pressure on Environment

There are 10 gases that make up clean air: in order of highest to lowest concentration they are nitrogen, oxygen, argon, carbon dioxide (CO_2), neon, helium, methane (CH_4), krypton, hydrogen, and xenon. Any gas could qualify as a pollutant if it reaches a high enough concentration to cause harm. Pollution is a prominent side effect of the urban sprawl if urbanization doesn't occur in a planned manner using eco-friendly technologies. Since the Industrial Revolution, the carbon dioxide content in the atmosphere has increased over 280 ppm (parts per million) to 400 ppm in 2013. It fuels the greenhouse effect, warming the atmosphere, and further disrupts the natural carbon dioxide cycle. Major sources of pollution are vehicular emissions, biomass and biofuel burning, long-range transports, combustion of CNG and LPG and industrial emissions.

Theoretically, there are dozens of different polluting gases. In practice, about ten different substances cause most concern:

- Sulfur dioxide
- Carbon monoxide
- Carbon dioxide
- Nitrogen oxides
- Volatile organic compounds (VOCs)
- Particulates
- Ozone
- Chlorofluorocarbons (CFCs)
- Unburned hydrocarbons
- Lead and heavy metals.

Water Scarcity

According to the National Sample Survey (NSS), an estimated 70 per cent of urban households in India reported being served by taps and 21 per cent by tube wells or hand pumps and 15 per cent of households did not get sufficient drinking water from their principal source, between April and June, May being the worst month.[24] Nine per cent still don't have regular access to drinking water, and in most of the cities the quality of supply water is not always ideal. Information provided by the Union Ministry of Health and Family Welfare shows that 285 people died of diseases caused by drinking water contamination in Karnataka, between 2010 and 2013. A ward quality survey done by Janaagraha in 2014 showed that 72 per cent of Bangaloreans get contaminated water, and 15 of BBMP's 198 wards get 100 per cent contaminated water.[25] A similar study carried out to gauge the extent of water contamination in Mumbai revealed that it was an issue in 77 per cent of the 596 households that were surveyed. In most of the cities, the drinking water available is often contaminated with total dissolved solids, hardness, chlorides and nitrates exceeding permissible limits, and toxic chemicals, arsenic, lead and disease-causing bacteria that were present in high numbers, causing the deadly diarrhoea and cholera.

The river Yamuna, the reason for Delhi's existence, has suffered heavily from pollution. Its dissolved oxygen (DO) content is 7.5 mg/l when it enters Delhi and falls down to only 1.3 mg/l at its exit, far below the basic minimum level of 5 mg/l. Roughly half of the entire city's raw sewage goes straight into the river. Fifty-five per cent of the city's 15 million people are connected to the city's sewer system and its treatment plants, but because of corrosion and clogging in the system, many of the treatment plants do not run at full capacity.

Urbanization has resulted in increased pollution in not just water and air but in all possible spheres of human life. The depleting green cover due to overcrowding, industries, development activities and urban sprawl further adds to the pressure on the environment. Hence proper provisions for the maintenance of green cover need to be made at the planning stage of urban development. Before the city expands further, a proper plan for greening in the city, especially with respect to land availability in the form of parks and gardens, forest patches and road-side plantation, should be in place.

Pressure on Energy Resources

Any increase in human population or human activities has a subsequent effect on the demands of the population on energy resources. The period of maximum population growth in 1955-2010 was accompanied by an increase in demand for coal to 7.1 billion tonnes, oil (10 million b/d to 88 million b/d), natural gas (8 Tcf to 113 Tcf) and nuclear power (nil to 2,500 TWh).[26] There was also an increase in the consumption of cement, steel, aluminum and other non-renewable resources.

The economic development of a country is often closely linked to its consumption of energy. Currently, India ranks fifth in the world in terms of commercial energy consumption. However, to keep pace with its development objectives for the projected population in 2030, it requires commensurate necessary growth in the requirement of commercial energy, most of which is expected to be from fossil fuels and hydroelectricity. India's vast coal reserves may last for 200 years, but the limited, known oil and natural gas reserves will last only a few more decades. The continued trend of increasing share of petroleum fuels in the consumption of commercial energy will lead to a higher dependence on imports and energy insecurity.

India's energy intensity per unit of GDP is higher than that of Japan, USA and Asia as a whole by 3.7, 1.6 and 1.5 times respectively due to its transition from an agricultural economy to an industrialized society. Most of the machine equipment and infrastructure used in the industrial sector are outdated and inefficient. To improve energy efficiency, the replacement of capital stock, process modification, and other technological changes are necessary. These would require large investments, however, and a scarcity of capital, the high cost of importing new technologies, and the country's shortage of foreign exchange hinder the introduction of energy-efficient technologies. In addition, because of the growing domestic demand for industrial products, investment for expanding production capacity is more financially attractive than investment to reduce costs by improving energy efficiency.

Conclusion

India's growing urban population over the last two decades has increased the expected problems of infrastructure, housing, education and health services, pollution and environmental degradation manifold. In addition, there has been an increase in the crime rates in urban areas due to the increasing urban poor population and socio-economic disparities. Urban sprawl and slums all add to the problems of agglomeration.

The rapidly declining livable status of Indian cities necessitates the requirement for smart and intelligently planned urban dwellings which would be the future centres of growth and prosperity.

These cities and urban areas need to be developed keeping in mind the utmost priorities of the population and the current socio-economic demands of the country. The cities should be planned in such a way that they don't burden the economic condition of the nation and are self-sustainable in all ways—social, economic and cultural. For developing such smart, intelligent future cities it is very necessary that proper metrics be developed. Some of the global cities which have paved the way for such smarter cities are Oslo, Barcelona, Vienna and Melbourne. These cities may be studied to take the best of the innovations they have applied along with the imminent socio-cultural requirements of the Indian scenario. This will help us develop the cities of the future.

NOW YOU KNOW:

- The world urban population is more than 50 per cent of the world population
- In 2013, there were 23 megacities (cities with a population of more than 10 million) with 10 per cent of world population
- Disparity in income and access to food, health and other resources is most wide between the urban poor and non-poor
- 55.3 per cent of India's population is multi-dimensionally poor

- Overcrowding has resulted in increased instances of accidents and crime in the urban areas
- More than 65 per cent of the people in urban Indian households with more than five members live in just one or two room houses
- Overcrowding has also resulted in increased number of slums, with 65 million Indians living in slums in 2014
- Urban sprawl leads to loss of forest land and forest cover of the city
- 71 per cent of the 1.3 billion Indians are mobile subscribers while only 47 per cent of 250 million households have latrines
- Other problems arising out of urbanization are water scarcity and pressure on environment.

3

Measuring Tapes: The Metrics for 21st Century Cities

This chapter traces the birth of democracy in the ancient city of Athens. It then discusses the various definitions for smart cities used worldwide and the proxies which exist in the world in the absence of a global Smart City index. The chapter further details the parameters on which the smartness of a city might be defined and tries to propose a metric for defining a smart city.

Athens, the Ideal City of Ancient Times

Inhabited from about 7,000 years ago, Athens is one of the oldest cities in the world. It was the leading city in ancient Greece in the first millennium BC, and the one to lay the foundations of Western civilization in both architecture and ideology. It has seen numerous ups and downs in its lifecycle—from the early Middle Ages, its rise under the Byzantine Empire and during the period of the Crusades, to its decline under the Ottoman Empire, and its later re-emergence in the 19th century.

Ancient Athens, located at the centre of Greece, was a very small area in the initial years, measuring only about 2 km from east to west. During the Iron Age, around 1200 BC, Athens was the leading centre of trade and prosperity in the region, having a stronghold in the Acropolis—an ancient citadel located on a high rocky outcrop above the city of Athens, and in close proximity to the sea. Such was the glory of Athens that a prominent Greek goddess, Athena, was believed to be its protector and shared her name with the city. She symbolized wisdom, justice, law and knowledge, a set of qualities which were also associated with Athens!

The city was one of the earliest to have a form of democracy—the Athenian democracy under Cleisthenes (510 BC), a radical politician with an aristocratic background. Before the time of Cleisthenes, Athens was ruled by four tribes. These tribes were based on family relationships and dominated the area, enjoying certain rights and privileges:

- Religious rights
- Common burial place
- Property succession
- Reciprocal obligations of help, defence and redress of injuries
- Right to intermarry in the case of orphan daughters and heiresses
- The possession of common property and a treasurer
- Limitation in the male line of descent
- Right to adopt into the family
- Right to elect its chiefs and depose them if required.

The ancient city of Athens was organic in its expansion yet ideal in its times. The city grew from its focal point, the Acropolis, which was also the ceremonial site dotted with temples, which included the Parthenon—the Temple of Athena; to Agora (the central market) and the community spaces for the Athenians. The infrastructure of the ancient town is still an inspiration for modern-day architecture like the building that houses the National Library of Australia, which is a modern version of the Parthenon. Despite many wars and invasions, Athenian buildings and monuments were left largely intact, with even their arch-enemies, the Spartans and the ruthless Persians, refusing to destroy the city's buildings and temples, acknowledging them as civilizational marvels. There was also, of course, the strategic advantage its geographical location played in the region.

But not all invaders were so moved by the city's beauty. It was first sacked by the Heruli, an East Germanic tribe, in 267 AD, who burnt all the public buildings, plundered the city and damaged the Agora, the Acropolis and other monuments. After this, the city was refortified on a smaller scale to the north of the Acropolis, leaving the Agora outside the walls. Athens, under the patronage of Roman emperors such as Nero and Hadrian, remained a centre of learning and philosophy.

Under the Byzantine Empire (roughly 330-1453 AD), the Roman Empire saw an era of Christianization. It was then that the city's old monuments like the Parthenon, the Erechtheion and the Hephaisteion (Theseion) were converted to churches, around the middle centuries of the 1st millennium. The 11th and 12th centuries saw the rise of Byzantine art in Athens, and it was during this period that most of the important churches in and around the city were built. Such was the beauty of the Athenian architecture that when the Ottomans raided Athens in 1458, Mehmed the Conqueror and the Ottoman Sultan, struck by the grandeur of the ancient monuments, issued a firman (royal order) forbidding their looting or destruction.

Modern Athens and its suburbs occupy much of the plain of Attica at the southern tip of Greece. In 1834, it was made the capital of Greece. The building of a modern city began during the reign of Otto I, modern Greece's first king (1833-62). Much of Athens as it is known today dates from the late 19th and the 20th centuries. The distant mountains of Aigaleas, Imittos, Pendeli, and Parnis ranges flank the city on three sides whereas the smaller hills, including the Acropolis lying within the walls of Athens, interrupt the plain. The

Acropolis, at 512 feet (156 m) above sea level, is still the best-known landmark of Athens.

With industrialization, Athens saw a growth in population and a transition from an agrarian economy to one which revolved around services and industries. As early as 1992, 69.2 per cent of the population of Athens was employed in the services industry and only 1.2 per cent in agriculture. Much of its employment in the services industry continues to be provided by the Greek government, which sometimes leads to nepotism in government jobs.

Ancient Athens—the seat of ancient democracy, with supremacy in economy, architecture and military prowess—was an ideal city in all the senses. Modern Athens has all the characteristics of a metropolis but has kept its unique ancient atmosphere intact. The birthplace of the concept of democracy also led to other cities putting together the factors which made it an attractive and smart place to live—the very same factors that we are going to analyse in this chapter, characteristics which will help us in developing a 'Smart City'.

Figure 1: Athens' Agora Market

What Went Wrong and the Way Forward

The 20th century saw a burgeoning global population thanks to better medical care, emerging nations in Asia and Africa, and overall increase in food supply due to modern agriculture. While the world productivity increased, our resource extraction was somehow able to match the growth in demand, albeit unsustainably. What the world was completely unprepared for was the agglomeration of large populations in very small spaces. Cities grew vertically, horizontally and often haphazardly. Delhi's population, for instance, grew almost 150 times in 100 years—a story replicated across most of Asia, Africa, South America and even the developed world.

Urban infrastructure was simply too strained to support such expansion. The situation was worse for the areas which were well inhabited and yet saw rapid growth. Plagued by poor technology and mediocre infrastructure, there was no room to overhaul the well-populated settlements—these cities became the epicentres of the global 'Urbanization Shock'.

Before 1800, almost all income was agricultural. This was dependent largely on a fixed factor of production, land. As production technology became better (which transformed at a very slow rate), wages increased, lowering death rates and increasing birth rates, which led to a growing population. As the population increased, less fertile land was brought into production, lowering per capita income in the rural areas. At the same time, with industrial production catching up, land was no longer the factor of production—it was machines, energy and capital. Soon, a small factory could generate multiple times the wealth that a large farm could—leading to economic-centric urbanization. Hence, as we highlighted in Chapter 1, the principal trouble of urbanization was that it did not happen by choice but by manufactured situations. And as we discussed in Chapter 2, this was plagued by many issues. In fact, by objective comparison, with no better healthcare in urban areas than their rural counterparts—urban life was far more perilous. To take an example, in London, 1580-1799, life expectancy fluctuated between 27 and 28 years (Landers, 1993). At the same time, in England as a whole, which was mostly rural, life expectancy was 35-40 years.

This is the worrisome trend which needs to be focused upon. Urbanization has been a consequence of wealth movement—and pursuit of income rather than a pursuit of happiness. Cities are unplanned entities, dangerously overburdened with human population and under-populated with all other species and plants. If the growth of the human race in the 21st century is going to be anywhere close to the rates that we saw in the previous century, urban planning is going to be the most important designing challenge ever. This is where cities need to become smart.

Let us focus on India for a while. Look at the modern towns which have come up. In no particular order and by no means an exhaustive list, we asked about thirty dozen professionals we met during different lectures and meetings to list all the modern Indian towns or cities which came to their minds and list one quality that they associated with them. Here is what they came up with.

Table 1: Indian cities and their recall value

Town/city	*Area (in sq km)*	*Population*	*Approximate developed area (in sq ft)*	*Key recall value as expressed by the interviewees*
Gurgaon (only the principal inhabited area)	About 250 (1/3rd of the total area)	650,000	1,000 million	Jobs, traffic jams, constructions, crime, concrete
Noida and Greater Noida	500	750,000	1,000 million	Jobs, crime, power cuts, metro
Faridabad	200 (only the newly developed)	200,000 (out of the total 1,400,000)	300 million	Automobiles, bad roads

Town/city	*Area (in sq km)*	*Population*	*Approximate developed area (in sq ft)*	*Key recall value as expressed by the interviewees*
Gandhinagar	177	200,000	150 million	Government offices, good roads
Navi Mumbai	162	1,110,000	1,000 million	Mumbai, local trains, pollution
Naya Raipur	200	About 100,000	20 million	Government offices, highways
Electronic City and Whitefield (Bangalore)	Less than 20. Add about 20 for nearby townships	Floating population. Townships will house about 250,000	40 million	IT, vertical risers, jams
Salt Lake city and Rajharat	60	1,000,000	100 million	Green cover, messy traffic, solar city
Chandigarh	114	1,000,000	50 million	Greenery, no industry, government offices, good roads and good traffic
OMR Chennai	Total about 100	1,000,000	400 million	Traffic issues, jobs, industries
Ambattur Chennai				
Oragadam Chennai				
BKC and Lower Parel	Part of Mumbai	800,000-1,000,000	200 million	Service sector, poor transportation
GIFT City (Ahmedabad)	4	Very small	20 million	Poor access, financial town

A few things emerge. First, India has added about 5,000 million sq ft of new development in about ten years—at an average of 500 million per year, which is phenomenal. Second, most of this has been unplanned and has not been administered by a vision—hence the problems of traffic, power, road and pollution are common.

Third, despite the growth, most of these areas are already under the stress of population. Fourth, most of these places are satellite towns of existing large cities—and hence limited manoeuverability was available to them in terms of innovation. Lastly, and perhaps as a grim reminder, none of them of were holistically planned.

Smart City Parameters

In recent years, many companies and nations have come up with smart city projects and propositions. The projects undertaken by Bellona, Siemens, Philips, Cisco, IBM, etc. are using different technologies for achieving smartness in different aspects of the cities—be it infrastructure, building, transport, energy generation, and greenhouse gas emissions. Figure 2 shows the Smart City model developed by IBM which incorporates the factors of human capital, infrastructure and planning, and management. Even the different stakeholders see the city's smartness in different ways.

In the private sector, city engineers and technology companies view the city as a complex system with multiple layers. Architects and non-governmental organizations (NGOs) see the city in terms of people, social inclusion and a sense of space. Government leaders, on the other hand, view the city in terms of economic growth and new or improved city services supported by policy initiatives designed to effect change.

There is also a difference in the enablers that the different stakeholders seek to achieve in the smart cities. Most smart city constituents agree that it's less expensive and easier to deploy Information and Communication Technology (ICT) than to replace existing city infrastructure. ICT is estimated to help 15 per cent savings in global carbon emissions by 2020, by facilitating innovations as well as social and economic restructuring.[1] Typically, a smart city will have sensors, integrated networks, multiple communication channels and a central monitoring and control station to provide

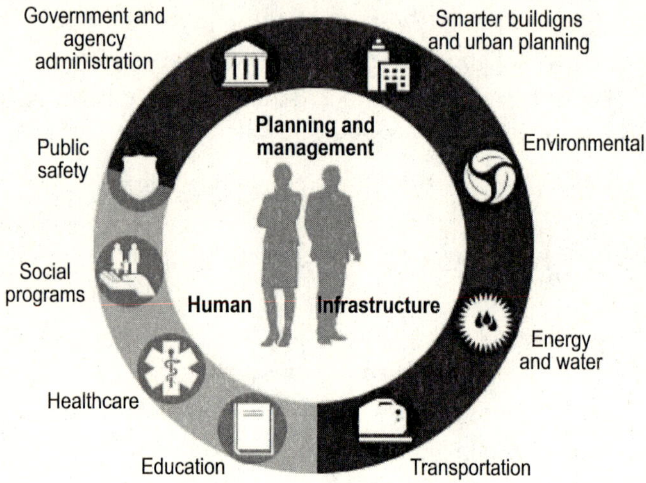

Figure 2: IBM Smart City Model

real time inputs to a control centre on all the public amenities, with information on clean water, public safety, energy, education, health care, traffic, emergencies and legal advice so as to help administrators and citizens manage and respond to emergencies quickly and make life easy.

Mercer's parameters for Quality of Living Survey:

- Economic environment
- Socio-cultural environment
- Medical and health considerations
- Schools and education
- Public services and transport
- Recreation
- Consumer goods
- Housing
- Natural environment.

Cisco defines smart cities as those which mitigate the challenges posed by the increasing population and rapid urbanization, through adoption of scalable solutions that take advantage of information and communication technology, to increase efficiency to reduce costs and enhance the quality of life. Many technology initiatives are being discussed and tried across the globe to integrate physical infrastructure parameters like utilities, transportation, real estate and city services to technology, to enable these cities to transform themselves into smart, intelligent cities. The difference in definitions across geographies, nations and organizations necessitates the need for a Universal Smart City Index which would incorporate the best practices of the developed nations, the problems and challenges of the developing and undeveloped nations, and would be the model for the future smart cities. Some of these factors have already been used to rank cities in terms of their livability and ICT usage.

The Quality of Living Survey by Mercer is one of the most reputed Global Livability Rankings for use by employers, assigning hardship allowances as part of job relocation. Mercer ranks the cities in terms of quality factors such as political, social, economic environment, health considerations and education. However, the index does not include the environmental livability impact. For the cities and buildings to be environmentally friendly, Boyd Cohen, who is an environmental strategist, has provided rankings for the different cities of the world. Boyd Cohen's[i] ranking of the European cities on their smartness and the comparison of the same is made in Table 2.

Table 2: Comparison of Boyd Cohen's smart city ranking to Mercer's ranking for 2012

Mercer Quality of Living Ranking	*City*	*Country*	*Boyd Cohen Smart City Ranking*
9	Copenhagen	Denmark	1
2	Amsterdam	Netherlands	2

[i] Boyd Cohen Ph.D., LEED AP, is a climate strategist helping to lead communities, cities and companies on the journey towards a low carbon economy. He has developed an index for measuring the smartness of cities and his results are shared on http://www.boydcohen.com/smartcities.html and http://www.fastcoexist.com/1679127/the-top-10-smart-cities-on-the-planet

Mercer Quality of Living Ranking	*City*	*Country*	*Boyd Cohen Smart City Ranking*
1	Vienna	Austria	3
40	Barcelona	Spain	4
29	Paris	France	5
19	Stockholm	Sweden	6
38	London	United Kingdom	7
17	Hamburg	Germany	8
16	Berlin	Germany	9
32	Helsinki	Finland	10

The top-ranked Copenhagen in Boyd Cohen's ranking led the Siemens Green City Index[ii] for Europe in 2014 and has also been selected as the European Green Capital for 2014. It has one of the lowest carbon footprints per capita in the world (less than 2 tonnes per capita against 4.3 tonnes per capita globally). In the second-ranked Amsterdam, 67 per cent of the commute is done by cycling or walking instead of the use of motored vehicles. It has an Amsterdam Smart City project, a Public-Private Partnership, focused on using the city as an urban laboratory for the use of open data, new mobility solutions and, ultimately, improved quality of life for all residents and visitors.

Mercer's top-ranked city for living, Vienna, has developed a 'Citizen Solar Power Plant' in partnership with the local energy provider, Wien Energy, which is a crowd-funded project whereby individual citizens can buy half or whole panels and receive a guaranteed returns of 3.1 per cent annually.

[ii] Siemens Green City Index was a research project conducted by the Economist Intelligence Unit with focus on the issue of environmental sustainability in the cities. It helps cities benchmark their performance and share best practices. The series began in 2009 and covers more than 120 cities in Europe, Latin America, Asia, North America and Africa.

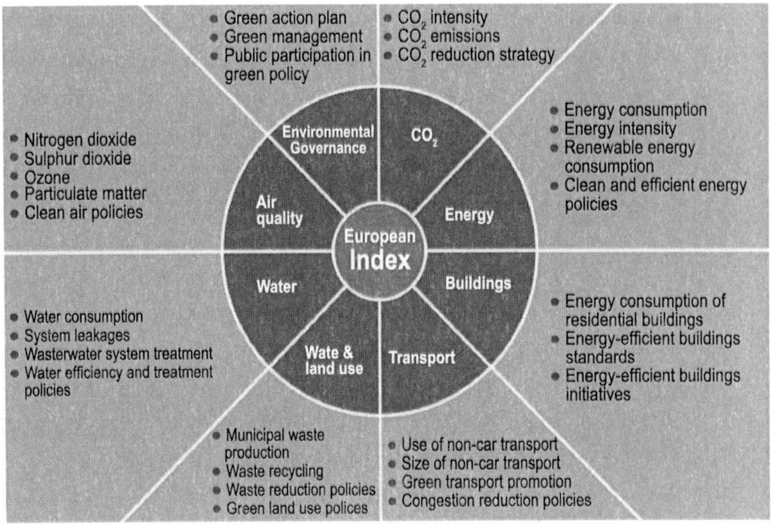

Figure 3: Siemens Green City Index parameters for Europe[2]

Many such innovative projects are being developed and run globally in partnership with energy and technology companies. Compiling them and indexing them on their smartness into a universal index would help measure the smartness of the initiatives in other cities all over the world. The comparison would be irrespective of their socio-economic and political situations.

Environment

One of the main value propositions of a smart city is its reduced impact on the environment. The smart city will have its infrastructure designed efficiently and productively without damaging the environment. Only when the environmental and social objectives are integrated with the city's economic and societal goals will the environmental sustainability of the city be possible. This requires commitment from all the stakeholders of the city, and includes environmental awareness campaigns with institutions and grassroot leaders collaborating on community outreach programmes.

The use of renewable energy resources for electricity generation, heating and cooling of a building, water heating, refrigeration and lighting will help in increasing the environmental sustainability of cities. Sewage disposal facilities and sanitation facilities covering entire city areas is another smart city requirement. Green buildings add to environmental sustenance and reduce the pressure on the resources. In conjunction with all such initiatives in infrastructure development, there is also the requirement of connecting all the systems with ICT for real-time monitoring of the different factors which would define the intelligence of the cities.

The factors which would be measuring the smartness of a city's environmental sustainability would be:

1. Smart Buildings
   a. Percentage of LEED[iii] or BREEAM[iv] sustainability certified buildings in the city
   b. Percentage of buildings/houses having access to sanitation facilities
2. Resources Management
   a. Annual Total Electrical Energy Consumption (in Mega Watt hr or MWh)
   b. Annual electricity consumption per capita (MWh)
   c. Annual Average PM10[v] concentrations (in µg/ cubic metre)
   d. Annual CO_2 emissions per capita (in tonnes)

[iii] LEED (Leadership in Energy and Environmental Design) is an ecology-oriented building certification programme run under the auspices of the US Green Building Council (USGBC).

[iv] BREEAM is the world's foremost environmental assessment method and rating system for buildings, with 250,000 buildings with certified BREEAM assessment ratings and over a million registered for assessment since it was first launched in 1990.

[v] Particulate matter concentrations refer to fine suspended particulates less than 10 microns in diameter (PM10) that are capable of penetrating deep into the respiratory tract and causing significant health damage.

   e. Percentage of renewable energy in the total energy production (in MWh)
3. Waste Recycling
   a. Annual household waste per capita (in kg)
   b. Percentage area covered with sewerage system
   c. Percentage area covered with ICT-enabled sewage disposal system
4. Sustainable Urban Planning
   a. Percentage of Forest Land allotted for urban development (in sq km)
   b. Urban green open areas per capita (in sq m)
   c. Percentage of city area with respect to total metro area
   d. Percentage of unused arable land
   e. Arable land per capita (in sq m)
   f. Percentage of houses left vacant

Mobility and Transport

Road traffic congestion is a chronic problem in the cities of the world currently, which the smart cities seek to reduce or resolve. Building transport infrastructure, improving public transport facilities and inducing road culture are some areas in which the governments need to work. These include the development of bus rapid transit systems, metro rails and mono rails to reduce the use of private vehicles and link the growing urban ends of the cities. As development of a mass rapid transit system is capital intensive, the government should try to implement Intelligent Transport Systems (ITS) which are much cheaper and help turn the existing systems smarter. These may include road sensors, mobile phone sensors, traffic classification and prediction, traffic signal management and other such parameters.

ITS applications can help in traffic management by:

1. Intersection control: For deciding the total signal cycle and the split of green times among different flows at intersections

2. Accident detection: Pinpointing locations of accidents or vehicle breakdowns
3. Monitoring: Pollution and road quality monitoring
4. Historical traffic data: For current and future developments.

ITS applications for commuters would aid them with congestion maps, travel time estimates, public transport information, vehicle management and accident handling. All such data would be provided by static sensors, mobile sensors, and hybrid sensors which would relay information regarding chaotic traffic, public transport real-time information, empty parking spaces, detection of road anomalies, etc. The technologies used would be RFID, GPS on vehicles and smart phones, images and videos and acoustic sensors. Social media, with the quantum of information that it generates, might be helpful in pooling the data and providing it in comprehensible formats. Incentives can be devised for commuters and social media users to provide correct information—or there could be some games or apps through which the data is collected.

The criteria to measure the smartness or the intelligence of the transport system could be as follows:

1. Clean-energy Transport
   a. Percentage of clean-energy transport use (electric train, subway / metro, tram, cable railway, electric taxis, bicycling)
   b. Percentage of bio-diesel or battery-operated vehicles
2. Road Density
   a. Road density per sq km of city
3. Travel Speed
   a. Average time required to travel 1 km by motorized transport
4. Accidents
   a. Incidences of pedestrian / non-motorized users accidents or deaths
   b. Incidences of road accidents

5. Public Transport Usage
   a. Average trip cost (per km)
   b. Average number of changes in a public transport to reach a destination (say 10 km)
   c. Percentage of public transit trips / Total trips
   d. Number of people travelling in public transport per 100,000 inhabitants
6. Access to real-time information
   a. Percentage of ICT-enabled public transport to offer real-time information to passengers

Use of ICT along with good traffic infrastructure provides a congestion-free traffic environment to commuters and ensures their safety and security while travelling. The challenges in the developing countries and developed countries would be different for solving the problems which require innovation in technologies and systems, according to local problems and challenges.

Governance

Policies form an important role in ensuring prosperity of a city and in defining its smartness, as they govern strategic thinking and conscious planning policies. They govern the developmental activities of a region or city as well as the investments a particular city may attract in comparison to others. Special Economic Zones and the ease of Public-Private Partnerships enhance infrastructure development, restoration of a city's historic core and the development of tourism industries.

For the city to be smart, it is imperative that the services be essentially provided online. Essential services like passport or driving licence issuance or applications should be offered online to keep administrative services on track. Mobile penetration has done wonders to include the common citizen in the technological race, but services like broadband or Wi-Fi are yet to connect many regions. Creating Wi-Fi hotspots, revamping public spaces, rehabilitation of architecture and historic landmarks, recreation of the street as part of the soul of the city, shaping a 'sense of place' with monuments, city squares, marketplaces and streetscapes as open venues for arts and cultural expression, and monitoring all these with ICT, are part of infrastructure development and integrating them with governance. It can also include monitoring and control of pollution by using sensors and ICT.

E-governance is a basic component of a smarter society as it provides a strategic interface between the local government and the public. The focus here is on facilitating the use of integrated e-services between the city governments and the stakeholders, which in turn impacts the competitiveness of the city, the citizen's participation, and their engagement in policy-making processes for driving change. Implementation of an e-governance system provides better services to citizens, more effective government, enhanced local democracy and improved decision-making processes.

ICT in the present day is showing a shift towards community-based interactive models of services, participation and innovation. Nations, regions and organizations are being assessed by their e-readiness index, viewed as the degree to which a community is prepared to participate in the networked world. It mainly measures the links and interactions within government, between government and citizens, and within and between NGOs and communities. This empowers them in the decision-making process beyond the traditional role of being a mere service provider, extending to overall social and economic urban development. This will make them more proactive and innovative.

The following governance factors would determine smart governance:

1. Online Services
   a. Percentage share of online procedures performed to total procedures
   b. Percentage of the digitally literate population
2. Infrastructure
   a. Internet coverage
3. Open Government
   a. Total number of open data sets (excluding regulations/laws) with information for the last three years
   b. Number of publicly available applications utilizing open data

Economy

The ITC[vi] e-Choupal infrastructure created for farmers to have access to information regarding prices and agriculture-related information, is a very good example of how technology can transform the lives of stakeholders by increasing their income, hence boosting the economy. The system was configured for the farmers to make them productive and to make the supply chain efficient—which was a win-win for both the farmers and ITC.

The Amul cooperative is one of the largest profit-making cooperatives in India, which discards middlemen and has an efficient supply chain. The cooperative today uses smart logistics which helps them in managing the inventory of their milk stocks without the requirement for packaging, by directly supplying milk through dispensers located at the milk counters. The system also reduces inventory and storage costs involved with perishable milk products.

Such innovations in manufacturing, production and agricultural spaces could be used to reduce the burden on the economy and make the cities self-sustainable. Removing middlemen would result in the

---

[vi] ITC is a leading FMCG company in India which produces a variety of food and processed food products.

manufacturers and the consumers getting the benefit of the price control—not the aggregators. This would also help in the efficient management of supply chain and logistics, leading to a reduction in the wastage of goods and products.

The factors to measure smartness in an economy would be:

1. Employment and Opportunities
    a. Rate of unemployment per 100,000 inhabitants
    b. Number of new opportunity-based start-ups in the past one year
    c. Percentage GDP invested in R&D in the private sector
2. Productivity
    a. Gross exports
    b. Gross imports
    c. Gross regional product per capita (in INR)
3. Local and Global Connection
    a. Percentage of ICT companies based in local clusters
    b. Opportunities for vertical integration and value addition (average level of vertical integration/value addition achieved)
4. Innovation
    a. Number of local events for citizens' participation in innovation
    b. Number of innovative ideas per capita (innovation coefficient)
    c. Number of international congresses and fairs attendees
5. Human Resource
    a. Percentage of labour force up-skilled in the past one year
    b. Customized vocational curriculum (number of customized curriculum and their student count)
    c. Inclusiveness of the economy (employment rate amongst women and underprivileged sections of society).

Society

Apart from ICT implementation in the societal processes, there would be the necessary integration of societal values by imparting education and promoting creativity and innovation. Education is an important facilitator in enhancing the status of society, and smart schools instead of traditional schools would be the requirement of the future smart cities. Smart schools can not only improve the physical performance of the city but also prepare students for life in the increasingly complex and the technological world of the future.[3] These smart schools will not only manage their energy consumption, security, communication and transportation intelligently, but will also have intelligent systems to help connect departments to enable virtual and online learning.

Another important aspect of smart cities would be their corruption factor. Corruption has existed in cities and societies since ancient times and takes any form like bribery, graft and nepotism. A corruption-free business environment and culture is imperative for a smart city, as corrupt politicians, citizens and middlemen will not let the societal benefits percolate to the citizens of the city.

Smartness of a society would be measured by:

1. Integration
   a. Percentage of Internet-connected households
   b. Gini coefficient of inequality
   c. Percentage implementation of ICT in e-participation and voting
2. Education
   a. Number of students per 1,000 inhabitants
   b. Number of university graduates per 1,000 inhabitants
   c. Number of unemployed per 100,000 college graduates
   d. Number of schools/colleges with online and virtual learning
   e. Number of schools/colleges with connected campuses
3. Corruption
   a. Number of cases registered with the vigilance department
   b. Number of convictions for corruption per 100,000 population
4. Creativity
   a. Percentage of labour force (LF) engaged in creative industries

b. Number of artists, architects, craftsmen, painters and other such creative full-time professionals practising in the city.

Equity and Justice

Equitable development would be an important factor for smart cities to foster equitable, healthy, and sustainable communities. Equitable Development strategies are 'ones that help low-income, minority, tribal and overburdened communities to participate in and benefit from decisions that shape their neighbourhoods and regions'.[4] The Medellin Declaration of World Urban Forum's 2014 session argues that the integration of equity into the development agenda can help to better address '*deep structural problems and challenges of cities*'.[5]

Equity comes from the concept of moral equality—'treating everyone as equal', the core of human development approach. Dr Amartya Sen, Nobel laureate, the pioneer of the concept, stated that 'human development, as an approach, is concerned with what I take to be the basic development idea: namely, advancing the richness of human life, rather than the richness of the economy in which human beings live, which is only a part of it.'[6] This would entail the application of equity-based urban development policies and initiatives to maximize equality. It has two important aspects—'generation of economic value' and 'to increase fairness'. Smart cities as future centres of entrepreneurship and economic activities have an important role in committing to gender equity, economic equity, social equity and social justice.

Factors to measure equity and the justice-readiness of a smart city:

1. Gender equity
   a. Number of households with working women
   b. Number of women at top management
   c. Share of women in local political positions
2. Urban poor
   a. Constructed roof area per urban poor
   b. Percentage of people living in slums

   c. Incidence of child labour, child abuse or molestation and child trafficking
   d. Variance in life expectancy at birth of BPL population and non-BPL population
3. Law and order
   a. Number of cases registered per 100,000 inhabitants
   b. Number of cases resolved
   c. Number of cases pending for more than one year
   d. Percentage of cases pending for more than one year, where the victim was BPL or from a socially backward segment (burden of poverty in justice delivery).

Quality of Life

Quality of life is the general well-being of individuals and societies, and is measured in the context of international development, healthcare, politics and employment. The standard indicators of the quality of life include not only wealth and employment but also the built environment, physical and mental health, education, recreation and leisure time, and social belonging along with freedom, human rights and happiness.[7] Mercer's 'Quality of Living Survey' and the *Economist's* 'Where-to-be-born index' measure and rank the cities globally according to these factors.

Smart cities are visualized as centres for business growth with high performance, environmental sustainability, economic competitiveness and quality of city services. All these factors also result in a better quality of life in such cities with a highly qualified, educated and mature population, citizens and government. Smart cities, with their better governance and public services, will be better equipped to provide safety, security and health infrastructure to their citizens, making them attractive places to live in.

ICT implementation in urban security systems can reduce the crime incidences in a city by 80 per cent and criminal activity by 35 per cent.[8] This urban security system would include aerial drones, CCTV cameras, gunshot sensors, automatic number plate recognition cameras, city-wide emergency phone network, public address speakers, vehicle location application, mobile data terminals and PDAs for police officers.

Factors:

1. Culture and Well-being
    a. Percentage of inhabitants with access to potable water
    b. Percentage of inhabitants with access to sanitation
    c. Percentage of inhabitants lacking electricity
    d. Theatrical and musical performances per year (or per capita)
    e. Sports and leisure activities per year (or per capita)
    f. Household spending on recreational activities (percentage)
    g. Percentage of municipal budget allocated to cultural events
2. Safety
    a. Number of violent crimes
    b. Number of homicides
    c. Number of kidnapping and abduction
    d. Number of crimes against women
3. Health
    a. Death rates due to diarrhoea, typhoid
    b. Death rates due to HIV
    c. Death rates related to heart disorders
    d. Death rates due to respiratory ailments
    e. Life expectancy at birth.

Conclusion

Smart cities would be the future of nations with their enhanced standards of living and quality of life. Most of them can be created by improving the infrastructure or by implementation of ICT which would integrate the existing physical factors with technology to make them efficient and real-time. Such real-time information would ease the lives of the citizens, the government machinery and the businesses

—making the smart cities attractive places to live in and invest. Intelligent and capable networks and communication technologies will be critical to the basic functioning of such cities globally—be it governance, amenities or services—in a world increasingly defined by new digital infrastructures and the interactions they empower. Such developments require a broad dialogue between stakeholders from all sectors of business and society. These also need innovative models of development which will be discussed in the next chapter.

NOW YOU KNOW:

- Athens was one of the earliest cities to have any form of democracy
- There are many indices to measure a city's livability or greenness like Mercer's Quality of Living Survey and Siemens' Green City Index
- Technology companies like IBM, Bellona, Philips have tried to define a smart city in terms of technology, but it is not a holistic approach to smart city modelling
- Boyd Cohen's smart city ranking is one of the most comprehensive rankings developed yet for smart cities. It ranks Copenhagen as the smartest city
- Environment friendliness of a city is one of the agreed measures of a smart city
- The smartness of a city is defined by its infrastructure development, environmental impact, IT integration and access to societal needs like health, education and justice.

4

Beyond Just Smartness: Making Cities of Wisdom and Happiness

Three Case Studies of Planned Cities in India

Jamshedpur

Jamshedji Nusserwanji Tata,[i] an Indian pioneer industrialist, while attending a lecture by Thomas Carlyle[ii] in Manchester, was struck by a bold declaration:

> *'The nation which gains control of iron soon acquires the control of gold.'*

This gave him the idea of building a steel plant and he started his search for a site which was rich in iron, coal, limestone and water. The search took his team to inhospitable regions of modern-day Madhya Pradesh, Chhattisgarh, Jharkhand and Odisha where they spent three years exploring. Then in 1907, they came across the village of Sakchi in the dense forests of Chota Nagpur Plateau. The

---

[i] Jamshedji Nusserwanji Tata founded the Tata Group, India's biggest conglomerate.

[ii] Thomas Carlyle (4 December 1795-5 February 1881) was a Scottish philosopher, satirical writer, essayist, historian and teacher during the Victorian era.

village, located near the confluence of the rivers Subarnarekha and Kharkhai, was rich in all the parameters they had zeroed in on and was decided upon as the site for the steel plant, the first one in India.

The construction of the steel plant and the city began in 1908. Jamshedji envisioned the city as one having all the comforts and conveniences of a modern industrial city and hence insisted on planning it well. In addition to the steel plant and the residential buildings, the city was to have public leisure places, wide streets with shady trees, open spaces for lawns and gardens, areas earmarked for developing sports activities and religious buildings—all planned in advance. When the first ingot was rolled out in the steel plant in 1912, it was not just the start of industrial India but also a milestone in the history of planned cities of India.

The brilliance in the planning and development of the city of Jamshedpur is reflected in its current status in the Indian scenario. It is the largest and the most populous city in Jharkhand and a major industrial region in eastern India. The city boasts of being the greenest and the most well-planned city in India. It has acres of parks and gardens dotting the city, with the most noted one being the Jubilee Park, spread over an area of 37.75 acres in the heart of the city. The park is known for its collection of varieties of roses and other flowers, and hosts an exhibition every year during the month of March. It also has the Tata Steel Zoological Park located near the steel plant that houses varieties of animals and birds.

The city's Tata Main Hospital is more than a century old and forms the backbone of the city's medical infrastructure along with other modern hospitals and medical facilities. This city has close to 200 schools and 13 colleges apart from renowned institutes like the Xavier Labour Relation Institute (XLRI), National Institute of Technology (NIT), Shavak Nanavati Technical Institute (SNTI), R.D. Tata Technical Education Centre and M.G.M. Medical College and Hospital (associated to Tata Main Hospital). The city is well regarded for producing hundreds of engineers, doctors and managers every year and enjoys a high literacy rate of 85.94 per cent. It is also known for its world-class sporting facilities and houses the renowned JRD Tata Sports Complex, which is one of the best sports complexes in India.

Jamshedpur is a good example of how visionary thinking and planning ahead of time can result in a world-class city with all required amenities in place. Despite being a major industrial centre housing many of the Tata group of companies and other corporates, it has managed to maintain a balance with the environment. Jamshedpur was declared the seventh cleanest city of India for the year 2010[iii] and has been predicted as the 84th fastest growing city in the world for 2006-2020.

Navi Mumbai

From the crowded station of the Chhatrapati Shivaji Terminus (CST)—a UNESCO World Heritage Site—local trains for two suburban lines can be caught. One is the Central Line which connects the historic site to the centrally located Kalyan and bifurcates from there towards the northeast and southeast directions. The other is the Harbour Line running from CST to Panvel, crossing the beautiful mangroves and swamps to reach the eastern trans-harbour of Mumbai and the city of Navi Mumbai.

Navi Mumbai is one of the largest planned townships in the world. It was built in the 1970s to ease the increasing congestion in Mumbai city, which was fast reaching its physical expansion limits. It was to serve as an alternative dwelling place for the millions of people who dreamt of making Mumbai their home. The city stretched along 150 km of the Konkan coast and was built on land acquired from 86 villages spread over an area of 159.54 sq km. A major part of the city covers portions from adjacent Thane (Thane taluka) and Raigad (Panvel and Uran) districts. The City and Industrial Development

---

[iii] http://pib.nic.in/archieve/others/2010/may/d2010051103.pdf

Corporation (CIDCO) was formed on 17 March 1971 to supervise the planning, development and maintenance of Navi Mumbai, which in turn developed the city as 14 smaller townships.

Despite plans to open railway stations in all the 14 towns, and the construction and opening of Vashi Bridge and the Sion-Panvel Expressway to the public, the city had a lukewarm response initially. Of the 14 planned towns, only three—Vashi, Nerul and CBD Belapur—had housing, schools and community centre roads till 1990. The opening of a wholesale agricultural produce market at Vashi, and the construction of the Mankhurd-Vashi commuter railway line in the early 1990s, led to a growth in economic activities and the subsequent growth in population, as well as the development of the other towns of Navi Mumbai. Post-1990, CIDCO allocated private builders to take care of housing projects, and concentrated only on basic infrastructure and their maintenance. In 1992, local self-government started with the Navi Mumbai Municipal Corporation (NMMC) being constituted for maintenance of nine developed nodes of the city: CBD Belapur, Nerul, Vashi, Turbhe, Kopar Khairane, Ghansoli, Airoli, Digha, and Sanpada.

The city is connected with Mumbai through the Mumbai suburban railway network and has stations at all the major railway junctions. Other modes of transport include the Brihanmumbai Electric Supply and Transport (BEST) and the Navi Mumbai Municipal Transport (NMMT) buses, with autorickshaws being the preferred mode of transportation. The city also boasts of the most advanced port of India, the Jawaharlal Nehru Port, which is well connected by road to Mumbai and all parts of India. The port handles 65 per cent of India's container traffic. The city is also slated to have its own international airport in the proposed Navi Mumbai International Airport to be built in the Panvel area.

The city has excellent supply of electricity from various private and public players and has numerous flyovers, broad roads and parking lots. The connectivity to the city of Mumbai is only through two road links and a single rail line which leads to huge traffic congestion. It is well served with utility services, banks, restaurants, malls, multiplexes and supermarkets. It also has an international cricket ground—D.Y. Patil Stadium in Nerul, which is one of the best cricket stadiums in India and has already hosted a few IPL T-20 matches.

Table 1: Land use pattern for Navi Mumbai[iv]

Land Use	*Area (sq km)*	%
Residential	132.68	38.64
Commercial	5.75	1.67
Industrial	43.14	12.55
Port area	22.7	6.6
Wholesale markets and warehousing	4.6	1.33
Regional parks	66.54	19.35
Institutional	1.09	0.31
Fishing & Allied	3.44	1
Transportation	29.73	8.65
No Development Zone (incl. Defence)	34.03	9.9
Total	343.7	100

The offices of many national and international IT and software companies are located in the city's numerous software parks. The proposed Navi Mumbai SEZ located in Dronagiri and Kalamboli are expected to further boost commercial growth and generate employment in the city. A mini SEZ is also being developed near the proposed airport which will be developed specially for the IT and ITES industry. It is proposed to have an integrated township of residential and commercial buildings, education institutes and recreation facilities. The city gets registrations for around 500 new

[iv] *The Making of Navi Mumbai* by Annapurna Shaw

and start-up companies in and around the region on a monthly basis. With so much development taking place in and around the city, it is all set to emerge as the new hub for newly incorporated companies and start-ups.

Naya Raipur

Naya Raipur is located 17 km away from the current capital city of Raipur in the Raipur district of Chhattisgarh. It is proposed to be the new capital city of the state to ease the pressure of the population increase and urbanization on the current capital city. Spread over 80 sq km of area, it has acquired land from 41 villages, out of which 27 villages serve as the core city. Almost half of the acquired land areas for Naya Raipur would be used for constructing public amenities—parks, roads, public conveniences, canals, green belts; and for reforestation. Twenty-three per cent is earmarked for educational institutes, government offices and public auditoriums and the remaining 30 per cent for residential and commercial buildings.

The city is proposed to be home to around 4.5 million people, as against the current population of 0.6 million in Raipur city. The satellite city would be a servicing hub to the manufacturing industry, the information technology and bio-technology sectors and serve as a centre for economic activities—be it trade, hospitality, cultural services, medical services or educational facilities. The authority constituted to supervise the planning and development was named Naya Raipur Development Authority (NRDA). The city is slated to have 225 km of roads, of which construction for 71 km has already been started. The city will be generating about 2.2 lakh jobs with an assumed workforce participation rate of 40 per cent. Modelled after Chandigarh, the planned capital city will have the following areas and buildings:

- Software technology park
- Gems and jewellery and other similar industries
- Business offices

- Health, education and research services
- Regional recreational activities
- Nandanvan zoo and safari
- Shaheed Veer Narayan Singh International Cricket Stadium
- 7-star and 5-star hotels
- 18-hole golf course and golf villas
- Museums
- Art gallery and library
- Garden
- Botanical garden
- Lakes
- Underground water system.

The city would be one of the first smart cities in India to be planned and developed on sustainability, where the emphasis is on both world-class physical infrastructure and social infrastructure. The city is planned to be constructed in three phases, of which the first one began in 2007 and is currently ongoing. Naya Raipur is slated to be completed by 2031.

Planned City and Smart City

A planned city is generally one which has areas earmarked for specific development—residential, commercial or industrial and for public infrastructure and open spaces if any. It is more inclined towards achieving the economic sustenance of the city. The last three examples of Jamshedpur, Navi Mumbai and Naya Raipur illustrate the numerous benefits of developing a city in a planned and phased manner.

Smart cities, with their balanced focus on physical, environmental and economic sustenance, need to be developed on similar lines as planned cities. Such cities will have planned infrastructure, efficiently designed energy resources and usage, ICT connectivity, sources for recreation and entertainment, avenues for education and research and smart buildings with reduced construction material. This will require integration of research, policy and construction technologies.

The basic components of a smart city have already been discussed in detail in the earlier chapter. They are listed in Table 2.

Table 2: Smart city components—their significance and measurement

Components	*Significance*	*Measurement*
SMART Infrastructure	• Includes transport and real estate • Efficient and optimal design • Sustainable • Integrated with technology	• Reduction of construction material • Reduction of emission • High speed, low accident transport
SMART Energy and Water Management	• Energy sources are limited and depleting • Renewable sources are not yet fully utilized • Potable water is scarce	• Extent of smart grid • Use of renewable resources • Water runoff and harvesting • Water supply
SMART Information and Communication Systems	• Use of technology to ease systems and processes • Real-time data transfer and monitoring	• Extent of ICT usage in public systems • Smart metering for controlling the usage
SMART Education and Research	• Literacy is an important societal element • Level of education reflects the societal development • Research is important for innovation and development	• Extent of literacy amongst the population • Connected educational institutions • Participation of population in research and innovation

Components	*Significance*	*Measurement*
SMART Building and Building Materials	• Buildings contribute 37 per cent of GHG emissions • Proper building materials reduce the emissions and energy usage of buildings • Proper design is important	• Heating and cooling systems • Building certification • Building material usage • Retro-fittings in the buildings
SMART Recreation and Public Spaces	• Open public spaces promote citizens' well-being • Recreation is important for stress-free life	• Extent of open spaces in city • Land usage pattern • Recreational activities and events in the cities • Stress-related ailment incidence
SMART Economy, Entrepreneurship and Financial Systems	• The Indian economy has slowed down in past decade • Manufacturing industry in a downward spiral • High rate of unemployment	• Tax waivers for creation of jobs and contribution to the economy • Employment creation both for skilled and unskilled labour • Creation of cities would help in creating employment
SMART Healthcare	• Urbanization has led to high incidence of stress-related ailments • Healthcare should be available to all	• Common diseases and their incidence • Healthcare accessibility
SMART Environment and Waste Management	• Waste management in cities through traditional methods of dumping in landfills • Rapidly increasing pollution levels and GHG emissions	• Levels of PM10 particulate matters within WHO guidelines • Green cover and open space for the city • UV-treated waste management system

Components	*Significance*	*Measurement*
SMART Governance	• Local governance accountability is essential for improving the situation of urban amenities • Transparency in the process and system crucial for making the system corruption free	• Open information policy by the government • Integration of ICT in the government processes • Making systems and processes citizen friendly
SMART Security and Safety	• Rapid increase in homicidal and terrorist incidents in the last three decades • Indian cities fare badly when it comes to women and children safety • Incidence of rapes, murders, thefts increasing in urban areas	• Innovative solutions to train citizens, especially women, in safety measures • Special squad for handling incidents of rape and murders • Monitoring of cities with helplines, GPS, CCTV and traffic police

The construction of smart cities would require urban planners, architects, energy scientists, engineers, construction workers, transport planners, road builders, nano-material scientists, economists, social infrastructure planners, etc.

While the smart cities are in operation, there will be demands for industrial workers, skill developers, teachers, professors, healthcare givers, utility managers, security services, transport services, hospitality industry, supply chain management, energy managers, water managers, waste disposal experts, etc.

Smart cities would expand over time to include more and more catchment areas, a large part of which shall be rural or semi-urban. This will push the demand for skilled workers, agro technologists, rural development experts, ecologists, social scientists, governance and administration experts, policy analysts, lawyers, etc.

In education and research, there would be bachelors and masters courses covering city designing, architecture, aesthetics, ecology, smart building, nano-material science, social infrastructure, education, medicine, hospitality management, rural management, agri-business, urban legal frameworks, etc. Additionally, there would be certificate programmes in skill development and skill upgradation in electrical works, construction, plumbing, logistics, driving, as well as industry-specific training.

Each smart city would be built around a critical product or service, e.g. electronic goods, washing machines, mobile phones, software services, BPO, agro processing, fishing and processing, ship building, soaps, textiles, education, tourism.

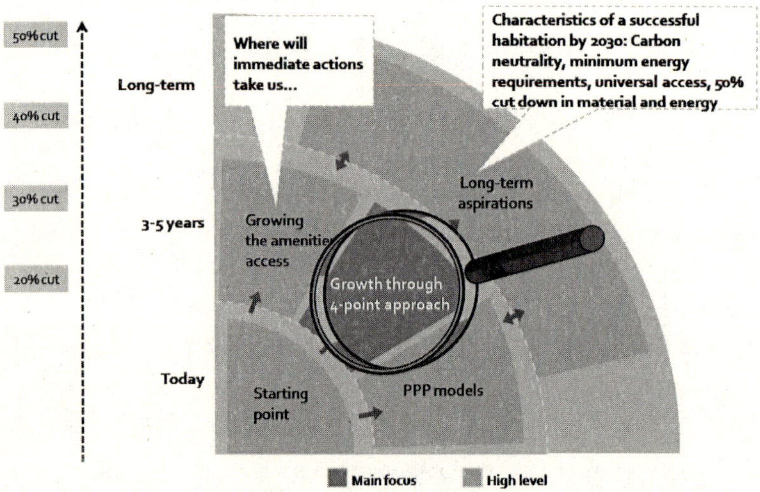

Figure 1: Focus areas in development of smart cities

Table 3: Land usage in smart cities

Land use Type	*Traditional cities (in %)*	*Present cities (in %)*	*Smart cities (in %)*	*Emerging trends and concepts for future development*
Residential	40-60 %	20%-40%	10%-20%	High-rise development within 50 storeys
Commercial	5%	5%	5%-10%	Commercial spaces will be integrated within residential spaces as multiple nodes
Social amenities	10%-15%	10%	5-10%	Technology advancement resulting in less usage of space
Industrial	10%-20%	30%-50%	10%-15%	Automated industries will go vertical and pollute less
Roads	10%-20%	15%-20%	5%-10%	Less vehicular roads, more pedestrian movement, walk to work with multiple node concept
Water bodies	5%	5%	10%-20%	More spaces covered by water bodies—for harvesting, reuse and recycle, energy generation
Recreational spaces	5%-10%	10%	30-40%	More green spaces, integrated development, land-based recreation

But a smart city goes beyond just numeric planning and balancing.

Beyond Smart: Cities of Wisdom and Happiness

A city is a habitable area physically demarcated by geographical boundaries. It has a population demography, infrastructure, civic amenities, governance, judicial systems and political system. These are the physical components of a city. There is another component of a city which is purely subjective. It pertains to the soul, the community, and the cultural, social and ethical values of the city.

Today, cities are characterized by booming population density, with millions of humans literally stacked on top of each other—in vertical structures. Cities, especially in Asia, can pack up to 50,000 people in a single square kilometre. Much of the urban lifestyle is about reaching office, school or business on time, weaving through congested traffic, living and working in artificially cocooned and air-conditioned environments.

Table 4: Average time taken between workplace and home

City	*Average commute time back and forth from office to home*
Mumbai	95 minutes
Delhi	87
Bangalore	80
New York	63

Uneven pricing and unplanned zoning have led to homes being far away from work, and sometimes even farther away from commercial and entertainment centres.

A resident of Mumbai on an average takes 95 minutes to travel back and forth between home and office—about 10 per cent of the total time awake is hence spent on the road. The number is not different from one megacity to another. The *Economist*, in a 2011 research, had discovered that commute time is one of the primary reasons for unhappiness in the urban professional population.

In most of the developing world, rising rent rates, soaring pollution, job stress, and falling health standards coupled with the constant hassle between essential supply of clean water and electricity are a source of risk and hence fear. The truth is cities are being reduced to emotionally rudderless entities, with little to observe and admire, and becoming a breeding ground for four concerns—mistrust, fear, anxiety and aversion.

How to replace these concerns to support human development is the key question to address in designing modern cities. How do we convert despair to hope, fear to belief, anxiety to ease and human aversion to compassion and love. These are the soft measures which need to be part of urban planning. This is what we term as 'city with a soul'—a city which offers not just amenities, but also happiness; not just economics, but also values. How do we measure this?

There is a difference, however, between measuring a city's happiness and its prosperity. While a fast-paced city like Bangalore would have a higher income level for its working population, the problems of high cost of living, congestion, traffic problems and long travelling distances would undermine the positives of the city. Further, the frequency of accidents, crime and socio-economic disparities is of greater concern to the city's population than the industrial and economic prosperity of the city. These are the reasons why a person might like to work in a city but might not prefer to live in the same city.

A city's well-being can be defined by a happiness index. Bhutan has prepared a comprehensive study on Gross Happiness Index (GHI) and has made it a part of its social policy on Gross National Happiness (GNH). It comprises socio-economic factors such as psychological well-being, standard of living, good governance, health, education, community vitality, cultural diversity, ecological diversity and time. Some of these factors are subjective, which are measured by proxy factors like level of income, career performance and social and personal relationships. The GNH has six strategic objectives—

1. Setting an alternative framework of development
2. Providing indicators to sectors to guide development

3. Allocating resources in accordance with targets and GNH screening tools
4. Measuring people's happiness and well-being
5. Measuring progress over time
6. Comparing progress across the country.

CWI: City Wisdom Index

Emanating from the need to transform planned cities into smart cities, and further, to make smart cities into cities of wisdom and happiness, there is a need to revise the performance matrix of cities. We will call it the City Wisdom Index which will be a multi-dimensional weighted average along parameters of sustainability which go beyond just the finances, and along investment beyond conventional assets of infrastructure, health and education. Our stress would be on developing a holistic and multi-dimensional indexing for cities which can be a benchmark to rate one city against another, and more importantly, guide the development planning in urban design.

A New Vision for Cities

Based on our discussions with town planners, environmentalists, architects, social workers and public policy makers, we have formed a profile for smart cities of the 21st century in a 10-point vision:

1. Smart cities have to be based on a core economic activity which adds value to the national economic objective and at the same time provides quality infrastructure to all at affordable prices.
2. Smart cities preserve and protect local culture and enhance it to bridge understanding between societies and people.
3. Smart cities are areas of equity of opportunities for all segments of the society. They provide an enviornment conducive to enterprise and to original research to develop new products and services.

4. Smart cities provide quality infrastructure, healthcare and education to all.
5. Smart habitations are zones of environment protection and their hallmark is to reduce, recycle and reuse along with the use of clean energy.
6. Smart habitations are a reflection of human diversity, different regions and even nations—they are zones of biodiversity and celebrate their multiplicity.
7. Smart cities are based on effective and cost-efficient usage of information technology and communication systems for smart governance and smart citizenship. They also promote electronic monetary transactions.
8. Smart habitations provide equal justice to all and dignity to all economic classes—treating all labour and professionals with respect.
9. Smart habitations co-exist with nearby rural areas and provide value additions to the lives and professions of these rural area—in the form of human development and value-addition activities.
10. Smart cities are clean, transparent, provide good governance, have zero corruption and are places which give happiness to the residents and visitors alike.

Developing a New Measurable Index

The issue is how to capture the above ten points into a single measurable index which can guide and rate cities—what we call the City Wisdom Index.

The figure on the next page shows a 10-dimensional City Wisdom Index based on the vision we discussed. Let us delve further:

1. **Economics:** Cities have to be designed around core economic activities which are cornerstones of job creation, research, skill development and general wealth creation in the area. This is the work horse of habitation. The economic sustainability of a city can be judged along the sub-parameters like:

Parameter	*Score (1= lowest, 10 = highest)*
Gross production of city in terms of net economic movement in Rs per year	
Per capita income level of the city in terms of income per capita per year	
Alignment of the economic production of the city with the overall vision	
Supporting **skill development** for growth	
Research and innovation environment towards economic activities to ensure future growth path	
Export versus import balance	
Average Economic Sustainability Score	Average of above

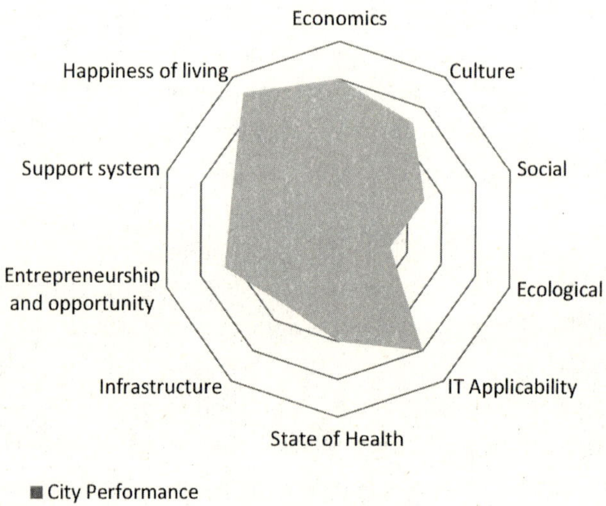

Figure 2: A typical City Wisdom Index based on a 10-dimensional rating

2. **Cultural Sustainability:** Cities need not become deathbeds of local culture—human civilizations are founded in strongly bonded cultural ties, avenues and reasons for community engagement where humans share ideas, visions, fears, friendships and emotions. Cultural sustainability is the **relationship and belongingness** factor of the city.

Parameter	*Score (1= lowest, 10 = highest)*
Performance of avenues for cultural exchange such as music, dance, creative pursuits and sports	
State of democratic values and spirit of scientific enquiry and the freedom of media and independence of critical analysis	
Universal awareness of the national, international and planetary issues in the citizens of the city	
Spirit of **service and compassion** in the citizens—measured by simple measures such as donations from salaries, CSR activities, donation of organs and blood, state of care centres for old, orphans and even animals	
Frequency of **community celebration** of diverse festivals and carnivals in the city	
State of multiversity of the city, composition of its inhabitants and sense of global citizenship	
Average Cultural Sustainability Score	Average of above

3. **Social Sustainability:** Cities have to emerge as centres of high service levels of human development and public good—basic amenities for equal development need to be universal and economically feasible for all. Social sustainability represents the **equity of opportunity** for all in a city design.

Parameter	*Score (1= lowest, 10 = highest)*
State of education for different economic classes and for including a diversity of learning streams—measurable in standard terms such as teacher-student ratios, quality parameters, access issues and gaps between high and low income social assets	
Safety and security situation of the city—measured in terms of perceived risk, actual crime, remedies and response rate, and security for risk-prone segments like women, underprivileged and children	
Justice and dignity to the citizen regardless of their economic class and social order. Dignity for lower income class and socially backward professionals and classes—dignity for women, and those who are socially alienated, such as those holding non-conventional viewpoints and orientations	
Income distribution across the population, the Gini coefficient (income gap measure) across the city and the avenues to invest wealth even as smaller investors	
Cost of living in the city—measured in terms of basic amenities such as rent for spaces, food and living expense, amenities, emergency service expenses and the difference in cost of living in city centres and peripherals	
State of NGOs and social organizations in terms of their working culture, impact factors, funding, employment, support from the government and public	
Average Social Sustainability Score	Average of above

4. **Ecological Sustainability:** Cities have established a notorious reputation for their negative effects on environment, for their air, water, soil and noise pollution arising out of uncontrolled and unmanaged disposal and pressurized transport networks. Ecological sustainability is hence a measure of a city's 'planet friendliness'.

Parameter	*Score (1= lowest, 10 = highest)*
State of water in terms of the quality of water and quantity of water available per capita—and advanced measures such as organic and oxygen content in water. The percentage of water recycled and reused.	
Air quality is a stress factor which needs to be monitored and factored as a measurement criteria—this would include typical pollutant concentration such as a CO_X, NO_X etc.—and their spread in terms of space and time.	
Carbon neutralization avenues operational in a city—including plantations, reduction of vehicles by introducing mass transit, usage of IT to reduce travel needs, solar and other green sources of power as a household and industrial mission to reduce emissions	
Waste disposal including reduce, recycle and reuse prevalence. Usage of non-biodegradable material in per capita terms.	
Green cover in the city—measured by tree concentration per acre and private and public gardens	
State of local biodiversity including preservation and nurturing of locally known fauna and flora	
Average Ecological Sustainability Score	Average of above

5. **IT Applications:** 21st century cities have to be established on the pillar of IT, to reduce transportation, improve governance and delivery, to create universal access to knowledge and connect people and ideas. In essence, this is a measure of the seamless connectivity of a city.

Parameter	*Score (1= lowest, 10 = highest)*
Quality of communication—in terms of cost and coverage and quality as available in different parts of the city	
Universal access to information—creating public access points to the Internet, coverage of such free or low cost internet access in the city	
IT applications in different sectors—measured in terms of the number of sectors fully IT-enabled, and the penetration level of IT in such sectors. They may include healthcare (e.g. central patient database), education (e.g. e-learning), etc.	
E-governance—including the transparency of the government and its services over a wide array of IT tools such as Internet and mobile phones. Availability of grievance redressal on IT tools and reduction in corruption due to it	
IT education in the city—measured in terms of e-literacy levels in the citizens and the usage of IT tools in day-to-day life	
Digital payment system—measuring the share of e-payments and digital transactions in the overall economic transaction—which leads to a reduction of the 'dark economy' and eliminates corruption	
Average IT Application Score	Average of above

6. **State of Health:** A core human habitation's goal is to enable quality and long life to its citizens. In essence, this is the measure of well-being of the city.

Parameter	*Score (1= lowest, 10 = highest)*
Critical parameters in generally acceptable measures like institutional delivery, infant mortality, maternal mortality, average life expectancy, burden of diseases—including communicable and non-communicable, etc.	
Access parameters such as hospitals, doctors and nurses per 1,000 population and average distance from medical facilities	
Preventive healthcare such as awareness, vaccination and seasonal measures to reduce disease burden	
State of nutrition measured in terms of malnourishment rate in children and women. Also measured in dietary habits	
Overall cleanliness and hygiene in the city—measured in terms of cleanliness in public places and hygiene in civil spaces like eateries, public and private kitchens, water consumption points, etc.	
Condition of the differently abled in terms of medical services and the community available to them—also includes hospice care centres	
Average State of Health Score	Average of above

7. **State of Infrastructure:** Infrastructure is the artery of any modern city and it governs how the economic and social growth progresses. Thus this is an assessment of the core connect of the city.

Parameter	*Score (1= lowest, 10 = highest)*
Roads in terms of road length per capita and quality aspects of it. Cost of movement in terms of tolls is also a criterion.	

Electricity in terms of quality and time-space access to power. Will also measure the usage of community power generation, measures to reduce power consumption and availability of green power	
Access to sewage and sanitation in both private and public areas. The coverage rate and processing and treatment of the waste generated in them is also measurable	
State of public buildings measured in the density of public buildings like community spaces, commercial spaces and government buildings and their state of construction	
Connectivity with nearby areas measuring how well the city is connected to its suburban areas and other cities	
State of mass transit networks measuring the quality and coverage of mass transit networks such as metros, BRTS, trains, sea ports and airports	
Average State of Infrastructure Score	Average of above

8. **Entrepreneurship, Innovation and Opportunities:** Fundamentally, cities are centres of growth and migration because they present opportunities to their population. Citizens believe that great cities can give them the chance to showcase their talents and rise rapidly in life—and hence they think, innovate and display enterprise. Smart cities need to work on how they can attract this innovation energy—which is the hallmark of any great city. Thus this is the aspiration quotient of the city.

Parameter	*Score (1= lowest, 10 = highest)*
Entrepreneur density measured in terms of the number of new start-ups per capita, in the direction of the core economic activity identified	

Centres for innovation and incubation which may be available with colleges and research facilities to nurture new enterprises	
Capital supply for entrepreneurship including access to regular commercial banks, equity investors (venture funds), investment banks, public-sourced funding and stock issue-based fund creation	
Cost of enterprise is a major factor which governs whether an enterprise is feasible or not in a particular area. This includes commercial rents, taxations, other costs and their comparison with other cities	
Policy support available to new start-ups in terms of subsidies, waivers, training, spaces for operation, etc. Measurable in number of enterprises benefitting from policy initiatives.	
Cities which are considered more favourable for enterprise attract **migrant enterprises** which help boost economic growth	
Average Entrepreneurship, Innovation and Opportunities Score	Average of above

9. **Support System:** Cities are seen as centres of hope for nearby regions. They see them as both a market and supplier of quality goods and services. Cities also support heritage, in terms of 'hardware' such as buildings and monuments, and 'software' such as arts, languages, dances, music and cuisine. Hence we measure the benevolence of the city here.

Parameter	*Score (1= lowest, 10 = highest)*
Economic activity with villages measured in terms of export and import which a city centre does with the nearby suburban areas and villages surrounding it	

Research and development for societal and rural growth including those done for agriculture and other nearby rural professional or social needs	
Preservation of places of historic and cultural relevance which lie within the geographical boundaries of the city	
Average Support System Score	Average of above

10. **Happiness of Living:** Eventually, the citizens pursue happiness. Cities have to be designed to provide this goal. This happiness is derived from all the previous parameters, but here we will also consider some additional parameters. Hence we measure the temperament of the city here.

Parameter	*Score (1= lowest, 10 = highest)*
Spiritual pursuits measured in terms of the avenues for spiritual well-being and their access in terms of time and expense	
Weather around the year is a prominent reason for the mood and happiness of the population—measurable in time of year when the temperature is optimal (around 17°C)	
Resilience of the city to natural calamities. Citizens living in areas prone to earthquakes, floods, hurricanes, etc. have a sense of fear, hence leading to unhappiness.	
Quality of family life measured in time spent with family, time spent in commuting and the opportunity to live in joint families	
Average Happiness Score	Average of above

Thus, we have designed ten pillars for smart and wise city creation and have created a measurement framework around it. The overall City Wisdom Index would be an average of the scores along the ten pillars. Depending on the overall urban planning objective, different weights can be given to these pillars.

As an example of the application of these scores, let's take some sample cities from India and summarize them along these pillars.[v]

Name	*Good performance in*	*Poor performance in*
Chandigarh Overall: 6	Culture (7), ecology (9), health (8), infrastructure (8), happiness of living (6), IT (5)	Economics (2), social sustainability (3), entrepreneurship (2), support system (2)
Naya Raipur Overall: 4.4	Ecology (8), infrastructure (8), health (6), support system (6), IT (6)	Happiness of living (2), culture (3), economics (1), social sustainability (3), entrepreneurship (1)
Gurgaon Overall: 4.1	Health (6), IT (6), economics (8), entrepreneurship (7)	Ecology (2), infrastructure (3), support system (1), happiness of living (3), culture (3), social sustainability (2)
Gandhinagar Overall: 5.2	Ecology (8), infrastructure (8), health (7), support system (7), IT (7)	Happiness of living (3), culture (4), economics (2), social sustainability (4), entrepreneurship (2)

We envision that smart cities should exhibit the following in the City Wisdom Indices:

a) Minimize the variation of scores across sectors—hence equitable performance across all pillars
b) Exhibit an average score of 7.5 or above.

How can we build such cities?

What are the elements that we need to consider in order to achieve these results? The following chapters will discuss each of these parameters, the examples that we can learn from and the innovations that we can implement in order to make planned cities—smarter and smart cities—wiser.

[v] Based on actual surveys from selected individuals in each of the cities under consideration—values based on perception as expressed by the samples.

5

Power Equations: Smart Energy for New Habitation

This chapter discusses the energy situation in the world and its consumption. It would explore the side effects on environment and hence the requirement for cleaner fuels. The chapter would further detail the different sources of renewable energy and their current production trends. The chapter will also discuss alternative technological innovations for monitoring and controlling energy consumption.

Globally, cities account for about 75 per cent of the total energy consumption and 80 per cent of greenhouse gas (GHG) emissions.[1] Of this, 40 per cent of the energy consumption is accounted for by the buildings used for housing, commercial or industrial application. In such a case, there is a requirement for the cities to reduce their energy consumption. The smart city projects in Europe majorly focus on making their systems energy 'SMART' or efficient.

The smart city project of Norway by the Bellona Foundation in partnership with Siemens reduced energy consumption by 20 per cent in the three largest cities of Norway, viz, Trondheim, Bergen and Oslo, by using proven, modern technology during the test period in 2011-2012. The production of electric energy in Norway for 2012 was 147.8 TWh,[i] an increase of 15.8 per cent compared to 2011, of which renewable and greener hydel-power accounted for 96.7 per cent.

Oslo is one of the cities in Norway which has been part of the smart city project and has shown commendable progress in reducing its energy consumption. It is the economic and governmental centre of Norway and is also a hub of Norwegian trade, banking, industry and shipping, not to mention its status as an important centre for maritime industries and maritime trade in Europe. The city is considered a global city and termed as a 'Beta World City'. This is a term used for cities that link moderate economic regions into the world economy in studies performed by the Globalization and World Cities Study Group and Network in 2008.[2] It was ranked number one for 'quality of life', among European large cities in the European Cities of the Future 2012 report by fDi Magazine.[ii] The city of Oslo has committed itself to reducing its energy consumption with the aim of becoming a city with the lowest energy consumption per resident in the world.

The dynamic street lighting on all relevant streets in Oslo—in line with the approved lighting plan (Action Plan for Environment and Climate 2012-2015)—aims at bringing down electric consumption by 70 per cent. Dynamic street lighting or intelligent lighting adapts to changing conditions by varying the amount of light according to the time of day, season, weather conditions and amount of traffic.

The upgrade involves replacing old lamp fixtures with new ones that contain energy-efficient bulbs and electronic drivers. Each lamp contains an electronic chip with a unique address, enabling

---

[i] Terawatt-hour (TWh), a measure of electrical energy, 10^12 watt-hours or 10^9 kWh (1 unit of energy)

[ii] fDi Magazine is an English-language bi-monthly news and foreign direct investment publication, providing an up-to-date review of global investment activity.

individual control of any lamp via a computer application (tele-management). Commands may be sent either to a series of lamps or to a single one. The key benefit is the ability to manage street lighting efficiently in keeping with changing conditions. A combination of tele-communication (GPRS) and the existing cable network is used to manage the lighting system. Today, more than 20 per cent of street lights in Oslo are dynamic.

The technology employed uses sensors to regulate the amount of lighting needed relative to the surrounding conditions. The technology is being developed by PHILIPS. With funding from Enova, a state entity promoting environmentally sound energy production and use in Norway, Oslo started to use this technology in 2004. The EU has also contributed through two projects such as E-street, and ESOLi[iii] in which Oslo had a leading role.

Following implementation of Streetlight Vision's solution, Oslo now benefits from the following advantages:

- 62 per cent reduction in energy consumption for its urban lighting network due to installation changes and reduced lamp burning hours[3]
- Significant maintenance savings, due to automatic breakdown detection
- Improvement of lighting in sensitive areas, and thus, improved security
- Option of using the public lighting network as a backbone network to install and control electric vehicle recharge stations, environmental sensors, information panels and other measuring and traffic control equipment.

[iii] ESOLi (Energy Saving Outdoor Lighting) is a project funded by the Intelligent Energy Europe programme of the European Union, aiming to increase the awareness of intelligent street lighting and accelerate the use of the best available technologies across Europe.

If all the 75,000 streetlamps in Oslo were dynamic, this could lead to a yearly reduction in electricity consumption totalling 20 GWh.[iv] This would mean a saving of [1.112 NOK * 20 *1000]. A reduction of this magnitude would also reduce CO_2 by approximately 7,000 tonnes annually.

Need for Smart Energy

Carbon dioxide's global atmospheric concentration till 1700 was around 280 parts per million (PPM). The levels have risen in 2012 to 392.6 PPM, which is a 40 per cent increase in the 262 years since the Industrial Revolution. It is one of the main components of the GHG emitted by human activities. Other gases include methane (CH_4), nitrous oxide (N_2O) and fluorinated gases. Fossil fuels, agricultural activities,[4] municipal solid waste, fertilizer usage, industrial processes, and refrigeration and consumer products are the main sources of these greenhouse gases. Categorization of global GHG emission sources has been represented in Figure 2. Figure 3 shows the increase in temperature with the rise in CO_2 levels.

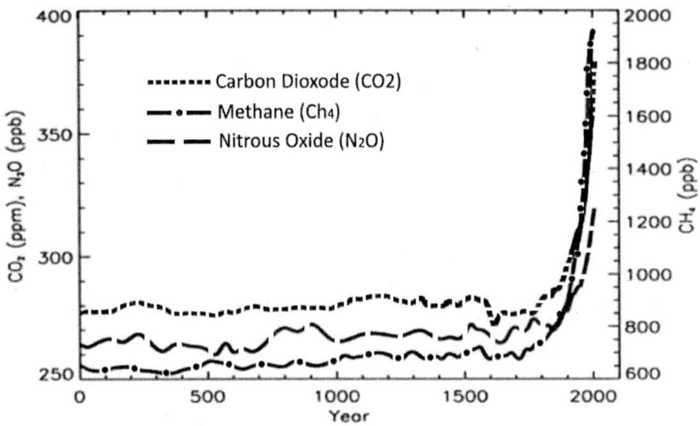

Figure 1: GHG concentration level in atmosphere

[iv] 1 GWh $=10^6$ kWh

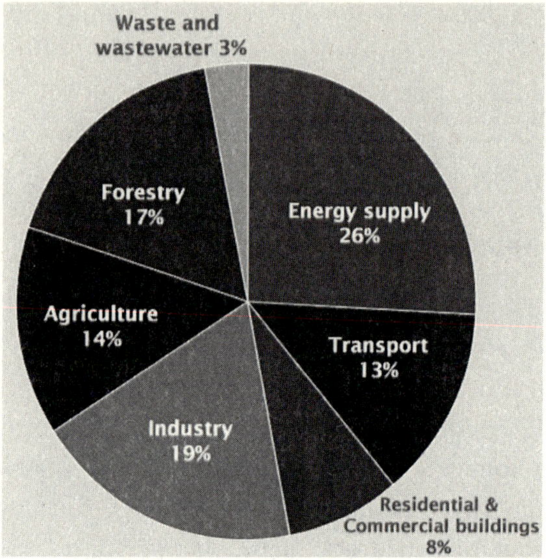

Figure 2: Global GHG emissions in terms of activities

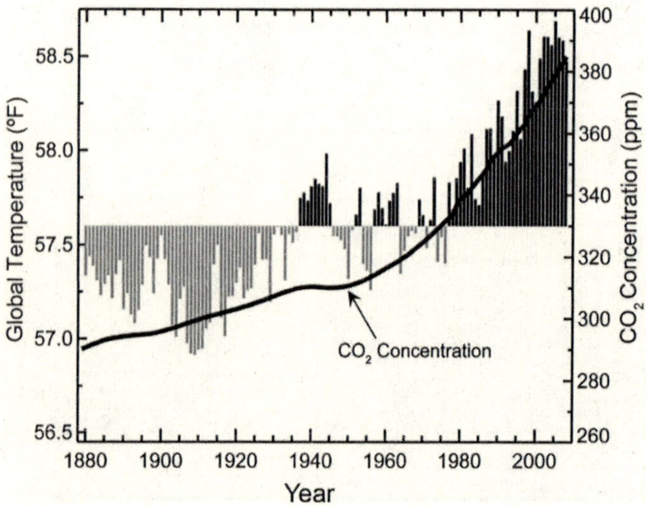

Figure 3: Increase in global temperature and CO_2 levels

The greenhouse gases can remain in the atmosphere for different amounts of time, long enough to become well-mixed. It means that the amount of greenhouse gas that is measured in the atmosphere is roughly the same all over the world. For each greenhouse gas, a Global Warming Potential (GWP) has been calculated to reflect how long it remains in the atmosphere on an average, and how strongly it absorbs energy. Gases with a higher GWP absorb more energy per pound than gases with a lower GWP, and thus contribute more to warming Earth.

GLOBAL WARMING POTENTIAL

The Global Warming Potential (GWP) for a gas is a measure of the total energy that a gas absorbs over a particular period of time (usually 100 years), compared to carbon dioxide. The larger the GWP, the more warming the gas causes.

GWP—CO_2—1
GWP—CH_4—21
GWP—N_2O—300

With the increasing impact of the GHG emissions and energy usage on the environment, along with the depletion of fossil fuels, it is imperative that sustainable development be linked with smart energy usage. It not only involves the usage of renewable and sustainable energy resources like biofuels, but also using these energy resources efficiently and optimally to reduce the overall energy consumption and the carbon footprint.

Today, India's energy consumption is the fourth largest in the world after China, USA and Russia.[5] The energy policy of India is largely defined by the rapid increase in the energy deficit in the country and increasing the main focus on developing alternative methods of power generation, that is, solar, wind and nuclear sources.

The power sector in India had an installed capacity of 250GW[v] as of June 2014[6]. India became the world's third largest producer of electricity in 2013 with a global share of 4.8 per cent in electricity generation, surpassing Japan and Russia.

India's energy sector has a mix of all the resources available, including renewable resources. The dominance of coal in the energy mix is likely to continue in the foreseeable future, which at present is 61 per cent. India plans to add till 2017 88.5 Giga Watt (GW) of capacity, of which 69.3 GW will come from coal. The renewable energy capacity addition is planned to be around 30 GW (5 GW of wind, 10 GW of solar and 2.1 GW of small hydro power).

Table 1: Energy resources in India

Traditional Sources (in GW)	Coal	Gas	Nuclear	Hydro
	152.3	22.6	4.8	40.8
per cent of total	60.4	9	1.9	16.2
Renewable Resources (in GW)	Small Hydro	Wind	Bio Power	Solar
	3.8	21.1	4.1	2.6
per cent of total	1.5	8.4	1.6	1

In this chapter, we will first talk about the different forms of smart energy sources available, which will help us solve the problem of the energy crisis that follows increasing urbanization. We will also look into the different sources which can be used in the smart cities, sources which have lower carbon emission by employing innovative solutions for energy generation, and thus reducing energy consumption.

[v] 1 GW = 1,000 Mega Watt (MW)

Smart Energy Resources

To solve the current energy problems and the issue of depleting non-renewable energy sources, research is being done all over the world to identify renewable and environment-friendly energy resources. Of these, of notable mention are solar, tidal, wind and biofuels.

Solar Energy

The solar energy absorbed by the earth's atmosphere, the oceans and the landmasses is 440 ExaJoules[vi] (EJ) in a single day, which is almost the same as that used by the entire human population in a year, which was about 474 EJ in 2013.[7] Despite this, the actual solar energy which has been trapped by living beings is mostly in the form of photosynthesis by plants. The actual scales of solar energy trapped for storage and direct usage by human beings have been very limited. Technology advancement in this field has been slow, but increasing focus on alternative energy sources poses tremendous possibilities for energy harnessing in future.

Since the invention of the first solar energy trapping device by Frank Shuman in 1897, solar energy has been harnessed using technologies such as solar heating, solar photovoltaic, solar thermal electricity, solar architecture and artificial photosynthesis. According to the International Energy Agency,[8] 'The development of affordable, inexhaustible and clean solar energy technologies will have huge longer-term benefits. It will increase countries' energy security through reliance on an indigenous, inexhaustible and mostly import-independent resource, enhance sustainability, reduce pollution, lower the costs of mitigating climate change, and keep fossil fuel prices lower than otherwise. These advantages are global. Hence the additional costs of the incentives for early deployment should

---

[vi] The exajoule (EJ) is equal to one quintillion (1018) joules or 277 TWh or 277x106MWh

be considered learning investments; they must be wisely spent and need to be widely shared.'

Through the transition which took place over a century, solar energy has come a long way from the first solar engine. It is now used for water heating, HVAC systems, water treatment, process heating, cooking, and electricity generation through photovoltaic cells. Solar chemical processes use solar energy to drive chemical reactions or photoelectric effects, which can also convert solar energy into storable and transportable fuels like photovoltaic (PV) cells; or through concentrated solar power (CSP), by using lenses and tracking systems to focus a large area of sunlight into a small but powerful beam. In the US, 30 per cent of the energy used by commercial buildings and 50 per cent of the residential buildings' energy consumption comes from heating, ventilation and air-conditioning (HVAC) systems which can be shifted to solar heating, cooling and ventilation technologies.

Wind Energy

Wind power is one of the renewable sources of energy which is clean, plentiful, and renewable and results in no greenhouse gas emission.[vii] Wind power has been one of the earliest forms of energy which was harnessed successfully by mankind in the form of sails in boats and ships, and later for grinding grains and pumping water. Today, wind power is used for electricity generation and has found wide applications in wind-powered generators available in all sizes. These are used for small tasks such as battery charging at isolated residences and larger projects like near Gigawatt-sized offshore wind farms that provide electricity to national electrical grids.

[vii] According to the World Wind Energy Association, in 2010, wind power generated was 430 TWh or about 0.33 per cent of worldwide energy usage. Between 2005 and 2010 the average annual growth in new installations was 27.6 per cent.

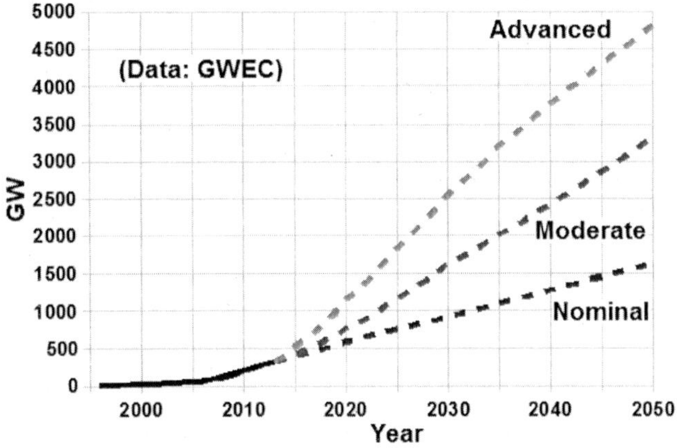

Figure 4: Global wind energy installed capacity at different levels of electricity generation

Wind power, though consistent over the years, suffers from variation over shorter time scales on a monthly basis. This can be mitigated for the wind farms, by better modelling of the dynamic electromechanical characteristics, to ensure predictable and stable power generation. The latest power management techniques can increase the stability of power generation. Some of these techniques are:

- Excess capacity storage
- Geographically distributed turbines
- Dispatch-able backing sources
- Storage such as pumped-storage hydroelectricity
- Exporting and importing power to neighbouring areas
- Reducing demand when wind production is low.

The global installed capacity of wind power generation in 2012 was 282,482 MW. In 2012, the European Union had 100,000 MW installed capacity, while the the US surpassed 50,000 MW, and China's grid-connected capacity passed 50,000 MW. Several European countries have relatively high levels of penetration—in 2011 Denmark had 28 per cent of stationary (grid) electricity production by wind power, and the same for Portugal and Spain for 2011 were 19 per cent and 16 per cent respectively. Wind power market penetration is expected to reach 8 per cent by 2018.

Many wind power companies work with local communities to reduce environmental and other concerns associated with wind farms. In other cases, there is direct community ownership of wind farm projects. Appropriate government consultation, planning and approval procedures also help to minimize environmental risks. Some may still object to wind farms but, according to the Australia Institute, their concerns should be weighed against the need to address the threats posed by climate change and the opinions of the broader community.

In America, wind projects are reported to boost local tax bases, helping to pay for schools, roads and hospitals. Wind projects also revitalize the economy of rural communities by providing steady income to farmers and other landowners. In the UK, both the National Trust and the Campaign to Protect Rural England have expressed concerns about the effects on the rural landscape caused by inappropriately sited wind turbines and wind farms.

Some wind farms have become tourist attractions. The Whitelee Wind Farm Visitor Centre in Scotland has an exhibition room, a learning hub, a café with a viewing deck and also a shop. It is run by the Glasgow Science Centre.

Tidal Energy

Tides are the periodic rise and fall of sea levels occurring at around a particular time in the oceans, and have a large amount of energy within them. Tides are the largest source of short term sea-level fluctuations and have a potential for electricity generation. As compared to the other sources of renewable energy, tidal power is more predictable than wind energy and solar energy, but has not been harnessed much due to the relatively high cost and limited availability of the sites which have the required range of high tides. The major factors in determining the potential of a tidal power station are the size (length and height) of the barrage required, and the difference in height between high and low tide.

There have been many technological developments and improvements in design and turbine technology recently that aim at bringing down the economic and environmental costs to the competitive levels of other energy sources. Tidal power can be generated by tidal stream generator, tidal barrage, dynamic tidal power and tidal lagoons. The world's first large-scale tidal power plant was built in 1966 in the Rance tidal power station in France. Despite the fact that four decades have passed since the installation of the first tidal power plant, there have been very few plants which were operational in 2014. It is estimated that tidal stream energy capacity is more than 150 TWh per annum, which is in excess of all domestic electricity consumption in the UK.

More than 75 per cent of Europe's tidal energy potential resources come from only the UK and Scotland, with Pentland Firth in Scotland being considered the world's best site for the generation of tidal power. The water flow is rapid there because the tide that is shifting from the Atlantic into the North Sea is forced through a narrow eight-mile channel. Pentland Firth is estimated to supply a maximum of 1.9 GW of power on a fortnightly tidal cycle, which equals 16.5 TWh of electricity a year.

Canada has a potential of 30,000 MW of energy and the same for China is 3.5 GW, according to China Ocean Energy Resources Division. In India, Asia's first commercial scale tidal power station is scheduled to be installed at Mandvi in the Gulf of Kutch, Gujarat. The construction began for the tidal power station in 2012 and is in the final stages of completion. The 50 MW project is awaiting Coastal Regulation Zone clearance.

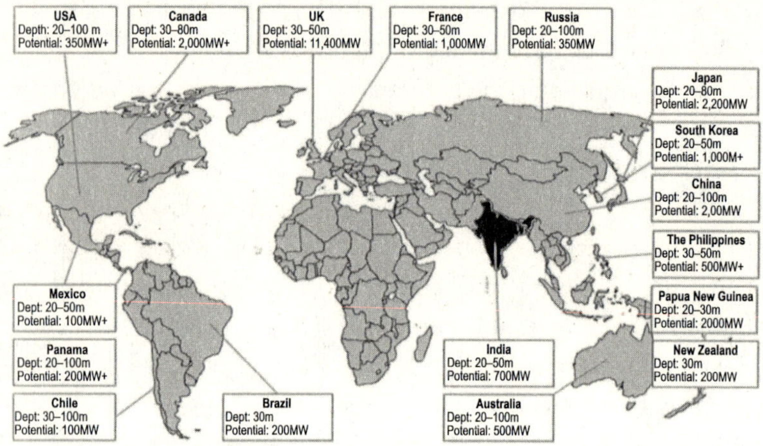

Figure 5: Tidal energy global resource

The main problem behind harnessing tidal power is that the turbines lose efficiency at low operating rates, and the time available for power generation is brief. Additionally, there is debate on the considerable damage to marine ecology due to tidal power stations. The historical problem of protecting the infrastructure when the seas get rough adds to the installation and maintenance cost of the tidal power stations. Despite this, with the technological advances, it is possible to build generators which can withstand the choppy seas and preserve marine biodiversity in the near future.

Biofuels

Biofuel is a fuel extracted by biomass conversion from geologically recent carbon fixation in living organisms and plants. Bio-ethanol is a popular biofuel produced by fermenting sugar or starch found in corn, sugarcane, or sweet sorghum. It can also be derived from cellulosic biomass derived from non-food sources. The ethanol thus produced can be used as a fuel in its purest form. It is widely used in the US and Brazil and both nations lead the world in biofuel production. The European Union is another big market for biofuel production and consumption. According to the International Energy Agency (IEA), in 2010, the biofuel production percentage for Brazil, US and the EU were 20.1 per cent, 4.4 per cent and 4.2 per cent respectively.[viii]

BIO-ETHANOL AND PRIVATE COMPANIES

Cosan is a public listed company, a Brazilian conglomerate producer of bio-ethanol, sugar, energy and foods. The company operates in Brazil, Uruguay, Paraguay, Bolivia and United Kingdom. On 1 February 2010, Cosan and Royal Dutch Shell announced the creation of a joint venture, Raízen, that merged their operations of sugar, ethanol and the distribution and marketing of fuels in Brazil. It formed the third largest distribution company in Brazil and the world's largest bio-energy operation.

To raise crop yields, Raízen uses new technology. For example, its own advanced geographical information system draws on a number of sources, such as official soil records, public weather stations and real-time imaging of its 800,000 acres. Then advanced mathematical modelling calculates how conditions affect crops. The results better inform agricultural managers who, for example, add more fertilizer or target pest control to help boost productivity.

[viii] Total cane production in Africa is approximately 90 million tonnes and the total potential for electricity export using state-of-the-art commercially proven technologies in Mauritius is estimated at 10,000 GWh. However, not all the countries have the investment potential and indigenous skill to tap this potential.

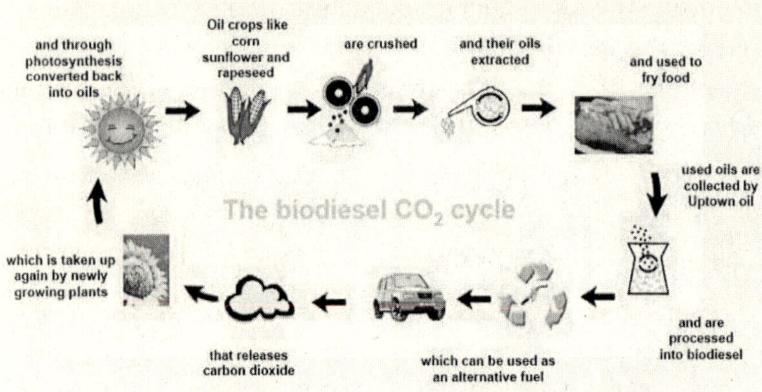

Figure 6: Bio diesel CO_2 cycle

Running road vehicles with bio-ethanol produced from sugarcane reduces CO_2 emissions from transport fuels. From cultivation to use, ethanol made from sugarcane produces around 70 per cent less CO_2 than petrol. As it grows, sugarcane absorbs more CO_2 than other biofuel crops. The savings also come from factors such as transport and processing. Despite these, some experts claim that if the end-to-end CO_2 emission for biofuels is considered, they perform worse than sand tar. There are studies being conducted regarding the same globally, and it has remained one major factor for the slow adoption of biofuels in day-to-day energy requirements.[9]

The global production of biofuels has grown sevenfold—up from 16 billion litres in 2000 to around 90 billion litres in 2013,[10] and provides for 3 per cent of fuel for road transport. Brazil produced 24 billion litres of bio-ethanol in 2013 and most of it was absorbed in the domestic market where bio-ethanol was either used directly as a fuel or in blended form with gasoline to increase the octane percentage in the fuel. Major oil companies like BP estimate that the biofuel consumption in Brazil in 2030 would be around 38 per cent for road transport, and that in the US would be 24 per cent. With the US and the EU moving towards biofuel legislation and production

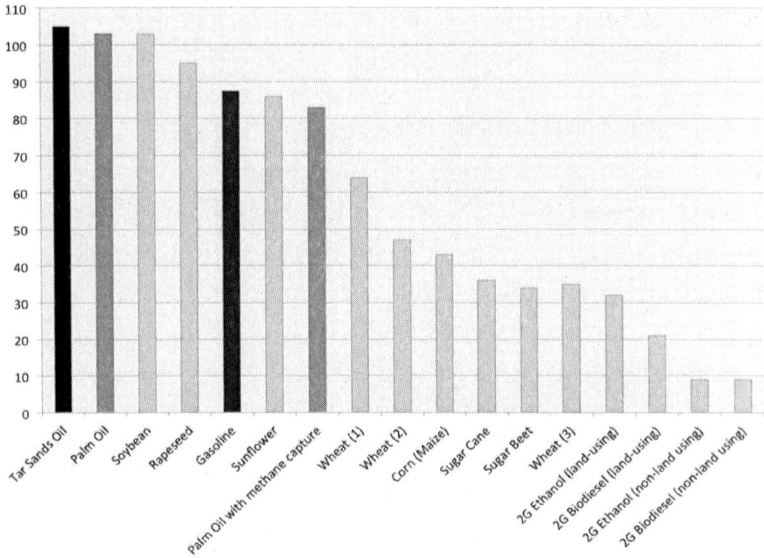

Figure 7: Default value (CO_2 /mj) of various fuels according to EU Data

of second generation or advanced bio-fuels by cellulosic biomass, there is expected to be an increase in its production and consumption.

Table 2: World bio-ethanol production in 2013[11]

Region or Country	*Billion litres*
United States	50
Brazil	23.7
Europe	5.2
China	2.6
India	2.1
Canada	2
Rest of the world	2.8

In the US, bio-ethanol production is shifting from the traditional sources of sugarcane and sorghum. Much research is being done in algae biofuels, which may provide a viable alternative to fossil fuels once it overcomes the challenges of strain identification, cost efficiency and improvement. The greater San Diego region, including the Imperial Valley, is actively pursuing becoming a leading producer of renewable fuels and petrochemical products from algae and other bio sources. A study conducted by the San Diego Association of Governments (SANDAG) found that the direct, indirect, and induced economic impact of the algae biotechnology research and manufacturing industry generated a total of approximately 1,020 jobs, $80 million in wages, and over $175 million of economic output to the San Diego region from 2008-2013.[12]

Sugarcane bagasse[ix] is another important energy source for electricity production. In the process of the recovery of sugar, the fibrous fraction of the cane stalk in the form of bagasse composed of 50 per cent fibre, 48 per cent moisture and 2 per cent sugars is normally burnt to generate steam and electricity to meet the energy requirements of the cane sugar factory. Over the years, sugar factories in a number of countries have adopted energy conservation and efficiency measures with a view to generate either surplus bagasse for use as raw material for pulp and paper and particle board, or surplus electricity for sale to the grid. By the end of 2015, it is expected to reach the production levels of around 26,000 MW, and about half of it will be from India.[13]

Biofuel development in India centres mainly around the cultivation and processing of the jatropha plant seeds, which are very rich in oil (40 per cent). Jatropha oil has been used in India for long as biodiesel for fuel requirements in remote rural and forest

[ix] Bagasse is the fibrous matter that remains after sugarcane or sorghum stalks are crushed to extract their juice. When burned in large quantities, it produces sufficient heat energy to supply all the needs of a typical sugar mill, with energy to spare. The resulting CO_2 emissions are equal to the amount of CO_2 that the sugarcane plant absorbed from the atmosphere during its growing phase, which makes the process of cogeneration greenhouse gas-neutral.

communities and can be used directly without refining. The jatropha plant has the ability to grow in non-arable and fallow land and has the unique property of transforming alkaline land into cultivable land. The plant bears fruit in only two years of cultivation and the high quality diesel produced from it has lower carbon content than the fossil fuels. Each hectare of jatropha plantation has the ability to offset 20 tonnes of CO_2 per year for forty years.[14]

The government of Chhattisgarh is actively pursuing jatropha plantation. It has already planted jatropha in 160,000 hectares of land. It plans to extract 2,000,000 tonnes of biodiesel annually with further plantation.[x]

Smart Technology Usage

Along with reducing the consumption of fossil fuels and increasing the consumption of energy produced from renewable sources and biofuels, there is also the inherent need to integrate them with technology to make for optimal use. In this respect, Information and Communication Technology applications and devices are being developed, which will add a digital layer of real-time information gathered on consumption and power generation. They will then relay both power and power distribution data to the consumers, giving them options to cut down their carbon footprints.

Smart Grid

Smart grid is a class of technology that uses the management of electricity consumption based on computer-based remote control

---

[x] 1 hectare of land under jatropha gives five tons of jatropha seeds annually (two years after planting) which can generate 0.75-2 tonnes of biodiesel depending on the conditions. If the ideal production is 1.4 tonnes of biodiesel per hectare, the wastelands of the nation have the potential to generate more biodiesel than our present demand.

and automation processes. The 'grid' here is the network that distributes electricity from the solar, wind and tidal farms, nuclear power plants and other electricity generation power plants to energy users' homes, offices and businesses. It includes wires, substations, transformers, switches, central control centre, power meters, voltage sensors and fault detectors. All the parts of a smart grid are connected through a two-way digital communication technology between the field systems and data viewing device with the user and the utility's network operations centre. The system is equipped with automation technology which allows the central utility network operations centre to adjust and control each individual device or million devices simultaneously.[15]

The benefits of the smart grid go beyond just the monitoring and controlling of energy consumption, GHG emission, carbon footprints, or reducing electricity tariffs—it extends to enhanced cyber security, handling renewable and variable power generating sources and integrating electric vehicles into the grid.

Smart Meters

Smart metering is adding the two-way data network to the metering system so that it does not require the utility handling companies to check the consumption levels and records usage in real time. Part of the Advanced Metering Infrastructure (AMI), these meters are different from the automatic meter reading devices on the front, in that they enable two-way communication between the device and the utility and not just record the total consumption. These meters have inbuilt real-time or near real-time sensors, a power quality monitoring system and power outage notifications.

Aiming at actively changing users' energy consumption patterns, these smart meters have the added benefits of off-peak time tariffs for offsetting the electricity consumption patterns, selling electricity back to the grid, and carbon emissions (like carbon credit selling) to other users with higher electricity consumption. Some of the cities that are already using smart metering systems include Victoria (Australia), British Columbia (Canada), (Italy), (Japan), Netherlands and Vienna (Austria). AMI has the end goal of building future-connected homes and creating utility control systems to manage energy exchange between buildings, and optimizing energy consumption locally.

Smart Energy Appliances

The Integral Resource Management Optimization Network (IRON) focuses on systems which adjust or control the load in normal grid operation. This could include load adjustment so that the electricity can be stored in some other energy form like cooling systems, heating system and pump systems. IRON would lead to transmission cost minimization by load balancing, time-of-use tariffs and balancing energy provisions.

Energy-efficient refrigeration of food in supermarkets is another area that traditionally uses a large amount of energy and where technological intervention can lead to considerable consumption reduction. It uses the time-of-use mechanism and the storing of energy at off peak hours to be used for cooling during the peak hours. It is like a thermoelectric battery in the smart grid, which can be used at the user's will, and can help in balancing the consumption levels.

Public lighting, though very important, is a heavy energy-consuming service. Using intelligent systems monitored over real time for public lighting would improve the quality of lighting and increase the energy saving, as the systems will switch the public lights on or off based on the lux[xi] levels, and dim them depending on time. Also, changing the existing traditional light fittings with

---

[xi] Lux is the unit to measure lighting intensity (Lux levels). It is a measure of the level of lighting in a building or area of a building. Lighting levels are task dependent, with higher levels of illumination required for more detailed tasks.

modern light fittings will not just improve the light quality but will also save energy and be sustainable in the long term. The aim of smart lighting would be to integrate smart metering systems with the public or individual usages so as to improve energy efficiency, system maintenance, energy accounting and lighting control.

Green Mobile Telecom

As India has risen in its mobile telecom coverage, with over 700 million connections in 2013, the expansion has taken a heavy toll on the environment. Estimates say that as much as 2 billion litres of diesel is being burnt and hence over 4.5 million tonnes of CO_2 are being generated in order to keep the 310,000 mobile towers alive in the nation. Often, these towers are located in the middle of densely populated areas, compounding the harmful effects.

This is another area for smart planning. The answer to this challenge is both solar and wind-powered mobile towers. Equipped with height and earmarked space, cell phone towers have excellent access to sunshine and wind power. Some major telecom operators, including BSNL and Airtel, have already begun their work in bringing solar-powered cell phone towers. Smart cities need to be planned to cater to this challenge.

Cloud Computing

Twenty-first century cities will be settlements powered by computers. Whether it is industry, government, homes or personal use—computers will be the life-thread of all activities. We need computing power to process problems, store and retrieve data and perform computations. In the US, the Lawrence Berkeley National Laboratory investigated the energy impact of cloud computing. Their research indicates that 'moving all office workers in the United States to the cloud could reduce the energy used by information technology by up to 87 per cent.'[16]

This energy saving is due to increased data centre efficiency when using cloud services (email, calendars, contacts, etc.). The cloud supports many products at a time, so it can more efficiently distribute resources among many users. It means that we can do more with less energy.

Smart habitations need to be designed to operate on cloud power—cloud processing, cloud storage and computing. Individual devices would be smaller then, require less power and be flexible. Big data technology needs to be deployed to ensure that maximum saving in energy and cost happens at the cloud level. Our target should be to cut down the energy used by information technology by at least 75 per cent.

One such city moving towards smart IT for energy saving is Shanghai. Key developments include a) upgrading information infrastructure—high-speed optical broadband network with full coverage of all the urbanized areas and 22,000 WLAN Hot Spots throughout the city; b) information sensing and intelligent application to facilitate management of city construction, operations safety, intelligent transportation, and e-governance; c) new generation of IT industry such as cloud computing, Internet of things and Internet of vehicles; and d) integrating ICT with society to enable the Shanghai way of life.[17]

Nano-material-based Energy Generation and Saving

One of the most promising sectors in modern material science is that of nano-materials. These materials are showing tremendous application potential in the sector of energy efficiency in smart city planning—and hence warrant significant efforts in research and development. The following table highlights some of the potential uses of nano-materials in the field of energy generation and saving.

Table 3: Potential uses of nano-materials

Field	*Potential uses of nano-materials*
Energy Sources	1. Regenerative • Photovoltaic's non-optimized cells (dye, thin film, multiple junctions), anti-reflective coatings • Wind energy: Nano-composite materials for lighter and stronger blades with wear and corrosion protective nano-coatings for bearings and power drives. • Geothermal: Nano-coatings for wear-resistant drilling equipments • Hydro/Tidal Power: Nano-coatings for corrosion-free parts • Biomass energy: Yield optimization by nano-based precision farming, i.e. nano-sensors which control the release and storage of nutrients and pesticides
Energy Change	1. Gas turbines: Heat and corrosion protection for turbine blades for better efficiency 2. Thermo-electrics: Nano-structured compounds for efficient thermo-electrical power generation, e.g. usage of waste heat in automobiles 3. Fuel cells: Nano-optimized electrodes for more efficient fuel cells for use in automobiles/mobile systems 4. Hydrogen generation: Nano-catalyst for more efficient hydrogen generation, e.g. electrolysis 5. Combustion engines: Nano-composites coating for resistance from wear and tear of engine parts 6. Electrical motors: Nano-composites for super conducting components in electrical motors
Energy Distribution	1. Power transmission • High voltage transmission: Nano-fillers for electrically isolated systems, soft magnetic nano-material for current transformation process • Super conductors: Optimized super conductors based on nano-scale interface design for efficient power transmission • CNT power lines: Super conducting cables (nano-tubes) • Wireless power transmission: Energy transmission based on electromagnetic, laser or microwave based in nano-optimized components

Field	*Potential uses of nano-materials*
	2. Smart grids: Nano sensors for intelligent grid management systems capable of withstanding highly decentralized power inputs 3. Heat transfer: Efficient heat transfer based on nano-optimized heat exchangers and conductors
Energy Storage	1. Electrical energy • Batteries: Nano-structured electrodes for optimized lithium-ion batteries with ceramic foil separators. These can be useful with solar equipment • Super capacitors: Nano-materials for electrodes and electrolytes for higher energy densities 2. Chemical energy • Hydrogen: Non-porous materials like metal hydrides for application in micro fuel cells • Fuel reforming/refining: Nano-catalyst for optimized fuel production • Fuel tanks: Air-tight nano-material fuel tanks for reduction of hydro carbon emissions 3. Thermal energy • Phase change materials: Encapsulated phase change nano-materials for air conditioning of buildings • Absorptive storage: Nano-porous materials for reversible heat storage facility in buildings
Energy Usage	1. Thermal insulation: Nano-porous materials for thermal insulation of buildings and industrial processes 2. Air conditioning: Intelligent and efficient management of heat and light flux in buildings by the application of electro-chromic windows, IR reflectors or micro mirror array systems 3. Light weight construction: Using nano-composites for construction purposes, e.g. nano-tubes, metal matrix composites, polymer composites 4. Industrial Processes: Replacing energy-intensive processes based on nano-tech innovation processes 5. Lighting: Energy-efficient lighting systems, e.g. LED

Conclusion

A sophisticated state-of-the-art energy infrastructure is required for the development of smart cities and for the maintenance of energy consumption and reduction of GHG emissions. Along with infrastructure development—energy grids, energy farms, ICT systems, modern energy-efficient devices—a key component for a smart city are policy makers and the decision makers who create suitable policies to help them implement strategic developments. Cities can also benefit by conducting urban simulation, scenario-planning models, experimentation with building and construction materials, installation of safety and security measures and making ready the ICT infrastructure for an 'Internet for everything' future.

NOW YOU KNOW:

- 40 per cent of total urban energy consumption is contributed by buildings
- Oslo reduced its energy consumption by 62 per cent by adopting dynamic street lighting system
- 80 per cent of the world's GHG emission is contributed by cities
- There has been a 40 per cent rise in the atmospheric carbon dioxide concentration since the Industrial Revolution
- Major GHGs are carbon dioxide, methane and nitrous oxide
- Energy supply contributes up to 26 per cent of global GHG emissions
- Solar energy, tidal energy, wind energy and biofuels are renewable energy resources
- Solar energy is the most uniform source of energy which has been proven for centuries and it can be harnessed and stored in battery banks

- Tidal and wind energy are potential sources of energy but fluctuate according to weather conditions
- Biofuels, especially bio-ethanol, are finding increased acceptance in America and Europe
- Biofuels' global production reached around 90 billion litres in 2013
- Use of smart technology innovations like smart metering, smart grid and smart energy appliances would further help in reducing the world energy consumption.

6

Connected Homes: IT-enabled Living and Working

This chapter will deal with the green building concept for environmental sustainability of construction in residences and commercial spaces. It will discuss different certifications for the buildings existing in India and the world. Further, the chapter will discuss the various components of constructing green buildings or of making existing buildings environmental friendly.

Green Buildings—the Smarter Way of Living

Green buildings or sustainable buildings are those that are constructed in an environmentally responsible and resource-efficient manner, which would be green and clean throughout their life cycle—construction, maintenance, renovation to demolition. This requires a close connection between design, planning, landscaping, building and construction, and energy generation and usage.

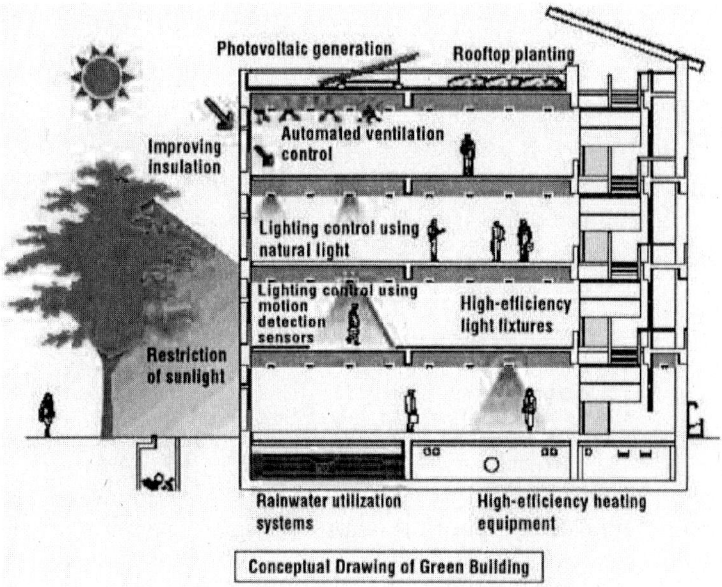

Figure 1: Conceptual drawing of a green building

As shown in Figure 1, a green building will have

- devices for energy harnessing and generation
- landscaping and passive design techniques to reduce the energy load of the building
- lighting control to allow maximum requirement to be met by natural light
- designing the building envelope and fenestrations in such a way that they allow or restrict sunlight and wind as required
- high efficiency heating or cooling equipment to maintain the building temperature.

The buildings are built of environment-friendly materials or recyclable and refurbished materials and are sustainable in their use of resources—water, energy, light, everything. These buildings with their efficient use of resources reduce waste, pollution and

BUILDINGS IN THE US

In the US, buildings account for:

- 36 per cent of total energy use and 65 per cent of electricity consumption
- 30 per cent of greenhouse gas emissions
- 30 per cent of raw materials use
- 30 per cent of waste output (136 million tonnes annually)
- 12 per cent of potable water consumption.

Source: US Green Building Council

environmental degradation, thus protecting the health and well-being of the occupants.

The green building concept integrates the aspects of sustainability and emphasizes the reduction of environmental impact through a holistic approach to land and building usages, and by applying construction strategies. It uses less energy, water and natural resources in comparison to a conventional building, creates less waste and provides a healthier living environment. Such buildings and constructions incorporate several sustainable features such as efficient water use, energy efficiency and eco-friendly construction materials, use of renewable or alternative energy sources and recyclable materials, effective use of landscapes, effective control and building management systems and improved indoor quality for health and comfort.

There are many components of green buildings, namely

- Air-conditioning and air quality
- Design efficiency
- Energy generation and conservation
- Environmental sustainability
- Materials used

- Safety and security
- Sewage treatment
- Water efficiency.

TERI'S RETREAT TRAINING CENTRE, GURGAON

Teri's Retreat Training Centre in Gurgaon is an ideal example of a green building, showcasing the application of passive design aspects to maintain the environmental sustainability of the construction. The centre has a biomass gasifier and a small solar panelled roof trap for its daily electricity consumption. A biomass gasifier can provide 50 kW of electricity which can be harnessed and trapped into battery banks. The solar panels have an additional capacity of 10.7 kW which is used during the day, the excess of which is stored in battery banks.

The building has solar chimneys which cool the building by providing vents for the warm air which rises upwards. The cool air from underground chills the inside air. The roof is insulated using vermiculite concrete and white finish China mosaic, making the roof surface reflective, thus reducing the requirement of cooling devices. Parts of the walls are insulated using expanded polystyrene. Parts of the parapet walls have 24 solar water heating panels that can provide up to 2,000 litres of hot water every day.

The campus has been planned in such a way so as to take advantage of the existing landscape and use it for the most efficient usage of the environment without polluting it. The deciduous trees on the southern side of the building that provide shade during summers let in winter sun after shedding their leaves, thus providing the much-needed warmth. It has a sewage treatment plant which stores the sludge and the first processing is done on the waste water by microbes. The partially treated water is then sent to the field where the reeds (special plants), whose roots act as filters, remove the toxic components of the water. The water thus treated is then used for irrigation and is also suitable for construction purposes.

Green Buildings—Ratings and Certifications

The Leadership in Energy and Environmental Design (LEED) rating system developed by the US Green Building Council (USGBC) is the most popular and globally recognized rating system for environment-friendly green buildings. LEED India, administered by the India Green Building Council (IGBC), has certified 540 buildings in India as green in 2013.[1] By 2014, India had more than 2,500 registered green[2] building projects (already constructed or in the building or planning stage) covering 1.54 billion sq ft[3] and is among the top five countries on the world green map. This means that Indian buildings adhere to stringent criterion in five environmental categories shown in Figure 2. For each of the broad categories shown in Figure 2, there are credits for each individual criterion which address the specific impact on the environment by the design and construction. Based on the total credits, the different levels of green certification are awarded. Additionally, the certification also lays emphasis on innovation and design process for sustainable building expertise and design measures, and the same are incorporated in the certification credits.

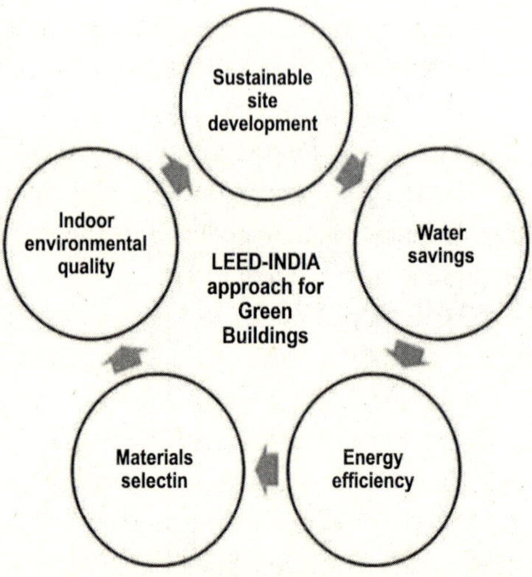

Figure 2: LEED parameters for green building certification

Table 1: LEED country rankings outside of US, 2014[4]

Rank	*Country*	*GSM* of LEED-certified space (million)*	*Total GSM of LEED- registered space (millions)*	*Total number of LEED-certified and registered projects*
1	Canada	17.74	58.66	4,068
2	China	14.3	96.22	1,638
3	India	11.64	66.22	1,657
4	South Korea	3.84	16.61	242
5	Taiwan	2.98	6.97	114
6	Germany	2.9	7.32	365
7	Brazil	2.85	23.24	829
8	Singapore	2.16	3.86	91
9	UAE	1.82	47.16	850
10	Finland	1.45	3.56	148

*GSM: Gross Square Metres

Table 2: LEED city rankings for India

LEED Rank	*City*	*No. of Registered Projects*
1	Mumbai	319
2	Delhi	199
3	Bangalore	198
4	Pune	197

The other rating system followed in India is the TERI-GRIHA Rating system. TERI's Green Rating for Integrated Habitat Assessment (GRIHA) is used to evaluate and rate the environmental performance of new and existing buildings, and its codes and guidelines are based on national and international energy and environmental principles, which are revised every three years for any upgradation or developments. It has derived inputs from the Bureau of Energy Efficiency, the Ministry of Non-Conventional Energy Sources, MoEF (Ministry of Environment and Forests), Government of India, and the Bureau of Indian Standards (BIS) and aims to achieve efficient resource utilization and better quality of life in the buildings.

LEED INDIA CERTIFICATION LEVELS

LEED certified: 23-27 credits
LEED silver: 28-33 credits
LEED gold: 34-44 credits
LEED platinum: 45-61 credits

Table 3 lists some of the greener projects in India and their LEED ratings.

Table 3: Green buildings in India and their payback periods[5]

Name of the Project	*Location*	*Build-up Area (sq ft)*	*Rating Achieved*	*Increase in Cost (%)*	*Payback Period (years)*
CII-Sorabji Godrej GBC	Hyderabad	20,000	Platinum	18	7
ITC Green Centre	Gurgaon	170,000	Platinum	15	6
Wipro	Gurgaon	175,000	Platinum	8	5
Technopolis	Kolkata	72,000	Gold	6	3
Spectral Services Consultants Office	Noida	15,000	Platinum	8	4
HITAM	Hyderabad	78,000	Silver	2	3
Grundfos Pump	Chennai	40,000	Gold	6	3

Green Buildings: Components

Air-conditioning and Air Quality

Air-conditioning is an essential component of buildings with a large amount of power requirement being used just for keeping indoor temperatures at comfortable levels. The traditional methods of air conditioning require air conditioners and coolers in summers and heaters in winters. Smart, clean and green methods use the principles

AIR-CONDITIONING AND ITS BURDEN

The number of US homes equipped with air conditioning rose from 64 to 100 million between 1993 and 2009, whereas 50 million air-conditioning units were sold in China in 2010 alone. And it is projected that the number of air-conditioned vehicles in China will reach 100 million in 2015, having more than doubled in just five years.

of geo-thermal heating and reversal of temperatures underground to maintain temperatures along with innovations in design to use perforated materials and thick walls which would reduce the amount of solar heat entering the building, thus requiring reduced heating power requirements.

The geo-thermal heating and cooling method requires rooms to be connected by underground tunnels and chimneys on the surface. The building can maintain a comfortable temperature of 20-30°C throughout the year by using this method. Such technology has been tried and tested in the Resource-Efficient TERI Retreat for Environmental Awareness and Training campus, TERI, located in Gual Pahari in Gurgaon, where it is used to keep the entire campus at comfortable temperatures throughout the year.

Another system uses water circulating through underground heat exchanger pipes, connecting them to a water air-conditioning system. This uses the basic principle of underground cellars being cooler than the outside surface during summer and the vice versa during winters. This allows the system to extract the colder temperatures below earth and then pass this to an air-conditioning unit. The air-conditioning unit extracts the cooler temperature and further cools it to finally supply it to the building during summers. This allows the buildings to maintain a single temperature inside the rooms throughout the year, achieving cooling temperatures between 22 and 27°C.[6]

HVAC (heating, ventilating, and air-conditioning) is a popular system used globally for providing 'conditioned' air[i] in the buildings so that they have a comfortable and safe working environment. It is a group of components for moving heat to where it is wanted (the conditioned space) or to remove heat from where it is not wanted (the conditioned space) and put it where it is unobjectionable (the outside air). The basic components of a central HVAC system are:

- Fans to circulate air
- Supply air ductwork for flowing the air from the supply fans to the conditioned space
- Air devices (air supply outlets and return air inlets)
- Return air ductwork to flow back the air from the conditioned space to the plenum[ii]
- Outside air device to allow entrance of outside air into the plenum
- Plenum
- Filter section to remove particulate matters from the mixed air
- Heat exchangers (hot water coil, steam coil, refrigerant evaporator, or chilled water coil)
- Auxiliary heating devices
- Compressors and condensers to remove heat from refrigerant vapour
- Controls.

Design Efficiency

Design efficiency contributes in large part to making a building clean and sustainable. The building should be designed in such a way that it harnesses the benefits of the surroundings, landscape and the natural resources available. It also affects the building's orientation to the sun, thus impacting its ability to optimize passive heating and cooling, as

---

[i] 'Conditioned' air means that the air is clean and odour-free, and the temperature, humidity and movement of the air are within comfort ranges.

[ii] 'Plenum' means air-mixing chamber.

THE TERMITE BUILDING

The East Gate Centre in Harare, Zimbabwe, largely made of concrete, has a ventilation system which is designed after termite mounds. The outside air is either warmed or cooled by the building mass depending on which is hotter—the building concrete or the air. It is then vented into the building's floors and offices before exiting via chimneys at the top. The complex also consists of two buildings side by side that are separated by an open space that is covered by glass and open to the local breezes.

well as natural ventilation.[7] Other factors of design which impact the building's performance are wall, roof and floor insulation, wall and roof colour, window covering, overhang depths, glazing types, openable windows, window-to-wall ratio, infiltration of air, etc.

Choosing the appropriate design according to the available land and surroundings is a vital part of the building planning and designing. Contrary to popular belief, a square or circular design might not always be the best layout for a particular site. It might include channelling the sunlight and wind for ambient temperature regulation, insulating walls against loss of inside heat during winters, or having the right kind of windows for lighting and ventilation. Some architects argue that the traditional architectures with underground tunnels and courtyard designs with large atrium kind of spaces in the central area might result in various energy-saving aspects of the buildings. Wipro Technologies Development Centre's[8] courtyard design, inspired by the traditional havelis, performs varied functions—its primary function being that of a light well, it acts as a micro-climate generator and reduces energy consumption; mutual shading of the courtyard walls keeps the inside temperature lower than that outside; and a big water body and vegetation in the middle of the courtyard keeps the building environment cooler by evaporative cooling.

Landscaping is another aspect of building design and planning. For the building to take advantage of its surroundings, the landscaping should be such that it allows passage of sunlight in winters and provides shade in the summers. The natural direction of wind flow, if considered during the designing phase, can result in the building walls being aligned so that they allow natural air for cooling and ventilation into the building, which results in energy saving by not using air-conditioners.

Proper design of the building—square, circular, L-shaped or any other shape—can also play a crucial role in keeping the temperatures lower by allowing or restricting the flow of air in the different seasons. Thick walls and double-glazed windows also lower the inside temperature along with high-reflective roof surfaces using insulated composite slab roof with extruded polystyrene. The platinum LEED certified buildings of ITC Green Centre and Wipro Campus in Gurgaon have used these innovative solutions to keep their buildings cooler during summers. The ITC Green Centre has an L-shaped design and a central atrium, resulting in glare-free natural lighting, and one area is always covered in shade to reduce cooling requirements.

Figure 3: ITC's Green Centre

ITC's Green Centre is a climate responsive building with its architecture designed so as to allow natural light to penetrate the building during the daytime. The high-reflective surface of the roof reduces the heat absorption to 90 per cent, thus reducing the roof surface temperature by 30°C and the air-conditioning energy usage on the top floor by 10 to 15 per cent.[9] The walls are 250 mm in thickness and the windows have high performance double-glazed glasses, which reduce the solar heat intake by the buildings by more than 65 per cent.[10] The building's annual energy consumption is 130,000 kWh per annum, which for a conventional building is 620,000 kWh per annum.[11]

'Building Envelope' is the building's outer surface, which takes the most heat from the sun and the surroundings. If it is designed properly to minimize the heat intake of the building, it can result in considerable energy saving for the buildings. These include use of Autoclaved Aerated Concrete (AAC) blocks,[iii] wall insulations, high reflective roof surfaces, hollow blocks for walls, double-glazed windows, etc. Some of such enveloping methods and the potential energy savings by their usage are shown in Table 3.

Table 4: Energy saving by envelope methods of passive designing[12]

Method	*Energy saving (%)*
AAC wall	3-8
Brick wall with 75 mm extruded polystyrene insulation	3-8
High albedo[iv] roofing material	2-3
Low-U[v] glass and glazing	6-8
Orientation	0.5-1
Roof garden	1-2

[iii] AAC is a lightweight, precast, concrete building material invented that simultaneously provides structure, insulation, and fire and mould-resistance

[iv] Albedo is the diffuse reflectivity or reflecting power of a surface

[v] U Value: Unit for heat transfer due to temperature difference (w/m^2 °C)

Method	*Energy saving (%)*
Roof insulation (extruded polystyrene)	5-6
Thermal break	1-2

Energy Generation and Conservation

Smart buildings can have many green sources of energy generation. The green sources for generating energy for a city or country have been dealt with in Chapter 5. The same sources, though at a smaller scale, can be used even for residential homes, buildings and apartments.

Most green buildings across the world use solar energy for heating purposes—even the temperature regulation of swimming pool water is done using solar energy. Solar energy is gaining more popularity with the advent of low-energy consuming CFL bulbs, LED lighting systems and low-voltage fans. For colder regions, solar space heating systems for buildings can be used to centrally heat the buildings for at least 80 to 95 per cent of the year when combined with a thermal storage.

ENERGY-STRAINED INDIA

In 2013, India saw a shortfall of 17 GW, with residential electricity being shut off for 16 hours per day in some areas. China fell short by 30 to 40 GW, resulting in energy rationing and factory closures.

Not all the buildings generate the electricity required for themselves—most of them rely on off-site renewable resources or vendors of green energy to meet their daily requirements. These vendors, in turn, generate the energy through greener methods using renewable resources like wind or solar energy. The biomass gasifier system, though around for a long time, is not yet being used for electricity generation for bigger complexes—it is mostly used as a back-up source of energy.

For conservation of the energy used in the green buildings, smart metering and smart grid systems are used, which can not only monitor but even control the electronic devices from a central, remote location. Additionally, retrofitting electrical devices with low-energy consuming devices like CFL and LED bulbs, low-voltage fans, dimmer switches, study lights modified for use as night bulbs and many more, can be used to conserve the energy.

RESIDENTIAL HOMES AND GHG EMISSION

Residential homes globally consume 29 per cent of the total energy and contribute to 21 per cent of greenhouse gas emissions.

An automated system integrated with IT and power line communication technology can help buildings make use of sensors for automatic switching on, dimming and switching off the lighting devices. It also switches off the electricity when the sensors detect that daylight is enough to light the rooms. The efficient designs would enable use of natural light instead of electrical lights during day. Phantom loads can have a surprising electric draw and thus TVs and other appliances should be unplugged when not in use or should be kept in 'standby mode'. Use of power strips can also reduce phantom loads, thus helping reduce the total load on the energy consumption of buildings.

Environmental Sustainability

Making a building environmentally sustainable means constructing it in such a way that it can sustain itself for future generations without degrading the environment. It also means that the inner surroundings of the building will be such that it will reduce pollutants from reaching the occupants and allow them to breathe fresh air. Additionally, it will reduce the emission levels for the buildings.

Indoor air quality of a building for the well-being of the occupants should reduce volatile organic compounds, or VOCs, and microbial contaminants. For this it requires a properly designed ventilation system for recirculation of fresh or filtered air. This is also dependent on the material chosen for construction which has zero or low VOC emissions. Cleaning and maintenance products also emit gases, some of them toxic, like formaldehyde, which can have a detrimental impact on occupants' health, comfort, and productivity.

Practices like providing soil with organic nutrients by converting waste and waste water into fertilizer would create carbon sinks which remove carbon dioxide from the atmosphere, thus reducing the GHG emissions of the building. The use of greener energy sources, HVAC systems, geo-thermal heating systems and underground tunnels also reduces the GHG emissions of the buildings. The idea is to reduce the GHG emission by reducing energy consumption and fossil fuel burning, which generate the most GHG in the households.

Material Usage

As evident from the environmental sustainability of the building, building materials are important in making the building actually green. It includes using renewable materials like bamboo and straw, dimension stone, recycled stone, recycled metal or using recyclable, non-toxic, reusable materials. Using materials which are extracted and manufactured locally at the building site can minimize the energy used in their transportation. For waste minimization, and for maximization of recycling, manufacturing the materials at one location makes the process optimal.

The following points need to be taken care of while choosing material and construction techniques:

- Foundations—use of composite foundation technique to stabilize the foundation and to reduce the energy content of the foundation
- Material with low embodied energy—use of soil stabilized blocks, prefabricated ferrocement channels, reinforced cement concrete framed structure
- Thermal insulation—use of thick expanded polystyrene insulation on walls and vermiculite insulation on roofs
- Non-toxic and recyclable materials—these include trass, linoleum, sheep wool, panels made from paper flakes, compressed earth block, adobe, baked earth, rammed earth, clay, vermiculite, flax linen, sisal, sea grass, cork, expanded clay grains, coconut, wood fibre plates, calcium sandstone, concrete

Nano-material Usage

An exciting recent research is around the usage of nano-materials. It has highlighted the potential use of nano-materials in various fields related to building construction, including material energy efficiency and water treatment. Nano-materials are defined as materials with at least one external dimension in the size range from approximately 1 to 100 nanometres. To understand one nanometre, take the measure of a single millimetre—the smallest division on an ordinary ruler. Divide each of the divisions into 1 million parts—one such part would be a nanometre.

The building materials domain is one of the main beneficiaries of the application of nano-materials that will improve the properties of concrete, steel, glass and insulating materials used for construction. Improving the materials' resistance and durability will reduce environmental pollution by reducing the carbon footprint of the building.

In general, the largest quantities of pollutants are due to the production of various construction materials and the energy required for their services. The use of nano-materials in the composition of some materials such as cement will result in significant reductions of CO_2 pollution and the use of performance thermal insulations will result in efficient use of energy for air conditioning. Moreover, nano-materials applied to the surfaces of structural elements of the building can contribute to environmental cleaning through photocatalytic reactions.[13]

The size of the particles being a critical factor, the material properties significantly differ at the nano-scale, when compared to those at the macro scale. Physical phenomena begin to occur differently below the boundary limit: gravity becomes unimportant, electrostatic forces and quantum effects start to prevail upon the other properties of the material. At the same time, the proportion of atoms on the surface starts to increase relatively in comparison to those inside, creating the so-called 'nano-effect'. All these nano-properties directly affect the properties of the materials at a macro scale and, from this point, the power of nano-technology is emphasized: if the elements are properly manipulated at the nano-scale, the macro-properties are affected and new materials and processes can be developed.

The most important nano-materials with potential use in construction process are:

- Carbon nano-tubes
- Titanium dioxide nano-particles (TiO_2)
- Silicon dioxide nano-particles (SiO_2)
- Zinc oxide nano-particles (ZnO)
- Silver-based nano-particles (Ag)
- Aluminium oxide nano-particles (Al_2O_3)
- Zirconium oxide nano-particles (ZrO_2)
- Wolfram (Tungsten) oxide nano-particles (WO_3)[14]

Nano-technology and nano-materials can be used in different areas of design and construction. Nano-materials have various unique properties which can significantly fix various construction issues, and may change the requirement and organization of the construction process.

These include products with the following applications:

- Lighter and stronger structural composites
- Low maintenance coating
- Improving pipe joining materials and techniques
- Better properties of cementing materials
- Reducing the thermal transfer rate of fire retardant and insulation materials
- Increasing the sound absorption of acoustic absorbers
- Increasing the reflectivity of glass[15]

Application of nano-materials for constructional purposes would not only help in prolonging their lifetime, but would also keep a check on the energy spent by them, at the same time gauging their reactions under different situations like fire, corrosion, water penetration, fractures, cracks, etc. Nano-materials also help improve energy efficiency and facilitate the ease of maintenance to provide increased living comfort.

The various products and applications in construction technology where nano-materials and nano-technology can be implemented are:

- Nano-technologies for concrete
- Nano-technologies for steel
- Nano-technologies for wood
- Nano-technologies for glass
- Nano-technologies for coatings and paintings
- Nano-technologies for thermal insulation
- Nano-technologies for fire protection
- Nano-technologies for structural monitoring

Sewage and Waste Water Treatment

For waste water treatment and management, the technologies available for green and clean alternatives require a traditional sewage system, but the treatment has a few added processes to make the resultant water usable for irrigation or construction. The retreat campus at TERI uses root zone techniques for the same. The sewage collected at the settling tank is partly decomposed by the microbes after the sludge settles down. The resulting water is then passed through soil containing reed (phragmites). These reeds are well-adapted to waterlogged soils. The roots of these reeds act as filters which absorb and remove the toxic substances from water. The treated water thus produced can be used for irrigation.

GREEN BUILDINGS AND WATER SUSTAINABILITY

Most of the Asian countries are water-stressed and in countries like India, the water table has reduced drastically over the last decade. Green buildings and architecture encourage the use of water in a self-sustainable manner through reducing, recycling and reusing strategies. By this, green homes can save potable water to an extent of 30–50 per cent.

Apart from innovative plumbing methods, techniques to conserve water include the use of waterless urinals in the building. These urinals use biological blocks containing particular bacteria that reduce odour problems and blockages in the urinals. The sewage treatment facility can use fluidized aerobic bioreactors, which not only assist organic processes but also significantly reduce the space necessary for the facility, as well as positively affect power and operating costs.

Water Efficiency

Green complexes employ modern methods to harvest and store rainwater and for efficient water conservation. The rainwater harvesting system mostly works on the concept of catchment area (located on rooftops, land surfaces, altering vegetation cover, collection devices—aquifers—and a conveyance system). Some buildings have dedicated rainwater harvesting pools which can prevent run-off by more than 60 per cent. Grass concrete pavers can help in reducing storm water run-off. Additionally, they also help in decreasing the heat island effect caused by asphalt pavers. Terrace gardens at various levels not only help in reducing the run-off but in also filtering sediments and pollutants from the storm water before it is stored in the aquifers.

Figure 4: Rainwater harvesting

The harvested water can be used for drinking, storage and irrigation. It can provide an independent water supply during heavy rains or can be used to supplement the main supply. It also helps in avoiding soil erosion by water run-off by mitigating flooding of low-lying areas.

Along with rainwater harvesting, efficient flushing systems and aerated taps to deliver water at preset rates can help in conserving water. Many buildings have waterless urinals or toilets with preset pressure flushes which reduce water consumption for such activities. Efficient plumbing fixtures and recycled waste water usage can result in more than 50 per cent less water consumption.

Recycling of water is another area which results in a large amount of water conservation. The grey water that is generated in the building complexes can be further treated to make it usable for cleaning and flushing purposes.

ICT and Green Buildings

Integrated Communication Technology is an integral part of today's technological boom. This is a major part of how the buildings of the future will be connected to each other through wireless technologies and smart cards. All the buildings will have smart meters controlling and monitoring the energy usage and emissions of each building, with the provision for shifting the load or selling it to neighbouring buildings to control demand and supply of energy.

Use of ICT also introduces the principle of smart grid and smart metering into the day-to-day management of building systems. Smart metering, used mainly for control and monitoring, in tandem with other policy measures such as load control, peak-load sharing and peak-load offsetting, can bring down the energy consumption and tariffs for residents by a significant amount. The system is already being employed in several cities of Norway and other countries of Europe as well. The dynamic system of sensors used in street lights, for controlling the dimming of the lights when not in use, can help automate building lighting devices in the common areas.

The buildings of the future will not have just the components built intelligently but will have devices and equipment which will have integrated intelligence in them to help in bringing down the emission and energy consumption of the buildings, thus resulting in construction which is not just green and efficient, but smart (technology-wise) too.

Policy Measures

In addition to using all the passive design techniques and modern technologies for making the buildings green, there is a requirement for intervention by the government—central and local bodies—to see to it that proper measures are taken for the promotion and adoption of green and smart buildings.

The Ministry of New and Renewable Energy or MNRE, under the 11th Five Year Plan, had granted the following incentives to various stakeholders under its 'Energy-efficient solar/green buildings' scheme to GRIHA-NRS projects. The various schemes and incentives are listed in Table 5. Most of such schemes are monetary at the moment. The government needs to introduce better policy measures to incentivize not only the building owners, design consultants and local bodies, but also the occupants. These should be monetary benefits as well as changes related to the improvement of lifestyles of all the stakeholders, resulting in long-term savings. Proper promotional programmes need to be organized to make people aware of the benefits of green buildings in terms of savings in electricity bills, reduced power cuts, as well as a comfortable and cleaner environment. All the components of a green building work in tandem to make the living environment fitter and healthier for the residents.

Table 5: Incentives to promote green buildings

Stakeholders	*Incentives*
Building Owners[4]	Reimbursement of registration-cum-rating fee for minimum 3-star rating
Architects/Design Consultants	Monetary compensation for minimum 3-star project rating
Municipal Corporations and Urban Local Bodies	• Monetary compensation for announcing rebates in property tax for green buildings • Mandatory ruling for new government buildings to adhere to GRIHA ratings • Annual awards for best performing body
Building communities	Annual awards to 5-star rated GRIHA buildings
Institutions	Monetary compensation for promotional activities like organizing workshops/ seminars/ training / publications/ awareness campaigns, etc.

NOW YOU KNOW:

- Green buildings are those that are constructed in an environmentally responsible and resource-efficient manner
- India has two green building certifications in use—LEED India and TERI-GRIHA
- Green buildings can maintain a room temperature of 20-30°C without air-conditioning by using geo-thermal heating and cooling methods
- HVAC system can reduce the energy consumption for maintenance of comfortable atmosphere in the buildings
- Buildings can adopt design features like ventilation system, passive designing, building envelope and open spaces to regulate the inside temperatures
- Buildings or campuses can use smart metering and smart grid systems for monitoring and controlling their energy consumption
- Use of organic and recyclable materials reduce the VOC emission in the buildings
- Use of phragmites for waste water treatment can recycle water for irrigation and construction
- Rainwater harvesting reduces water run-off, replenishes the water sources and provides water for future use
- The Indian government has introduced incentives for changing existing buildings to green buildings by adopting policy measures in the 11th Five Year Plan.

7

The Dynamic City: Infrastructure for the Smart City

This chapter will focus on the infrastructural aspects of building smart cities. It will discuss in detail Harappan architecture and how infrastructure like drainage, residential spaces, water systems and storage spaces were designed. The chapter will then discuss the various components of physical infrastructure for a smart city. The various components would be discussed in relation to their existing situation in India.

Harappan Architecture

The Indus Valley civilization was notable for its architecture. The excavations found in Harappa, Mohenjo-Daro, Lothal, Kalibangan and Dholavira show the granularity of the Harappan design and architecture which was way ahead of its time. The city plan conformed to standard rectangular forms with defined high and low public spaces and a citadel. The city had streets running parallel to the outside wall and the drainage system ran parallel to the street. The city walls were massive, built mainly to control trade and to prevent the city from getting flooded. City walls were also used to demarcate the various sections of the city. Harappan cities were built on a grid system with houses built in block form. The houses were mostly made of sun-dried or kiln-fired mud bricks strong enough to withstand natural calamities and regular wear and tear. The most elaborate buildings of the city were the great bath, the granary and the comprehensive water management system.

Figure 1: Mohenjo-Daro ruins

The great bath in Mohenjo-Daro was a public bath—a vast 12m-by-7m rectangular structure which could hold 140 cubic metres of water. The bath was filled with water from a well on the eastern side and had a corbelled drain of 1.8 metres in height.[1] A wooden superstructure surrounded the bath and a public street lay on the perimeter of the bath. The bath is said to be of religious significance, with bathing being an essential ritual cleansing act, but there is no proof of the religious connotation of the great bath.

The granary at Mohenjo-Daro lay to the west of the great bath, a huge building of 27m-by-50m built of brick plinths arranged in 9-by-3 rows. There was another granary at Harappa—a 47m-by-17m structure supported by a wooden superstructure. Both are impressive pieces of architecture.

Figure 2: Indus Valley civilization city layout

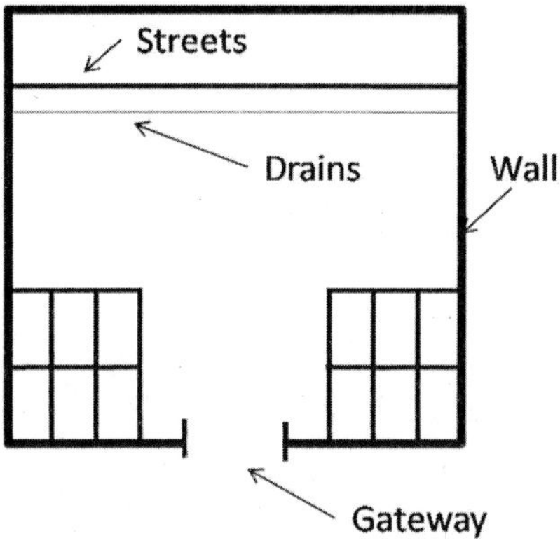

Figure 3: Indus Valley civilization city illustration

In Harappa, they had a sophisticated water management system. The domestic drinking water system had wells to draw water from reservoirs to store it during times of scanty rainfall; and drains—both open and covered—to move the dirty water from the bathrooms and toilets. The drinking water from the wells was drawn by an elaborate hydraulic system and was directly supplied to the households. At Dholavira, there was an extensive system of check dams and raised reservoirs to harvest fresh water from the seasonal channels of the Mansar and Manhar rivers. The city had an intricate network of storm water drains linked to an arterial drain with a variety of manholes, paved flooring and capstones. The waste water from the drains was channelled away to a reservoir around the city.

The architects of the Indus Valley civilization could be called 'smart architects' in terms of city planning, given their foresight in the use of architectural elements, taking into account the sustainability of their town structures. The sustainability of their buildings is evident in the excavations found at the different sites, which have withstood the wear and tear of over thousands of years. The city architects had a clear vision of what the city was required to withstand, given the smaller population and mostly agrarian economy. The present city planners need to take inspiration from these ancient examples of city planning to build sustainable infrastructure which is relevant over future generations.

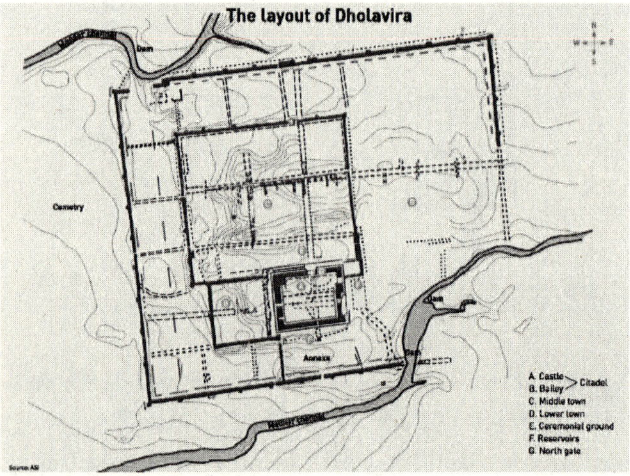

Figure 4: The Indus Valley civilization city layout for Dholavira

Urban Infrastructure in India

The urban infrastructure in India is managed by urban local bodies like municipal corporations of cities or towns, or the city development authority. In some cases, special bodies have been established to create urban infrastructure, often with a Public-Private Partnership model.

Urban planning can be categorized as a conglomeration of GRIDs covering all dimensions of urban planning and urban living. We will divide them as Hard GRIDs and Soft GRIDs. Let us elaborate this further.

A Hard GRID essentially refers to physical infrastructure, like roads, power lines, water works, transportation, sanitation network, etc. which form the core of the hardware in the city. A Hard GRID has to be planned and executed, at least partially, well in advance for the city. A Soft GRID, on the other hand, defines how this Hard GRID will be optimally utilized to maximize the returns—whether economic or social. It refers to the underlying quality standards which the Hard GRID should be able to deliver. Aspects such as source of the power used, fidelity and speed of telecommunication network, quality and recycling rate of water, transportation routes and modes will be some of the areas under Soft GRID.

As one would perceive, both these GRIDs work closely with each other and in an integrated manner lead to the overall economic growth of the city.

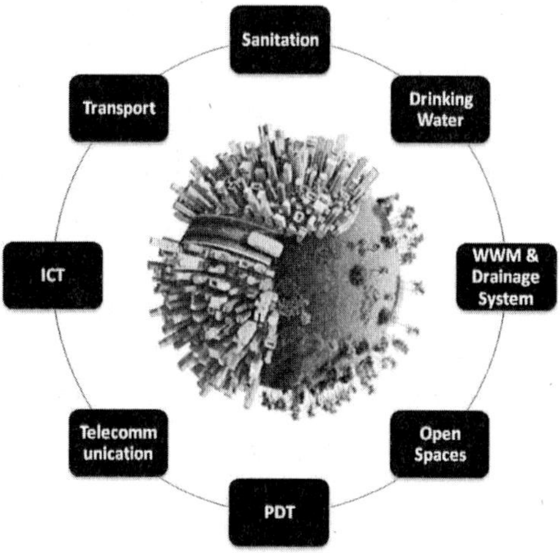

Figure 5: Typical urban physical infrastructure (Hard GRID)

Some typical examples under these GRIDs are:

- Water supply
- Sewerage and solid waste management system
- Waste water management and drainage system
- Construction of roads, highways, expressways
- Urban transport system—local trains, railways, buses, metro, waterways, airways
- Power distribution and transmission
- Mobile telephony
- Information and communication technology
- Parking lots and spaces
- Development of heritage areas
- Preservation of water bodies
- Health and educational institutions
- Governance and public services
- Employment generation

Part of the work is done under the PPP model with private parties as the stakeholders, part by private developers and the rest by the urban local bodies or municipalities. After the liberalization in 1991, power and telecom were a few of the sectors to be privatized. Health and educational systems, employment programmes, governance and public services will be discussed in detail in Chapter 8. Parking lots, open spaces and recreational sites development will be dealt with in Chapter 9.

Water

Access to water is not universal in India. Drinking water is generally supplied from surface water from rivers and if untreated contains agricultural pollutants, pesticides, contaminants, industrial chemicals, factory waste, and leach from pipes and storage tanks. Sometimes the pollutants in the supply water are the byproducts of the water treatment process. Even the groundwater might need UV treatment

WATER QUALITY IN INDIA

Biochemical Oxygen Demand (BOD) is the amount of oxygen required by microorganisms to degrade organic pollutants and higher BOD signifies higher level of organic pollution as more organisms in water would require more and more amount of oxygen. 15 per cent Indian rivers in 2005 had a high BOD greater than 6 mg/l, and 19 per cent had BOD between 3-6 mg/l whereas the acceptable level of BOD for drinking quality surface water before treatment is 3 mg/l.

to filter out the high levels of iron, chlorine, fluoride and other metals in the water.

Less than 50 per cent of urban households have drinking water sources within their premises and only 70 per cent of the urban households have access to tap water, that too for limited durations.[2] In the metropolitan cities with a population of more than 1 million like Ahmedabad, Bangalore, Delhi, Hyderabad, Pune and Allahabad, water supply is only for a few hours every day—one hour to 18 hours with the average duration being 4.3 hours.[3] The longest water supply was 12 hours for Chandigarh and the shortest for Rajkot at 0.3 hours per day.[4] Thiruvananthapuram and Kota were the only two Indian cities in 2010 to have continuous water supply for 24 hours.[5] Amongst 28 cities surveyed by the World Bank for supply water quality, none had performance indicators close to average international standards.[6]

Due to inadequate water supply, most of the households depend on at least one other source of drinking water, like groundwater through borewells or pumps. As a result of this, groundwater is being increasingly over-exploited whereas the surface water is mostly inadequately or inefficiently utilized. Even when the water is supplied through taps, the quality of the water supply is questionable with the presence of impurities in the water, or water having impurities and high levels of fluoride, nitrate, calcium, potassium and heavy metals. The government generally uses water testing kits to control the quality of water supplied through taps. Additionally the water supply is unmetered in most of the cities and the distribution losses of treated water range between 25 per cent and 40 per cent.[7]

The urban poor are the worst affected social class when it comes to water pollution. Almost all the urban poor do not have any access to potable water and the same segment is the worst affected by water-borne diseases, which ensures that they remain in poverty. As of December 2013, the Government of India defined the urban poor as those earning less than Rs 32 a day. The commercial rate at which clean bottled water is available in urban areas is up to Rs 20 per litre. With each adult requiring about two litres of drinking water per day, the urban poor in India are permanently marginalized for access to clean drinking water.

Table 1: Cost impacts of poor drinking water

Study	*Result*
Hygiene and Health in Developing Countries: A Cost-Benefit Assessment, Bjorn Larsen, The Second International Scientific Forum on Home Hygiene Conference, New Delhi, 15-16 April 2002	425,000 out of a total of 800,000 'preventable' child deaths per annum may be actually 'prevented' by improved water and sanitation
Environmental Health in India: Priorities in Andhra Pradesh, Environmental and Social Development Unit, South Asian Region, The World Bank 2001	Over 40,000 deaths amongst children occur in Andhra Pradesh every year due to lack of poor sanitation
The Global Burden of Disease 2000, World Health Organization, 2000	5.4 per cent of all deaths in the world are due to water-related diseases.
How Access to Urban Potable Water and Sewerage Connections Affects Child Mortality, Anqing Shi, Development Research Group, The World Bank, 2000	Child mortality rate is inversely correlated with access to potable water and sewerage connection.

Study	*Result*
The Cost of Inaction: Valuing the Economy-Wide Cost of Environmental Degradation in India, Asian Environmental Division, The World Bank, 1995	With the provision of safe water and sanitation, there will be a reduction of 47 per cent of water-related deaths

Drinking Water in Smart Cities

For treating water for the removal of microorganisms and bacteria, other than conventional ways of treating with chlorine, water can be passed through special microbes which kill the bacteria, clean it of toxins, and increase its oxygen content. To ensure the efficient distribution of the supply water, the controlling authorities need to properly supervise the maintenance of the distribution and service pipes. Use of stainless steel and other non-corrosive materials for pipes prevents a significant amount of water from being lost during distribution. Additionally, it is imperative that proper measures be taken for maintenance of the water and waste water treatment plants, pumping stations and household plumbing. This will reduce the levels of lead and chlorination byproducts in the supply water, thus reducing the risks of residual pollution (like increased risks of cancer) due to corrosion. This would also render the necessity to disinfect the water post-treatment for chlorination byproducts. Else the supply water can be additionally filtered at the final distribution point with a carbon filter for removing chlorine, lead and other impurities.

Another aspect of drinking water supply is its availability and access. Authorities should initiate measures so that 100 per cent of the households have access to continuous water supply. This can be achieved by renovation of the distribution networks, installation of meters, introduction of a commercial system to monitor and control the water supply and manage the revenues from it, and effective grass-root social intermediation programmes by the government, communities and NGOs. This was demonstrated in the cities of Hubli, Belgaum and Gulbarga in the state of Karnataka by a private operator, Veolia, which was successful in increasing the water supply from once every 2-15 days to 24 hours per day for 180,000 households of the three cities in 2006-2008.[8] In doing this, the bulk amount of water supplied remained the same. Metering the water supply not only increased the identification and legalization of illegal connections, but also increased the number of customers, thus helping the operator companies recover their operating costs thanks to the reduction of non-revenue water.

Waste Water Treatment

Waste water treatment mostly involves separation of solids from liquids by sedimentation and then treating the water with biological microbes or chemicals to make it fit for reuse. This treated water is then free from suspended solids, bacteria, algae, viruses, fungi, minerals such as iron, manganese and sulphur, and man-made chemical pollutants including fertilizers. Biological processes like aerated lagoons, activated sludge or slow sand filters can be employed in the treatment of waste water so that the water is fit for further use for irrigation, construction and flushing toilets. Many organizations use reeds such as phragmatis to treat the waste water and free it from microbes and toxic materials.

Waste water treatment should remove dissolved oxygen and maintain an optimal pH and alkalinity level to prevent the corrosion in low pressure industrial boilers, thus making the treated industrial waste water reusable for industrial purposes. This would also result in reduction of scale formation, corrosion and fouling and would not allow harmful bacteria to grow in the water. Maintenance of optimal pH and reduction in scale formation would help in better maintenance of the piping system and prevent any leakages.

Sewerage and Sanitation Systems

Availability of sewerage and sanitation systems is a big problem in Indian cities. Despite the fact that people in the subcontinent were perhaps the pioneers in creating the drainage system in the Indus Valley civilization as mentioned earlier, drainage is a common problem in Indian cities.

In the plains, poor drainage leads to rainwater accumulation in roads and ditches; in the hilly areas it leads to accumulation of rain and storm water in road side ditches, and in the coastal cities, tidal water may get accumulated on the ground. Additionally, poor drainage systems lead to inefficient disposal or harvesting of rain or storm water, thus resulting in water logging which hampers traffic, sanitation and health. Ideally, storm water drainage and the sewerage systems in a city should be kept separate for proper management and maintenance. Also, sewage water requires treatment before being discharged into water bodies, whereas no such requirement is there for storm water.

Fifty per cent of the families have to defecate in the open due to non-availability of toilets within the premises. More than 80 per cent have no drainage system or have to live in the vicinity of open drains.[9] According to UNICEF and WHO, there are 2.5 billion people in the world lacking improved sanitation facilities, of whom 1.5 billion defecate in the open and 665 million of them are Indians.[10] A recent study showed that effective sewerage systems typically reduce diarrhoea incidence by as much as 60 per cent.[11] This is of greater concern as 88 per cent of deaths from diarrhoea occur because of unsafe water, inadequate sanitation and poor hygiene.[12]

In the state of Karnataka, only half of its 52 towns were served by a sewerage system, while in Andhra Pradesh (before its division), two-thirds of the 124 towns had no sewerage systems.[13] In fact, a study made by the government's own Urban Development ministry concluded that out of the 1,405 cities surveyed only about 700 had a water supply or waste management system in place.[14] The sewerage networks in these cities lacks maintenance, resulting in the overflow of raw sewage in open drains due to blockage, settlements and inadequate pumping capacities.

Smart Sanitation

Since sanitation is still a taboo word among Indians, there have been initiatives from the government and from communities and NGOs for tackling the situation and to spread awareness. The government has initiated a National Urban Sanitation Policy or NUSP for urban sanitation awareness and to increase the user base. It includes the following initiatives:

- Awareness generation amongst households and institutions about sanitation and its effect on public and environmental health
- Promotion of behavioural changes for healthy sanitation practices
- National-level communications strategy on awareness generation on urban sanitation
- Promoting access to households with safe sanitation facilities
- Promoting community-planned and managed toilets
- Adequate availability and 100 per cent upkeep and management of public sanitation facilities in all urban areas.

Within the framework of NUSP, NGOs and communities have initiated Community-Led Total Sanitation or CLTS programmes which aim at achieving safe sanitation practices by CLTS interventions. First started in Maharashtra, it has been employed across Indian states and has resulted in better sanitation habits amongst the urban and the rural poor. In Himachal Pradesh and Haryana, CLTS has resulted in 60-70 per cent increase in sanitation coverage over a period of four to five years during 2006-2010.[15] The communities, through CLTS, can also engage in mobilizing themselves to stop open defecation, making their locality garbage free, and undertaking the responsibility of keeping the city drains clean, thus helping the authorities in formulating an overall city sanitation plan.

Smart Sewerage and Drainage

Proper drainage systems mean separate sewerage and drains systems in the urban areas. Closed drains should be built in and around the city, especially the nearby residential areas. Any open drains should be closed to avoid leaves, plastics and other solid wastes blocking and choking the drains, which during times of heavy rain cause flooding of roads and water logging. The drains constructed should be pakka, properly maintained and cleaned by the local city municipal corporation. Additionally, to avoid drains getting choked with solid wastes like plastics, the urban local bodies should ensure that wastes are not dumped in open grounds or near drains. Proper drainage systems would also help in rainwater harvesting, zero run-off, and in controlling water run-off.

Drainage for a smart city would lead to zero run-off and no water clogging or flooding of the streets. It requires the drains to be built of non-corrosive materials so that there is no leakage, and to be fully covered to avoid deposition of sediments, sand, soil and other solid wastes. The drains would be maintained by the local authorities. Revolutionary ideas can be used in drains—for example, 'belt of extruded PVC that is constructed with tiny micro siphons that literally pull water from the ground. These micro siphons are specially constructed to utilize the capillary and siphoning properties inherent in water in a high performance drainage material. Unlike ordinary perforated pipe and filter fabrics, it doesn't clog over time.'[16]

Another aspect of designing a proper drainage system for a city is to model a storm water or rainwater harvesting system. It mainly requires the collection of rainfall data for the city, city hydrology and the demand estimation for water, which can be met through rainwater harvesting. The rainwater harvesting that has been discussed in Chapter 6 is for a building or residential campus. The same can be done for the entire city with collection tanks located at appropriate locations.

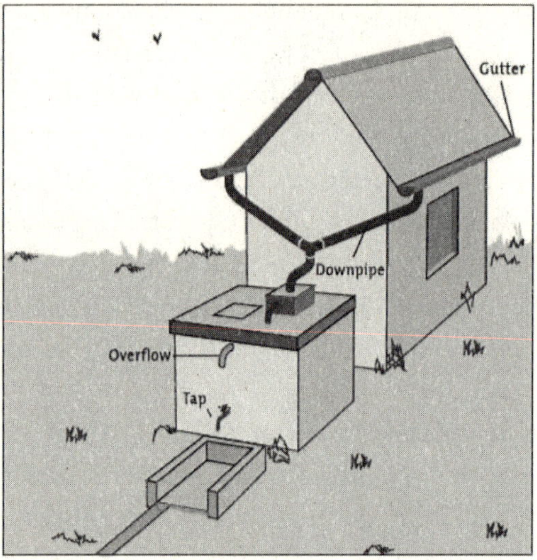

Figure 6: Rainwater harvesting system

Transport

Roadways

In 2011, India had a total road length of 4.7 million km, of which paved roads were 54 per cent.[17] The total road coverage when compared to the developed and developing nations was only behind the US, which has 6,500,000 km of roads but had all of them paved.[18] The road density in relation to area covered is greater than that of China, Brazil, Korea, Russia, South Africa and even the US (which had a road density of 0.67 km per square km). The situation in 2009-2011 is shown in Table 2.

The national highways are very important as even though these comprise only 1.5 per cent of the road network in India, they carry about 40 per cent of the total road traffic[19] and are the arterial roads for interstate movement of passengers and goods. All the national highways are surfaced and link national and state capitals, major ports and rail junctions. These are single lane (24.22 per cent), double lane (51.56 per cent) or four lanes (24.22 per cent).[20]

Table 2: Roadways comparison between a few developed and developing nations[22]

			Road length (km)		
Country	*Road Density (km/sq km)*	*Share of Paved Road (per cent) (year)*	*Total (year)*	*Motorways (per cent of total roads)*	*National Highways (per cent of total roads)*
1	2	3	4	5	6
Brazil	0.21 (2004)	NA	1,751,868 (2004)	0	93,071 (5.31)
China	0.40 (2009)	53.50 (2008)	3,860,823 (2009)	65,055 (1.69)	59,462 (1.54)
France	1.73 (2009)	100 (2009)	951,260 (2009)	11,240 (1.18)	9,020 (0.95)
India	1.42 (2011)	53.83 (2011)	4,690,342 (2011)	227 (0.005)	70,934 (1.51)
Japan	3.20 (2009)	80.11 (2009)	1,207,867 (2009)	7,642 (0.63)	54,790 (4.54)
South Korea	1.05 (2009)	79.25 (2009)	104,983 (2009)	3,776 (3.60)	13,819 (13.16)
Russian Federation	0.06 (2009)	80.06 (2007)	982,000 (2009)	NA	NA
South Africa	0.30 (2001)	17.30 (2001)	364,131 (2001)	239 (0.07)	2887 (0.79)
United Kingdom	1.72 (2009)	100 (2009)	419,665 (2009)	3,674 (0.88)	49,032 (11.68)
United States	0.67 (2009)	100 (2009)	6,545,839 (2009)	75,643 (1.16)	19,857 (0.30)

Source: CIA—World Factbook

Like the national highways, state highways are roads connecting the states' capitals to important cities of the states, linking them with national highways and state highways. They are important for within-state transportation. Their maintenance is undertaken by the state Public Works Department, unlike national highways, which are maintained by the Ministry of State for Surface Transport in India. The state highways are two-laned, four-laned or six-laned all-season, access-controlled expressways. Despite 98 per cent of the total state highways being surfaced with either black top or with cement concrete, most of the state highways suffer from poor maintenance.

The third category of roads in India is that of rural and urban roads, which connect the different districts, district headquarters and talukas. These roads are being maintained by the state PWDs and form a substantial portion of the road network. These roads are poor in quality, potholed and cannot withstand heavy vehicles. The quality and maintenance of the roads vary from location to location, but a majority of the roads miss out on proper maintenance, safety measures, pedestrian footpaths, and properly placed speed breakers. Studies suggest that about 60 per cent of the urban roads do not have footpaths in urban areas.[21]

The traffic on the urban roads is of a heterogeneous type comprising slow-moving bicycles, rickshaws, and fast-motorized vehicles like motorcycles, scooters, cars, buses and other public transport vehicles. Additionally, there are the pedestrians whose safety is also important for proper road management. Owing to variable space occupied by each of the vehicles and their speeds, design and safety measures should be properly planned for a smooth and safe flow of traffic and freight movement.

Public transport in India has historically moved at a slow speed at 20 km per hour but with the introduction of Bus Rapid Transit Systems with dedicated corridors, the speed has increased considerably. The buses used are low-floored AC or non-AC shuttles which are more comfortable for travel than the earlier prevalent high-floor buses. BRT systems used globally have specialized design, services and infrastructure which improve the quality of the public transport and reduce causes of delay. BRT systems have higher flexibility and lower operation and construction costs. The simplicity of the bus system makes them a convenient option for intra-city transport in comparison to other high-speed options like light rail, monorails or metros.

Smart Roadways

Smart transportation for the city would include roads to be built for future sustenance. The roads should be all-weather surfaced roads integrated with safety measures for road safety and sensors for monitoring and controlling road transport.

Creating a smart road network requires the following:

- Building optimally designed lanes for the road, keeping in consideration the future demand
- Tolling systems for traffic management on highways and expressways
- Extensive networks of flyovers and bypasses to prevent traffic congestion
- Rapid road transit lanes for speedy public transport and speedy emergency services
- Mass transit corridors
- Traffic control stations to divert the traffic in case of jams, accidents and other incidents
- Properly designed traffic signals for optimal traffic regulation
- Properly placed speed breakers to restrict high-speed traffic near residential areas, schools and public places
- Battery and solar operated vehicles and charging stations
- Footpath and pedestrian walks built on all roads to ensure pedestrian safety
- Bike rentals and deposit stations for providing facilities for short transports
- Adequately designed and placed parking lots
- Exhaust gas emission monitoring units
- Kiosks for street vendors so that they don't encroach upon public roads.

Use of GPS and ICT would enable the authorities to get real-time data on road traffic and help in management of signals using video

THE DIGITAL ROAD AUTHORITY—IJBURG

IJburg is a residential neighbourhood in the east of the city of Amsterdam in The Netherlands. It is being built on artificial islands recovered from low lying lakes.

The Digital Road Authority, a collaboration of the Department of Traffic and Infrastructure of the Municipality of Amsterdam, Amsterdam Smart City and Traffic Link, facilitates the cooperation between government bodies and private parties. It brings together various types of traffic data in order to provide the residents of IJburg with personalized travel advice and effective route management.

Residents receive advice through a mobile app. It is based on existing appointments in their phone's calendar, their destination and the current situation at the traffic lights, calculated on a real-time basis. The Digital Road Authority, thus, is not only in contact with departing travellers, but also with the traffic lights. It divides what it calls 'personal travel slots' based on current and expected traffic density, factoring in historic data. In case of an expected high traffic density, the Digital Road Authority can also increase the 'green time' at the traffic lights to improve traffic circulation—thereby improving the overall traffic situation.

cameras, CCTV footage and magnetic sensors. Through real-time data capture, GPS systems could be used to track the location of public buses, thus helping the traffic authorities to manage any incidents or urgent situations. Innovative management of social media solutions and applications would facilitate the 'management of potential traffic jams by changing bus routes, modifying traffic light sequences and delivering information to drivers via mobile apps indicating approximate driving times and giving alternative routes.'[23] Use of sensors to collect data regarding structural behaviour and corrosion of the roads, bridges and flyovers can help in proper maintenance of the roads and help prevent accidents and collapse of the bridges and flyovers.[24]

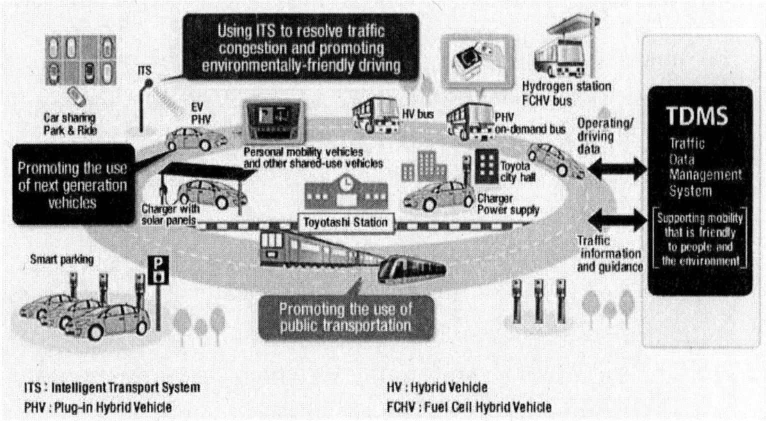

Figure 7: Traffic Data Management System in Toyota using smart applications

Railways

With more than 65,000 km of railway route, more than 7,000 stations, and more than 23 million passengers daily, the Indian Railways is one of the largest railway networks and the 9th largest employer in the world.[25] By the end of the financial year of 2011, the Indian Railways had carried about 1 billion tonnes of freight across the country for a meagre charge of less than a rupee per tonne km.[26] The suburban local trains transfer more than 10 million passengers daily in the urban areas.

The urban railway system operating within the city and the nearby suburban areas includes the suburban trains and the metro trains. These have unreserved seating accommodation and stop at all stations within the city. The metro, though introduced in India three decades ago in Kolkata in 1984, caught popular imagination as a mode of urban transportation after the success of the Delhi Metro, which commenced in 2002. After a decade of operation, the Delhi

Metro system has proved itself to be a world-class transport system, and a motivation for other Indian cities to have high-speed intra-city transport. Till July 2014, metros were operating in six Indian cities. Plans are under way to replicate this in 20 more cities. Though part of the rapid transport system, the metros run at a slower speed than their counterparts in other countries, at a maximum speed of 40 km per hour. The metros today are considered a very convenient mode of transport, which at a little more premium than the local suburban trains and buses, offer public transport at a greater speed despite too many stops.

Smart Railway Systems

Despite the success of the metro rail systems in providing speedier transit in the future smart cities and in connecting the neighbouring cities or suburbs, the conventional local suburban train systems and their utility cannot be denied for the time being. The Mumbai local suburban trains help in taking 2.64 billion passengers off the roads on a yearly basis.[27] The trains provide passengers a speedier mode of travel if not a more comfortable one than a road journey. The suburban railway system, with 2,342 train services and 7.5 million daily commuters, is the busiest rapid transit system in the world.[28]

The success of the Delhi Metro has resulted in the initiation of many metro rail projects in India, so as to provide high speed and comfortable transport systems to the public. The main merit of the metro system lies in its dense network and its separation from the conventional roadways so as to not affect the road traffic in any way, thus resulting in a significant reduction in travel time. The metro system, when designed properly, also results in considerable environmental savings and conservation along with a reduction in the release of harmful gases into the environment. By providing a speedier and more comfortable mode of transport, the metro system also helps in easing road traffic. The Delhi Metro operation has resulted in taking about 40,000 vehicles off the road as in 2011, resulting in savings of Rs 75,795 crore in fuel costs.[29]

Other forms of rapid transit system include monorails and light rails. Monorails are generally elevated, running on a single track and can be staffed or unstaffed. Modern monorails are separated from other traffic and pedestrians, leading to a faster mode of transport and one with reduced opportunity for collision or accidents. Riding on an elevated surface, the monorails avoid red lights, intersections, turns and traffic jams just like metro trains do. India is developing monorails in 15 cities for mass rapid transit with the Mumbai monorail being the first one to start in February 2014.

Waterways

Waterways, despite having been the preferred mode of transport in ancient and medieval times, have not been a preferred mode for intra-city transportation of passengers and freight in modern India. India has a long coastline of 7,517 km and an extensive network of inland waterways in rivers, canals, backwaters and creeks. The total navigable length is 14,500 km, out of which 9,000 km can be used by mechanized crafts. The inland waterway traffic is only 0.1 per cent of the total inland traffic movement in India.

Waterways, though not extensively used in Indian cities, can provide an eco-friendly way of transporting passengers and goods. Kolkata is one of the few Indian cities to use the inland waterways ferry system to a great extent for these purposes. Other than West Bengal, only Goa, Assam and Kerala use inland waterways for freight transport. Other than the commercial usage, the inland water bodies are mainly used for tourist purposes.

Smart Waterways

India has five waterways on its rivers, together constituting a total river length of about 4,500 km.

1. Allahabad-Haldia (Ganga-Bhagirathi-Hooghly system)

2. Saidiya-Dhubri (Brahmaputra river system)
3. Kollam-Kottapuram (West Coast canal)
4. Bhadrachalam-Rajahmundry-Wazirabad-Vijaywada (the Krishna-Godavari river system)
5. Paradeep-Talcher (the Mahanadi-Brahmani river system)

To use the inland waterways properly, infrastructure should be built for ferry systems to operate between different inter-city points and freight systems between intra-city points. The river systems require to be managed for deposition of silt and sediments, which would result in the grounding of the boats and ferries. Using the waterways has the benefit of relieving the roads and highways of the congestion of the freight cars. Additionally, shipping costs for water transport are lower than that for road or rail transport due to higher energy efficiency of the barges along with fewer emissions and lower accident numbers.

Airways

Post 1991, there was a surge in private companies operating in the airline sector in India. They introduced many flights for inter-city transportation. The infrastructure development for all Indian airports was till recently with the Airports Authority of India—now there are 125 airports and civil enclaves which are owned and operated by AAI; the rest are managed in Public-Private Partnership with private players such as GVK and GMR. There are around 350 airports and 100 airstrips in India, of which 16 are international airports. Indian airports had been planned for development to international standards by a projected investment of $8.5 billion in the 11th Five Year Plan. Mumbai, Delhi and Hyderabad airports have already been privatized. With the Open Sky Policy of the government, there has been a rapid increase in privately owned airlines and international airlines. It has also led to a higher frequency of flights, of both private and international airlines. With urbanization and the development of many new airport projects like Navi Mumbai International Airport, New Raipur Airport, etc., the proximity of these airports to Indian cities is constantly reducing. Inter-city distances and travel times are also being reduced drastically by the introduction of newer airports.

Smart Airways

Airports are another important component of the city's physical infrastructure. Airports connect the major cities of the country. Privatization of the airports in the first decade of the 21st century has resulted in better-equipped and cleaner airports. Around 40 AAI-operated airports in metros and non-metros have been modernized, and plans for modernization of the rest are being undertaken. About 110 tier-3 cities have been identified for development of airports or for upgrading airstrips, with 15 greenfield projects under way.[30]

Smart city airports need to have low-cost carriers for better connectivity to other cities, thus providing faster and cheaper connectivity to the neighbouring cities. There is a need to assess the demand and supply of the aviation industry to optimally use the existing airstrips, air routes and airlines for better consumer and freight transportation. Hence, there is a need to develop cargo hubs for handling the increased demand of the transportation industry. The airports need to be upgraded to the latest airport technology, have better designed and maintained infrastructure, and smartly designed terminals and operation processes with PPP, FDI or government provided investments.[31]

Some of the basic amenities and structures required at the sustainable airports of the future are listed below:

- Car parking
- Elevated road in front of the building
- Profile roof sheeting
- Internal and external electrification, lighting
- Power supply including DG sets

- Central air-conditioning system
- Traveletors and elevators, escalators
- Fire alarm and detection systems, fire-fighting systems with automatic hydrant
- Surveillance CCTV system and IT systems
- Security systems
- Flight information display system
- PA and car call system EPABX
- Water supply and sewage treatment
- Building management system.

Power Line Transmission and Distribution

Power is generated in the power stations and then transmitted to the consumers by a network of transformers, overhead lines, cables and other equipment. Some energy is lost during the process of distribution and is known as transmission and distribution losses—these losses may be of technical or non-technical nature. The technical losses are the losses due to energy dissipation by the conductors, transformers, sub-transmission line and magnetic losses in transformers. India loses about 30 per cent of its electricity during transmission and distribution with a peak shortfall of 13 per cent between 5 p.m. and 11 p.m.[32] despite an extensive transmission system network of 500 kV HVDC, 400 kV, 220 kV, 132 kV and 66 kV. Much of the commercial or non-technical loss is attributed to theft and pilferage, common in the urban areas, amounting to about 1.5 per cent of the GDP.[33]

Various factors leading to technical losses are as follows:

- Lengthy distribution lines
- Inadequate size of conductors of distribution lines
- Installation of distribution transformers away from load centres
- Low power factor of primary and secondary distribution system
- Feeder phase current and load balancing
- Load factor effect on losses

- Transformer sizing and selection
- Balancing 3 phase loads
- Switching off transformers
- Unequal load distribution among different phases
- Leaking and loss of power
- Overloading of lines
- Inefficient operating conditions at which power and distribution transformers are operated
- Low voltages at consumer terminals causing higher drawl of currents by inductive loads.

Power-line communication or PLC can carry data on a conductor, which when used in a network form is called power-line networking or PLN. This is used for a wide range of power-line communication technologies, from home automation to Internet access (through Ethernet). Power line communications can also be used in home to interconnect home computers and peripherals, and home entertainment devices that have Ethernet ports.

It enables in-vehicle network communication of data, voice, music and video signals by digital means over direct current (DC) battery power-line. Advanced digital communication techniques tailored to overcome hostile and noisy environments are implemented in a small-size silicon device. One power line can be used for multiple independent networks. The benefits would be lower cost and weight (compared to separate power and control wiring), flexible modification, and ease of installation.

PLC, when used together with smart grids, results in the integration of intermittent renewable energy sources into the electricity supply chain, thus securing reliable electricity delivery and efficient use of electricity infrastructure, though it is yet to be employed in India. PLC provides the natural upgrade from simple electricity conductors to hybrid and bidirectional electricity and data communication solutions.[34] This, when used with ICT and mobile telephony, has the potential to revolutionize energy control, automation and communication.

Smart Electricity Transmission and Distribution

The reasons for losses in power transmission and distribution have been explained earlier in the chapter. To reduce the losses, the load factor on the PDT along with the energy-use pattern, the intensity of load demand, the load density, capability and configuration of the transmission and distribution system that varies for the different system elements are important factors to be studied.[35,36] It is shown that if the load factor is lower than what the PDT is designed to handle, the losses are higher and hence proper load control needs to be maintained to reduce the losses.

For proper management of the PDT systems, the sub transmission and distribution system extension to new areas should be done with foresight. Improper load management and multi-staged transformations should be avoided for reducing losses. There is also the need for use of good quality of equipment for the urban residential and industrial loads to avoid load shedding, power failures and accidents. A detailed analysis of the PDT needs to be done for identifying the weakest areas in the PDT and measures should be taken to strengthen them.

The technical losses can be prevented by the following measures:[37]

- Converting low voltage lines to high voltage lines
- Serving large commercial or industrial consumers directly from the feeder line
- High voltage distribution service (HVDS) for agricultural customers
- Reduction in the number of transformers
- Replacement of old cables and infrastructure
- Feeder renovation
- Following preventive maintenance

For preventing commercial losses due to theft and pilferage, the following measures could be taken:

- Metered supply to all consumers
- Mapping of distribution lines
- Vigilance squads to check and prevent pilferage of power
- Penalties for tampering with the meter seals
- Energy audits for the local bodies and areas
- Installation of tamper-proof meter boxes and use of tamper-proof numbered seals
- Adequate meter-testing facilities which should be checked at regular intervals for replacement

ICT

No vision for a smart future and a smart city is complete without ICT or Information Communication Technology and Internet technology for advancing the scope of all devices and applications. ICT for governance, education and health will be taken up in the next chapter. The ICT and Internet infrastructure we will be talking about here is about integrating all other infrastructural elements with ICT to make them future smart. It includes GPS tracking of traffic, passengers, public transport systems, trains and metros, mobile telephony, metering systems and apps to connect the dots between the supply of water and electricity and their demand and distribution, and to build the city infrastructure to achieve all these.

A smart city strategically uses data, information and communication technologies to:[38]

- Provide efficient and enhanced services to citizens
- Monitor and track the government's progress towards policy outcomes
- Manage and optimize the existing infrastructure
- Plan for new and efficient infrastructure
- Reduce organizational silos and employ new levels of cross-sector collaboration

- Enable innovative business models for public and private sector service provision

With fast mobile Internet connections and a high penetration of smart phones even in remote locations, these devices are easy enablers of energy-efficient transport services. They can help in making the public transport system more flexible, providing services like driver support, safety and fuel optimization for smart vehicles and an intelligent transport management system which will help in emission management and optimization. Also, ICT would help in generating demand for responsive transport and introducing intelligent payment systems like virtual ticketing and Near Field Communication-enabled smartcards or smart phones. It can also help in route planning, driver monitoring, and provide eco-friendly or fuel-efficient guidance for routes so as to make the driving experience more efficient and comfortable.

ICT is also an enabler in smart water and electricity management in future cities. ICT can be used for:

- Rain/storm water harvesting by accurate weather forecasting
- Flood management by in-situ terrestrial sensing system
- Managed aquifer recharge
- Smart metering
- Process knowledge systems
- Smart pipes
- Maintenance and repairs
- Asset management by identification and electronic tagging of buried assets.

ICT will be more crucial with the advent of smart meters and smart grids. With the use of ICT, smart meters and differential tariffs, it would be possible for a consumer to use his smart phone to turn on the washing machine when electricity is cheaper, or switching on the heating or cooling system just before reaching home to ensure that it is at a comfortable level when he enters it. The flexible tariffs could be used to reflect the demand pattern and supply side constraints. Individual devices in the home will be networked, automatically or remotely controlled, and will help in managing the cost. For instance, imagine on a sunny day, the solar power generated would be abundant, and hence the Grid Power price would be lower. This information would reach all the consumers—who can then use their mobile phones to turn on or increase the power on their devices—such as electric stoves, chargers, refrigerators, etc., thereby making the best use of the additional power available. This will also reduce the need to store unpredictable power, such as that from solar or wind, in batteries—which is a significant cost and environmental hazard.

Conclusion

The physical infrastructure of a city comprises the bare necessities without which a city cannot be termed smart. It should be the mandate of the urban local bodies and the authorities to develop, construct, plan and provide this infrastructure to the public, as these are public utilities. It also governs what an individual may find attractive in a city, by making his life comfortable. The availability of these basic necessities affects the individual in the smallest of ways, and adds to the overall experience of living in a city.

The physical infrastructure of a city cannot be seen individually and hence there is a necessity to develop social and environmental infrastructure in the city, a subject which will be taken up in Chapters 8 and 9.

NOW YOU KNOW:

- Harappan architecture was a pioneer in its time in design and development of the infrastructural facilities of the city
- The physical infrastructure of a city includes drinking water supply, waste water management, drainage system, power distribution and transmission, telecommunication, information and communication technology, transport and sanitation
- Only 70 per cent urban households have tap water for limited duration, and which might not always be safe for drinking purposes, according to international standards
- The urban poor are the worst affected as they don't have water supply in their premises and thus suffer from water-borne diseases
- Smart drinking water solutions pertain to preventing leakages, the proper treatment of water, and a metering system. It also means access and availability of water to all.

8

Social Paradigm: New Models for Building Infrastructure

This chapter continues from the previous chapter that focused on infrastructural components of cities. It discusses the various parameters of education, health, social and economic equity, and employment. The various components are explained with their existing conditions in India. Further, the chapter recommends measures and metrics to use for adapting the existing components for a smart city, or for building a new city from scratch.

As discussed in the previous chapter, urban infrastructure comprises physical components along with social infrastructure and open spaces. The components of social infrastructure for a city are shown in Figure 1. It consists of social welfare and women and child welfare, as each component of social infrastructure needs to be analysed from the social welfare point of view and from women's and children's perspectives too.

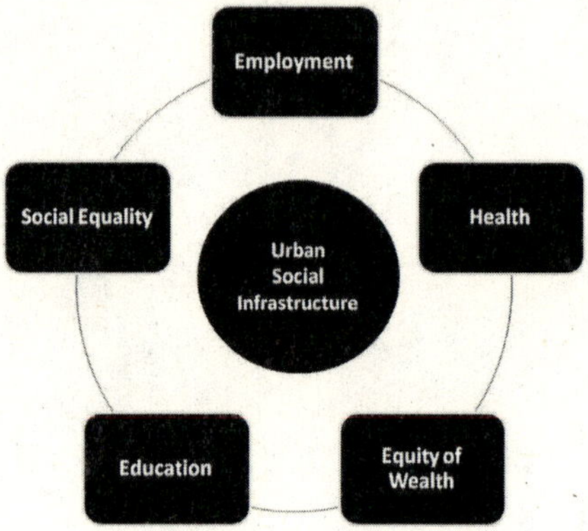

Figure 1: Components of social infrastructure

Education

It is one of the most essential components of social infrastructure. It not only impacts the quality of life of the people by providing livelihood but also influences health, social outcomes and the individual as well as household decision-making. Though educational quality available in a place and its access to the general public is a factor of the economic wealth of the occupants, vice versa is not true.

In India in 2001, of the children going to school, 58 per cent did not complete primary education and 90 per cent did not complete their secondary education. Less than 10 per cent of Indian children went to college for graduation level studies and higher studies.[1]

Table 1: Level of education amongst Indian literates

	Per cent to Literate		
Level of education	*Persons*	*Males*	*Females*
Literate	100	100	100
Literate without educational level	3.6	3.4	3.9
Below primary	25.8	24.1	28.4

Level of education	Per cent to Literate		
	Persons	Males	Females
Primary	26.2	24.8	28.2
Middle	16.1	16.6	15.3
Matriculation/Secondary	14.1	15.2	12.5
High secondary/Intermediate/Pre-university/Senior secondary	6.7	7.3	5.9
Non-technical diploma or certificate not equal to degree	0.1	0.1	0.1
Technical diploma or certificate not equal to degree	0.7	0.9	0.3
Graduate and above	6.7	7.6	5.4

Literacy, the simplest indicator of the educational status of a place, stood at a national average of 73 per cent in the Census 2011. The literacy rate for urban males and females stood at 89 per cent and 79 per cent respectively. In absolute numbers, there were more females added to the literates list than males in India during the decade of 2001-2010. Table 2 shows the literacy figures for India and its states in 2011. Kerala took the top spot in literacy, with urban youth literacy at 99 per cent and the total literacy rate at 94 per cent. Corresponding figures for male and female literacy in this state were 97 per cent and 93 per cent respectively—far above the national average. National urban youth literacy rate for the same period was 90 per cent.

There are three levels in education in the Indian system—elementary or primary education, secondary education and higher education. Primary education is till the age of fourteen years and is covered in the Right to Education Act of the Government of India which makes it free for all to access. This is provided by government-run or supported schools, thus constituting the bulk of the education system in the Indian scenario. Despite its high number of schools, this system suffers from a massive lack of infrastructure, which includes teachers, teachers' training and proper school buildings. In 2011, there were 5.8 million elementary school teachers in India[2] despite which many schools in the small towns and rural areas suffered from high pupil-to-teacher ratios. The all-pervasive government schooling system is slowly and steadily being replaced by private schools, which provide better amenities and a better quality of education to the students. Studies show that less than 50 per cent of the students studying in government schools in India can do basic mathematics calculations or read simple sentences in English or Hindi.[3]

Secondary education covers classes from 7th standard to 10th standard, i.e. till matriculation. Matriculation, still regarded as an important certification in the child's education, is now being continuously dominated by private schools. Government schools like Kendriya Vidyalaya, and a few Vedic and Christian schools, have been able to provide quality education to the students. These schools, if located in urban areas, have a lower dropout ratio than their rural counterparts. The reason lies mostly in the socio-economic differences in the student's family incomes.

Despite India having a highly developed higher education system offering learning opportunities in almost all aspects of creative and technical fields, only 6.7 per cent of the literates are graduates. As of 2012, India had 152 central universities, 316 state universities, and 191 private universities. Other institutions include 33,623 colleges, including 1,800 exclusive women's colleges, functioning under these universities and institutions, and 12,748 institutions offering diploma courses and 13 institutes of national importance. There were around 20,000 degree and postgraduate colleges, of which 14,000 were under UGC and the rest 6,000 were professional colleges under AICTE, ICAR or MCI. The national average of women enrolment in professional courses was as low as 12 per cent out of a total 40 per cent women enrolment for higher education and was the highest in Kerala at 66 per cent and the lowest in Bihar at 25 per cent.[4]

The reason for the gender gap in the literacy rates in most of the Indian states is the social conditions prevailing in the states.

A comparison between a few Indian metro cities for the literacy indicators is done in Table 3. It shows that the cities with lower populations fare better in literacy rates than their counterparts with higher populations. Most of the metro cities have both private and government schools. A city's status as an industrial or financial hub also acts as a factor in the better quality of educational infrastructure in the city. Prominent examples are the steel cities and the industrial towns set up by government-controlled PSUs like ONGC, SAIL and BHEL. In India, Bangalore and Mumbai form the IT and the financial hubs respectively. They act as forces attracting technological companies, telecommunications, aerospace and defence institutions.

The social and cultural heritage of a city also contributes a lot to the education infrastructure and the literacy rates of the city or the state. This is evident from the high literacy levels in the southern and eastern states of India which have been part of communist movements and have a history of art, culture and education. This is also true of Kolkata, which has a good literacy rate at 87.14 and was the hub of educational institutions during the 1900s.

Table 2: Comparison of city literacy rates in India

City	*Literacy Rate*	*Population*
Delhi	86.34	16,753,235
Mumbai	94.70	12,478,447
Bangalore	89.00	8,499,399
Hyderabad	82.96	6,809,970
Ahmedabad	89.62	5,570,585
Pune	86.15	5,049,968
Ghaziabad	93.81	4,681,452
Chennai	90.33	4,681,087
Kolkata	87.14	4,486,679
Nagpur	93.13	2,583,911
Thiruvananthapuram	93.72	1,687,406

City	*Literacy Rate*	*Population*
Jabalpur	89.13	1,438,777
Raipur	86.90	1,010,087
Kochi	97.49	595,575
Aizawl	98.80	228,280

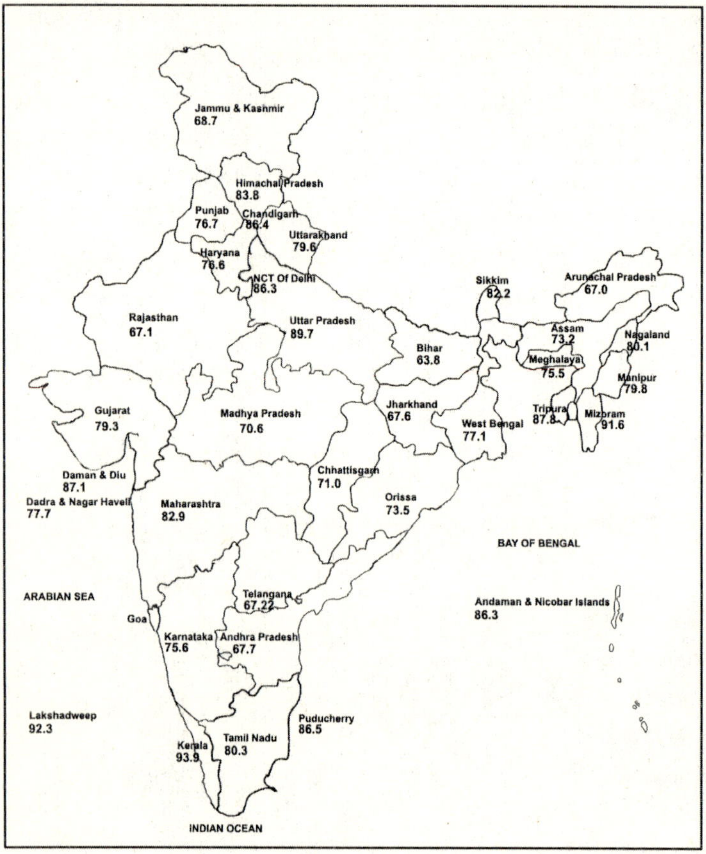

Figure 2: Literacy rates in Indian states

Smart Education

To tackle the situation of gender and to deal with the socio-economic gaps in education, future cities should be looking at developing proper infrastructure. The parameters defining the quality of education provided in the smart cities would be as follows:

Table 3: Smart education measures[5]

Parameters	*Current Scenario*	*Smart City Measures*
Pupil-teacher ratio	32:1	25:1
Gender Parity Index (Enrolment)	0.93	1
Literacy rate (2011)	Males: 82.1 Females: 65.5	100
Gender gap in literacy	16.6	0

The number of schools, the dropout ratio, attendance, the quality of literacy, the cost of education, the number of students passing 10th, 12th and graduation exams, quality of the city library, innovation, educational conferences, seminars and events, etc. are a few other parameters on which a smart education system is measured.

Along with other measures, it is crucial that policy makers know and acquaint themselves with the educational landscape and engage with school leaders, families and young people for coming out with innovative strategies in education. Policy makers should further devise metrics for linking high-quality education to the economic and social prosperity of the local communities.

It is also imperative that schools and institutions be constructed so that they can be accessed by all the inhabitants. As per the current education programmes in India, emphasis should be laid on the primary and secondary education which should be ample in the city and well distributed in its various localities. Education audits of all the schools—whether private or government—should be mandated to keep a check on the quality of the education imparted.

Along with these, schools should use innovative methods to bring down the costs of education. Distance learning and teaching through video or tele-conferencing is a way to do this. This would also help in maintaining the pace of education in different schools.

The teaching should lay emphasis not on rote education for getting through examinations, but on developing their aptitude in creative, intellectual and other personality development programmes.

A focal sector would be that of online education and also those based on mobile phone platforms. Globally, the revenues from e-learning have reached $35.6 billion in 2011, and given an estimated five-year compound annual growth rate of 7.6 per cent, are expected to grow to $51.5 billion by 2016. The growth rate from 2011 to 2016 is expected to be 17 per cent per annum for Asia, largely driven by India. As we have proposed smart cities to be centres of free and readily available Internet, it is imperative to streamline traditional education with online-based, especially open source, classroom models—where skill development can be readily available, round the clock. Entrepreneurship in e-learning should be encouraged to come from school teachers and colleges educators as a common community-shared pool.

Also there is a need for the education system to grow from being a competitive environment to one that helps in developing entrepreneurial traits in children. The modules should be defined such that they help students make a decision on their career choices—arts and humanities; natural, mathematical and social sciences, engineering; medicine; dentistry; agriculture; education; law; commerce and management; music and performing arts; national and foreign languages; culture; communications, etc.

Health

The healthcare quality varies from city to city in India, though urban healthcare is of adequate quality and occasionally meets Western standards. Despite a thriving healthcare private sector, the state of health in India, especially in childcare and neonatal care, remains dismal. According to a 2005 report, 42 per cent of India's children below the age of three were malnourished, which was greater than the statistics of the sub-Saharan African region that had 28 per cent. 'Malnutrition is more common in India than in sub-Saharan Africa. One in every three malnourished children in the world lives in India.'[6]

Malnutrition impedes motor, sensory, cognitive, social and emotional development. Malnourished children are less likely to perform well in school and other activities, and are likely to continue being malnourished even through their adult lives. They are at greater risk of contracting infectious diseases and thus face early death. Around one-third of all adult women, irrespective of their social or economic background, are underweight, which is majorly due to their childhood upbringing. Inadequate prenatal and neonatal care results in low birth weight babies.[7] Nearly 42 per cent of all newborns have a low birth weight, making them vulnerable to further malnutrition and disease.[7]

Infant mortality in India is as high as 43 deaths per 1,000 live births. Most infant deaths occur in the first week itself—around 47 per cent.[8] Maternal deaths are similarly high—190 per 100,000 births. The reasons for this high mortality are that few women have access to skilled birth attendants or quality obstetrics (the nursing and midwifery personnel density per 10,000 population was less than 10 in 2008 and only 57 per cent of the births were attended to by skilled health personnel). Additionally, only 15 per cent of the new mothers receive complete antenatal care and only 58 per cent receive iron tablets.

A few health indicators for India are shown in Table 4. The death rate of 7.35 per 1,000 people puts the country at the 118th rank globally and it is ranked 55th and 50th in terms of its MMR and IMR. The sex ratio at birth stood at about 1.12 males/females, which improved to 1.08 males/females when taken for the entire population in 2014.

Table 4: Health indicators for India. Source: CIA[9]

Median Age	
Total	27 years
Male	26.4 years
Female	27.7 years
Birth Rate	19.89 births/1,000 population
Death Rate	7.35 deaths/1,000 population
MMR	190 deaths/100,000 live births
IMR	
Total	43.19 deaths/1,000 live births
Male	41.9 deaths/1,000 live births
Female	44.63 deaths/1,000 live births
Life expectancy	
Total	67.8 years
Male	66.68 years
Female	69.06 years
Fertility Rate	2.51 children born/woman
Contraceptive prevalence rate	54.8 per cent
Health expenditures	3.9 per cent of GDP
Physicians density	0.65 physicians/1,000 population
Hospital bed density	0.9 beds/1,000 population

0.3 per cent adult Indians have HIV-AIDS and the total deaths due to HIV-AIDS stood at 135,000 in 2012. A majority of the population is at a high risk of infectious diseases like bacterial diarrhoea, hepatitis A and E, and typhoid fever, dengue fever, Japanese encephalitis, and malaria, leptospirosis (water-borne diseases), and rabies.

Table 5: Common disease incidences in India. Source: WHO

Indicator	*Year*	*No. of cases*
Diphtheria	2012	2,525
Japanese encephalitis	2011	8,247

Indicator	*Year*	*No. of cases*
Malaria	2012	1,067,824
Measles	2012	18,668
Neonatal tetanus	2012	588
Pertussis	2012	44,154
Poliomyelitis	2013	0
Rubella	2012	1,025
Total tetanus	2012	2,404

The urban public mainly relies on the private rather than the public sector due to the poor quality of care in the public sector. Other major reasons are distance of the public sector facility, long waiting times, and inconvenient hours of operation. The study conducted by IMS Institute for Healthcare Informatics in 2013 across 12 states in over 14,000 households indicated a steady increase in the usage of private healthcare facilities over the last 25 years for both out-patient and in-patient services, across rural and urban areas.

Smart Health

The first smart city in India will first need to improve the basic medical facilities available to all. It requires health institutions and dispensaries to be available to the population and at affordable prices. The population should have a medical insurance policy which helps them cater to emergencies and this should be provided to all low income populations. There should be centres where people can get free treatment in case of epidemics, and the hospital institutions should be well equipped to cater to the public in case of such emergencies.

Additionally there should be designated centres for childcare and mother care during pregnancies. The youth, especially girls, should be given sex education. The quality of health institutions can also be judged by the incidences and prevalence of diseases in the area, as these provide an insight into the health and sanitation practices at a particular location. Some of the indicators for judging the quality of the health facilities are listed below:

Table 6: Smart health parameters[10]

Parameters	*Current Scenario*	*Smart City Measures*
Number of physicians per 1,000 population (2012)	0.7	2 to 2.5
Number of nurses and midwives per 1,000 population (2011)	1.7	3
Number of hospital beds per 1,000 population (2011)	0.7	2 to 2.5
Health expenditure per capita (2012)	$61	120

As per existing norms, further metrics which could be used for measuring health-related infrastructure in the city are listed as follows:

- Number of doctors per 1,000 population
- Number of specialists for common diseases
- Number of hospitals per 10,000 population
- Number of hospital beds per 10,000 population
- Number of health educational institutions
- Disease incidences (per 1,000 population per year)
- Type of diseases (communicable versus non-communicable)
- Air quality and environment
- Medicine availability
- Distance between two health centres or dispensaries
- Healthy habits (e.g. incidence rate of smoking)
- Per capita healthcare spending
- Preventive healthcare spending
- Nutritional status and spending
- Provision for preventive measures against epidemics.

Further developments in smart city health administration could involve developing fundamentally new sensor technologies for monitoring individual health conditions and controlling healthcare needs simultaneously, through data-fusion and pattern-recognition from a common platform of non-medical/environmental sensors at homes. The system should be general-purpose, low-cost and accessible. The sensors will be entirely passive, requiring no action by the user and suitable for all patients, including the most vulnerable. There could be a home sensor system to detect an overnight stroke or mini-stroke on waking, by detecting small changes in behaviour, expression and gait. It could also monitor a patient's compliance with their prescribed drugs.

Smart health should deploy the power of electronic database and the Internet in ensuring better delivery of healthcare at lower costs.

Equity of Opportunity

Inequality of wealth or poverty is the biggest bane of society, which leads to other evils. Poverty not only leads to economic disparity but also to social disparity. Lack of basic necessities and physical infrastructure impacts the lives of the poor by impacting their health, nutrition and social status. The complexity of the issue is evident by the fact that there are different definitions and hence different levels of poverty in India. The World Bank estimates that 32.7 per cent of the Indian population was living below the poverty line in 2010, whereas the UNDP estimates the same at 29.8 per cent. The Indian Planning Commission puts the Head Count Ratio[i] for poverty estimation at 29.8 per cent, with rural poverty at 33.8 per cent and urban poverty at 20.9 per cent.[11]

---

[i]Head Count Ratio (HCR) is the proportion of a population that exists, or lives, below the 'poverty line'.

Eradication of Poverty in the Smart Cities

A major component in the eradication of the inequality of wealth from smart cities is employment to be generated for all. The employment schemes of the government, like the one that provides compulsory employment through MNREGA, works in rural India but does not add to the skills of the labourers in the long haul. Therefore there is requirement of employment generation schemes which would help the population by making them self-employed or industrious.

Another factor is food and health security for the poor. Food constitutes a major expense for the poor, and hence provisions should be made to provide food at affordable costs. This also requires keeping inflation in check, as food price fluctuations impact the low income and middle income groups the most. Health security is another area where households have been spending less due to lower incomes and higher costs. To provide accessible and affordable health facilities, the required measures were discussed earlier in this chapter.

Employment

In 2012, India had around 487 million workers, the second largest after China, and had an unemployment rate of 8.8 per cent. More than 90 per cent of these workers were employed in unincorporated, unorganized enterprises ranging from pushcart vendors to home-based diamond and gem polishing operations. The organized sector included 27.5 million workers employed by the government, state-owned enterprises and private sector enterprises.

Agriculture, dairy, horticulture and related occupations alone employ 52 per cent of the labour in India. Most of the rural population is self-employed in agriculture and non-agricultural activities. In contrast, almost 42 per cent of the urban population is employed in services or derives regular wages; and only 34 per cent are self-employed. In urban areas, female unemployment stood at 12.5 per cent as against national average at 6.9 per cent[12] in 2012.

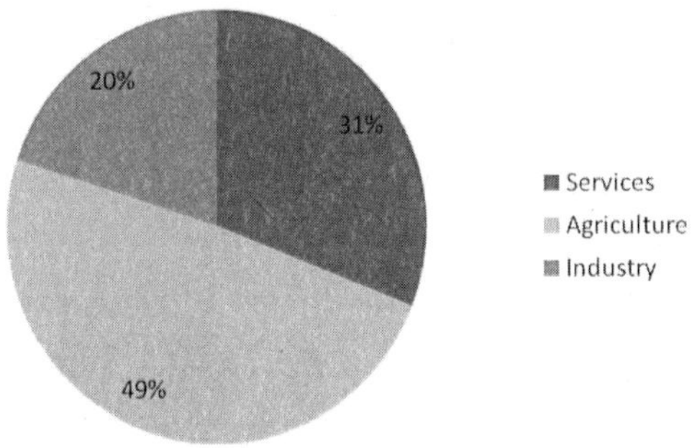

Figure 3: Sector-wise workforce, 2012

In 2014, the unemployment rate was expected to rise to 3.8 per cent, according to the report 'Global Employment Trends 2014'.[13] According to the ILO report, it has been argued that India was experiencing 'jobless growth' due to the fact that total employment grew by only 1.1 million from 2004-05 to 2009-10 (based on the National Sample Survey), representing an employment elasticity of almost zero. However, the total employment in India expanded to a much healthier 13.9 million from 2009-10 to 2011-12, 'though many of these jobs are in the informal economy,' it added. In India, the ILO report showed, 21.2 per cent of working men (aged 15-59) had a regular salaried job (in 2011-12 period).

Table 7: Indian cities' employment ratio (per 1,000 people in working age group)[14]

City	*Male*	*Female*	*City*	*Male*	*Female*
Agra	833	147	Indore	835	283
Ahmedabad	795	214	Jaipur	766	377
Bangalore	841	202	Kanpur	776	77
Bhopal	782	151	Kolkata	751	190

City	*Male*	*Female*	*City*	*Male*	*Female*
Chennai	749	168	Mumbai	786	267
Delhi	714	112	Pune	712	291
Hyderabad	770	190	Surat	876	182
Urban India	763	227			

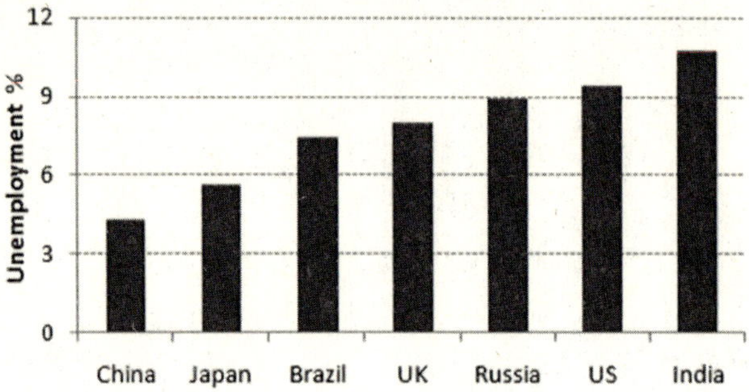

Figure 4: Unemployment rate in India in 2011 versus other major economies

Table 8: Employment type for Indian cities (per 1,000 people)

	Male			*Female*		
City	*Self-Employed*	*Salaried*	*Casual Labour*	*Self-Employed*	*Salaried*	*Casual Labour*
Delhi	413	518	69	226	762	12
Mumbai	403	517	80	321	542	137
Kolkata	368	435	197	388	299	313
Chennai	351	545	104	516	442	42
Bangalore	351	462	186	292	689	19
Hyderabad	447	427	126	239	672	90
Ahmedabad	369	525	107	335	650	15
Jaipur	450	466	84	450	466	84
Surat	294	682	24	294	682	24
Pune	291	596	113	238	634	128
Bhopal	533	413	54	533	413	54

City	Male			Female		
	Self-Employed	Salaried	Casual Labour	Self-Employed	Salaried	Casual Labour
Indore	519	390	91	519	390	91
Kanpur	441	434	125	441	434	125
Agra	603	341	56	603	341	56
Urban India	449	407	144	471	361	167

The major reasons for the dismal employment rates in India are its economic condition, rapid population growth leading to addition in labour force without similar increase in job opportunities, a certification-based education system which does not lay much emphasis on skills and industrial training, and inadequate employment planning. The ineffectiveness of the education system in providing employment is evident by the fact that Kerala, despite having the highest literacy rates, has the highest unemployment rates, with 73 out of every 1,000 people remaining unemployed in the urban areas.[15]

Creating Employment Opportunities in Smart Cities

The smart cities envisioned to sustain industries will become hubs for employment. The cities will have centres for promoting handicrafts, local artifacts and other MSMEs. The cities, with their satellite development areas for agriculture-related activities, will promote agricultural employment (both self-employment and casual labourers) in their immediate vicinities. Proper management of agriculture resources and operations would help in controlling the disguised unemployment in agriculture.

Additionally, there would be separate zones for IT, industrial manufacturing, and services in the smart city. Having industrial hubs along with the demand required for employment by controlling population would help in generating adequate employment opportunities for all. Other measures for increasing employment

ENTERPRISE DEVELOPMENT IN SMART HABITATIONS

Creating a culture of enterprise in smart cities:

- Incubation and enterprise development centres through educational institutions
- Platform for participation of venture capitalists and investors
- Public funding for enterprises
- Use open space events to create open source ideas and challenges
- Tax benefits for nurturing enterprises and small business
- Enterprise development incentives to be sector-specific and aligned to the overall economic core activity of the smart city.

are steadying the pace of economic growth, reduction in corruption and nepotism, skills and communication training, and introduction of government measures like fair wages and effective labour laws.

Another major thrust area of smart cities should be to create job creators rather than just job seekers. This would mean a thrust on creating modern technology-driven entrepreneurs, which will be a culture in smart habitations. Smart habitations, with their modern educational facilities, should stress on creating ideation and incubation centres in these facilities. Open-source discovery platforms and idea exchange forums should be part of the DNA and the Hard Grid of Open Spaces, and ICT should be deployed for this purpose. The urban local governance should be a host to venture-funding events and to public funding for enterprise incubation. It would be a worthy idea to incentivize large businesses that mentor smaller entrepreneurs in the form of tax benefits at the local body level—in this way each smart city can choose to be the world-class centre for incubation of ideas and enterprises for its chosen core economic competency.

Equity and Social Justice

'Equity derives from a concept of social justice. It represents a belief that there are some things which people should have, that there are basic needs that should be fulfilled, that burdens and rewards should not be spread too divergently across the community, and that policy should be directed with impartiality, fairness and justice towards these ends'.[16] It means a minimum level of income, social status and environmental quality for the population so that everyone has equal access to community resources and opportunities. It encompasses the idea of everyone having an acceptable quality and standard of living.

Equity not only includes reducing gender and social gaps but also emphasizes on providing justice and sustainable development. It includes equal rights to security, electorate, freedom of speech, property rights, and prohibition of forced labour and child employment. India has a set of fundamental rights which prohibit trafficking of human beings and forced labour and employment of children in factories, etc. It also recommends that the state provide equal justice and free legal aid to every citizen. For reducing the social gap between minorities and socially backward classes, states are directed to promote the educational and economic interests of the weaker sections and the scheduled castes and tribes. One prominent example is the discrimination made against Dalits in India—a socially backward caste—preventing them from entering many religious and social places managed by people of a higher caste.[17] While this system was prevalent in the past, it still lingers on in some areas. The rural system is still biased against such social classes and these attitudes lead to harassment, cruelties and exploitation of these weaker sections of society.

The state shall, in particular, direct its policy towards securing:[18]

- that the citizens have the right to an adequate means of livelihood
- that the ownership and control of the material resources of the

community are so distributed as best to subserve the common good

- that the operation of the economic system does not result in the concentration of wealth and means of production to the common detriment
- that there is equal pay for equal work for both men and women
- that the health and strength of workers, men and women, and children are not abused and that citizens are not forced by economic necessity to enter vocations unsuited to their age or strength
- that children are given opportunities and facilities to develop in a healthy manner and in conditions of freedom and dignity and that childhood and youth are protected against exploitation and against moral and material abandonment.

Sustainable Development and Social Equity

When considering social equity and sustainable development for smart cities, we would mostly be considering the measurable portions of the components of equity. These would include cases registered and verdicts delivered for social offences, reduction in indicators for social group and gender gaps for access to education, health facilities and employment, child employment, availability of legal aid to citizens, etc. Corruption, economic exploitation of labour, reduction in forced labour, fair wage policies and their strict implementation, and mitigating the impacts of poverty so that they do not affect the social lives of the citizens are also included in the same.

This requires the social and economically richer class of people to share their riches and assets with all and follow fair practices and just policies. The government needs to enforce the administrative machineries to eradicate processes which differentiate between citizens based on their social or economic classes, or that which favour the privileged classes of people in this access to services and facilities. The discriminations are not just restricted to social exploitation but extend to denial of economic and legal justice. Hence, there is a requirement of strict enforcement of laws against economic exploitations like benami, begari, deceptions and frauds. The laws should be strict not only for the offender but also for those who aid the offenders in breaking the laws.

A few indicators which can be used to measure the smartness of the social equity status of a city are as follows:

- Number of cases registered for social exploitation of weaker sections per 1,000 population
- Rate of cases resolved (against total number of cases registered) and prosecutions in them
- Dowry cases registered and resulting prosecutions
- Number of child labour cases being registered
- Cases of vigilance and corruption registered and resolved
- Economic exploitation cases registered against weaker sections
- Number of cases pending in the courts.

Conclusion

If physical infrastructure is the body of the city, then social equity and infrastructure is the soul of the city. Without proper development of the social infrastructure, the city would not be able to thrive and fulfil its potential for growth. It is imperative that the future cities develop measures and indicators for measuring the quality of the social life for a fully sustainable development.

NOW YOU KNOW:

- Literacy rate for India in 2011 stood at an average of 73 per cent, with Kerala having the highest literacy at 94 per cent
- India has three levels of education: primary, secondary and higher education

- India has a good number of educational institutes at all levels but suffers from a high drop-out ratio in the primary and secondary schools
- Smart education metrics should include pupil-teacher ratio, gender parity in both literacy and enrolment and total literacy rates
- For providing smarter education, changes are required in the policies and the infrastructural components of the institutes
- The Indian population suffers from multiple health ailments pertaining to women and children like malnutrition, infant mortality and natal mortality
- Most of the Indian population suffers from 'third world diseases' which spread through water, air and pathogen carriers like mosquitoes and flies
- Smart health metrics should include globally used health parameters like number of physicians, nurses and hospital beds per 1,000 population and average health expenditure per capita
- Equality of opportunity includes eradication of poverty and providing food and health security for the poor
- India has a high rate of unemployment, at 11 per cent in 2011, resulting from an increasing population and dismal economic conditions
- Smart cities would have separate economic zones for providing better employment opportunities to skilled labourers and agricultural and industrial opportunities for less-skilled labourers.

9

Green Cover: Ensuring Ecological Friendliness in the New Cities

This chapter introduces the concept of open spaces and green cover in urban spaces. It further talks about the benefits of open and green spaces. It analyses the scenario for green spaces in India and its cities and compares this to the global best practices. In the end, it recommends a few measures to improve the green cover of cities.

For the silver jubilee celebrations of the rule of Krishnaraja Wodeyar IV in 1927, preparations were made to improve the city of Bangalore. It included the construction of parks, public buildings and hospitals in the city. As a result the city had large parks, open spaces, tree-lined avenues, broad streets, greenery, palace grounds, golf courses and many public parks. The most notable ones among them were the Lal Bagh and the Cubbon Park. The gentle climate and the greenery gave the city its sobriquet of being the 'Garden City of India'.

The status of the city has changed since then. From being a 'Garden City', Bangalore has become a city with dwindling tree cover over the past few decades. The estimated tree cover of the city is about 15 per cent of the geographical area. This amounts to a per capita green space availability of around 17 sq m. In 2014, the city had not more than 15 lakh trees left. Around 66 per cent of the tree cover has been lost since the 1970s. There are about 17 trees per 100 people in Bangalore and some areas like Shivajinagar and Chickpet have less than one tree for every 500 people.[1] The WHO standard for green space is 9.5 sq m per person, which is about 1.2 trees per person.[2]

There are 705 small, medium and large parks in the city of Bangalore. Additionally, there are around 200 open spaces and green areas to be developed into gardens and parks and other community infrastructure. A majority of the plants or trees planted in Bangalore are of exotic species, planted for their high growth rates and decorative appearance. The city lacks trees that provide multiple benefits like providing edible pods, flowers, fruits and leaves.[3]

Green Cover, Open Spaces and Recreational Spaces

Open spaces in a city act as places for activity, engagement, peace, recreation, relief, and social and environmental health. The improve the quality of residents' lives with a wide range of health-related benefits, by providing them with an opportunity to exercise or walk, and access to sunshine and fresh air. They impact people's stress levels and overall mental health, and have a positive impact on healthcare and its attendant costs.

Definition of Open Spaces

Open space can be defined as an area of land which is not open for residential or commercial development. This does not include infrastructure such as roads, railways and transport systems. It does include recreation parks, sports grounds, natural areas, landscaped greenways, plazas, or other land used for community activity. Whilst open space does not include roads and related footpaths which are part of the transport system, well-landscaped boulevards or pathway systems can be considered as open spaces if their focus is on recreation or the public realm. A couple of examples include the MG Road boulevard in Bangalore and the premier boulevard of Rajpath in Delhi. Rajpath, designed by the British architect Edward Lutyens, is a tree-lined road with ponds and fountains. It is used for various annual national events such as Independence Day and Republic Day parades. Another such boulevard in India is the Marine Drive, also known as the 'Queen's Necklace'. It is one of the most famous tourist attractions of Mumbai and is frequented by locals for morning exercise or for enjoying the cool sea breeze. The posh and beautiful C-shaped coastal road, though considered an open space, has sparse tree cover.

There are three major types of open spaces when considered with respect to a city:

1. *Public Open Space:* This is community land accessible to the general population, including people who do not live within the development area. Such area is generally owned by the national or local government body. This may also be owned by private individuals or organizations, but it is made available for public usage. A few examples of public open spaces are public parks, town squares, greenways, highways, etc.
2. *Communal Open Space:* This is private land accessible to and shared by residents within a defined community or a multi-unit development, e.g. land set aside for the use of residents in one building or a cluster of buildings for common use. This land is privately owned by the residential development community or the agency and is part of a residential development project. These areas should be of sufficient size, dimensions and gradient to be functional and meet likely occupant needs (i.e. entertaining, clothes drying, refuse storage, recreational purposes and to accommodate landscaping).
3. *Private Open Space:* This is land or spaces (such as courtyards and

balconies) that are owned or controlled by the dwelling occupiers and are available for private use only. This may include small parks, landscaping, recreational spaces and entertainment spaces within the dwelling area. These days, such open spaces are mandatory in modern buildings.

> About six tonnes of carbon is sequestered by 1 hectare of forests annually, accounting for 20 kg of CO_2 per tree per year.

Benefits of Open Spaces

A few benefits of open spaces and green cover are listed in Figure 1.

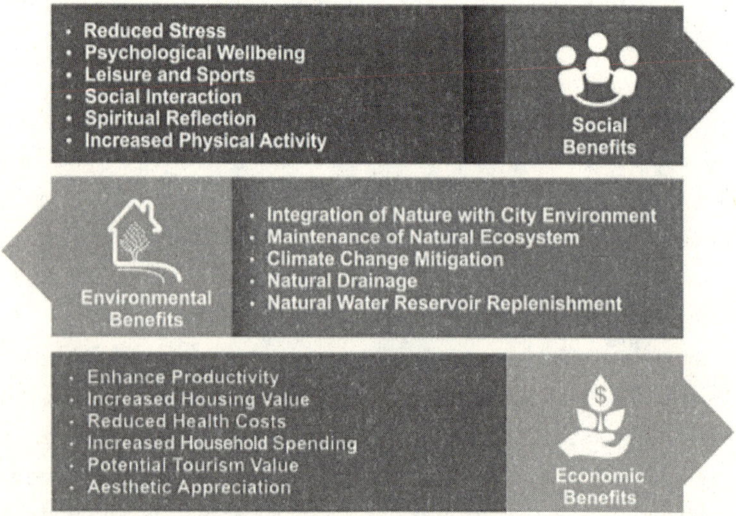

Figure 1: Benefits of urban spaces

Social Benefits

1. *Reduced stress and psychological well-being:* Open spaces are mainly used for exercise and other physical activities which are associated with improving psychological and spiritual health. Studies

show that physical activity in the natural environment leads to improvement in mental and physical well-being, increased life span, reduced cases of depression, smoking and substance misuse, and ability to function better at work and home.[4]

2. *Leisure and sports:* Open spaces in a community or within a building area are generally used by children and the elderly for sports and leisure activities like football, cricket, laughter clubs, discussion groups, meditation groups, etc. These help in binding the residents socially, helping to make a positive impact on the growth of the children.[5] Many residents use the gardens in the city for a break from their mundane daily activities and visit them on weekends for a getaway. Lal Bagh in Bangalore on weekends attracts hundreds of visitors who seek leisure in nature's lap.
3. *Social interactions:* In the present fast-paced world, there is little time for social chit chat and interactions. Lack of open spaces in the neighbourhood impedes any possibility of the same. Hence developers these days design the residential areas such that there is enough space for people to meet and indulge in social interactions with each other.
4. *Spiritual reflection:* Many of the residents in India—housewives and elderly people in particular—use the parks and gardens in the vicinity of their residential areas for meditation and yoga.
5. *Increased physical activity:* The local parks and gardens serve as an area for increased physical activity like running, jogging and walking, morning or evening exercises for residents.

Environmental Benefits

1. *Integration of nature with the city environment*: With increased tree cover and open spaces, the environmental burden on the city is reduced. Studies show that for every tree planted, around 20 kg of CO_2 is absorbed from the environment and 14 kg of O_2 is released into the atmosphere.[6] Additionally, there is the benefit of 'carbon sequestration', which refers to the process of changing of carbon

from its gaseous form (largely CO_2), to the leaves and trunks of the trees—where carbon occurs in solid form.

2. *Maintenance of the ecosystem:* Tree cover is essential for maintenance of water levels underground and O_2-CO_2 balance of the atmosphere. Additionally, natural habitats provide sanctuary to breeding populations of birds and scavengers, which help in keeping insect and pest populations under control in agricultural areas.[7]
3. *Climate change mitigation:* Climate change in local terms majorly concerns managing high temperatures, surface water and water supply, reducing soil erosion, controlling run-off, etc. Having dense tree cover results in added precipitation for the area, thus increasing the surface water levels and decreasing temperatures within the city. Reduction in green cover by 10 per cent is shown to increase city temperatures by 7-8°C.[8]

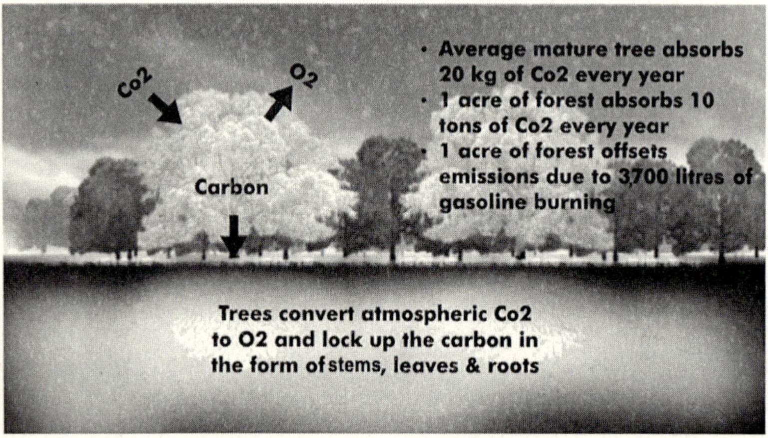

Figure 2: Carbon absorption and oxygen release by trees

4. *Natural drainage:* When it rains, most of the water is soaked by the topsoil, slowly making its way to the nearest water body by natural drainage. In the presence of trees, the flow of the

rainwater is slowed, thus leading to low run-off, which would otherwise be wasted when running off a concrete pavement, thus leading to better natural drainage.

5. *Natural water reservoir replenishment:* The roots of trees, by holding the water flow after rains, allow the soil to soak in more water than it can otherwise absorb on its own. The rainwater that seeps through the soil is collected underground below the water table by percolation, thus replenishing the natural water reservoir.

Economic Benefits

1. *Enhanced productivity:* Green spaces result in the enhanced mental and physical health of the residents, which positively impacts the productivity of the residents at their work spaces, as residents are less susceptible to depression and stress, e.g. Pune.
2. *Increased housing value:* With better landscaping and healthier environments, houses located in areas with low population and less traffic, boasting of calm and peaceful surroundings, are better economic investments than their counterparts in populated areas, e.g. Pune, Navi Mumbai.
3. *Reduced health costs:* With increased well-being, the health costs for residents are also reduced. Also, the recuperation time required after an illness is reduced if one stays in a greener and more open locality, e.g. Auroville.
4. *Increased household spending:* Residents of such areas have reduced costs on health and transportation. They can spend more on sports, recreation and commercial needs, e.g. Auroville.
5. *Potential tourism value:* The green tree cover, open boulevards, exotic gardens, natural habitats, local biodiversity—all add to the potential attraction of the city. Such areas, if developed and maintained properly, can generate substantial tourism revenues, e.g. the Great Himalayan National Park in Himachal Pradesh.

6. *Aesthetic appreciation:* Tree cover and local biodiversity not only add to the environmental sustainability of a city but make it beautiful as well, e.g. the Chandigarh Rock Garden, Lodhi Garden in Delhi.

Green Cover and Open Spaces in India

In 2003, India had 67.83 million hectares of forest and tree cover and open spaces, which accounted for 20.64 per cent of the total geographical land area. These included mangroves spread over 4,461 km of land area—0.14 per cent of the country's land area. The forest cover for major cities shows that Gandhinagar has 416 trees for every 100 people, followed by Bangalore with 17 trees, Brihanmumbai with 15 trees and Ahmedabad with 11 trees.[9] In Jaipur city, as per the existing land use analysis, the area under parks and open spaces is around 5.43 sq km for a population of 2.32 million, making the per capita availability of green space about 2.30 sq m.

Chandigarh city was built as a replacement for Lahore city, the capital of the undivided Punjab which went to Pakistan in 1947. The city has more than 35 per cent of its geographical area under forest and tree cover, making it one of the greenest cities of India. The population of the city was 0.9 million in 2001, making the per capita availability of green space around 55 sq m.

The enhancement of urban green spaces or urban forests is one of the ways which has the potential to mitigate the adverse effects of urbanization in a sustainable manner, making cities more attractive and comfortable to live in. The 'Best Practice Open Space in Higher Density Developments Project' has provided a list of some of the best practices used globally by the development authorities and agencies for maintaining optimal open spaces in the cities and the residential areas.

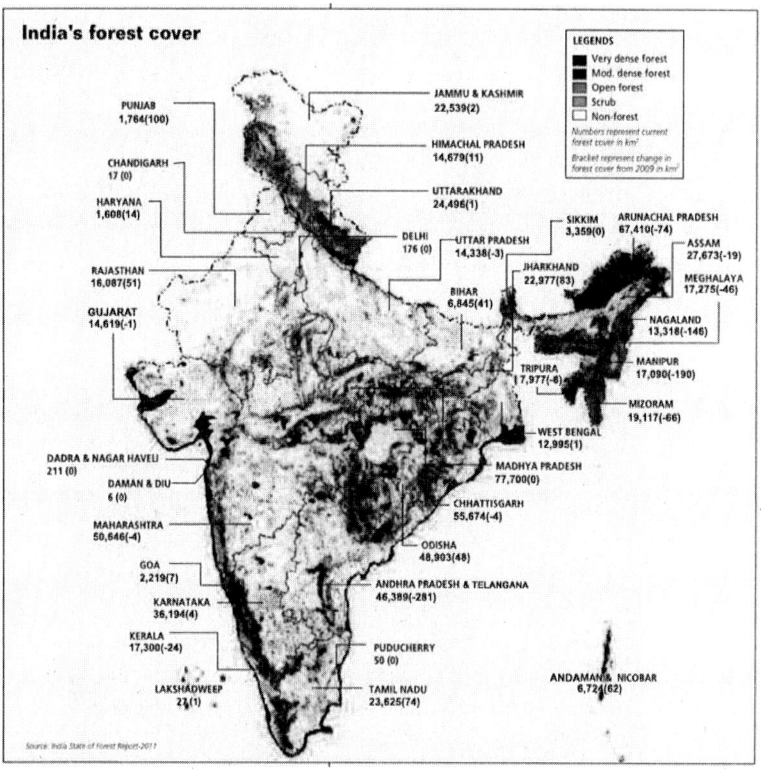

Figure 3: Indian forest cover

Table 1: Best practices in open spaces globally[10]

Features	*Description*	*Best Practice*
Open Space Provision	Area required to be earmarked as open space for a city	25-50 per cent of land allocated to open space (including communal and public realm such as plaza areas)
Diversity	Different categories of open spaces for development	A diversity of open space typologies including green space, linear connections, plazas, natural areas, and play and recreation spaces, as part of a hierarchy of provision
Open Space Features	Geographic and functional features of open spaces	Long linear public square (Loretto neighbourhood, Tübingen-Südstadt, Germany)

Features	*Description*	*Best Practice*
		Central square that offers a meeting, play and picnic focus (Lime Tree Square, Somerset, England)
Landscape Verges	Limits of landscaping areas	Wide verges (5 m to 12 m)
Road Widths and Shared Use	Road widths for different types of roads	Wide roads (5 m to 7 m)
		Central road verge (4 m)
		Shared streets, path widths, wide pathways (most are 3 m)
Communal Open Space	Area earmarked by the development agency for community usage	Large courtyards (0.2 ha)
Private Open Space	Private open spaces provided to the residents	Internal courtyards, useable private balconies and rooftop communal spaces that provide for the immediate needs of occupiers
Planning Considerations	Heritage, cultural and landscaping features of the open spaces	Reflection of the heritage, cultural and landscape features of the area and reflection of good health planning objectives
Renewable Energy	Usage of renewable resources in public spaces	Large-scale renewable energy through solar-roof panels (Vauban Freiburg, Germany)
Community Involvement	Level of involvement of communities in planning and development of open and green spaces	Widespread community involvement in planning and development (Vauban Freiburg, Germany)

The Indian Perspective

For the past few decades, Indian cities have been trying to increase their green cover. Delhi has been laying consistent emphasis on increasing its tree cover by planting more trees and enforcing the strict monitoring of tree cutting permissions. In 2011, the per capita green space availability in Delhi was 22 sq m, which was greater than the national average. For achieving this, multiple organizations and agencies like the Environment and Forests of National Capital Territory Delhi, the Municipal Corporation of Delhi, the New Delhi Municipal Council and the Delhi Development Authority have been working together. Under the Green Mission, these agencies try to plant and maintain parks and gardens like the Lodhi Garden, Deer Park, Buddha Jayanti Smarak Park, Indraprashtha Park and the Garden of Five Senses. Additionally, for all the building societies built by the DDA, the societies and colonies are accompanied by parks and gardens in the vicinity which can be used by the residents for relaxation and recreational activities. Other initiatives include the clubbing of archaeological conservation with creation of urban green spaces. About 100 monument sites have been resurrected with green spaces around them and 1,200 are aimed for the future. There is free distribution of saplings to schools, RWAs and NGOs, and financial assistance to RWAs to plant saplings, and maintain parks and gardens.

Measures Required for Increasing Open Spaces in Cities

Open spaces are breeding grounds for creativity, knowledge exchange and community organizations. They reflect the spirit of a city, the thoughts of its people. Smart cities need to have open air spaces dedicated to different segments of the society.

To manage the green cover of the global cities, the following measures need to be taken:

- Increase the share of green space in urban land use
- Emphasis to be laid on managing the quality of the trees planted
- Changes in tree cover patterns need to be monitored over time
- Conservation of the native flora needs to be stressed upon
- Active participation by the city administration and citizens
- Policies should be devised so that the green and open spaces are equally accessible to all.

Some of the measures are discussed in detail in Table 2.

Table 2: Framework for increasing public open spaces and green cover in the city[11,12]

Distribution of spaces	Spaces should be developed so that they are within 1 km reach for residents
	Park or recreation areas should be a minimum 0.25 hectares in area
	Optimal design to maintain the international standard of 9.5 sq m per capita
	Reduce traffic activities around the area
	Should be spread around the city
Types of green cover and open spaces	Mix of parks, gardens and recreational spaces
	Highest priority to green cover to maintain the environmental system
	Emphasis laid on spaces for residents as well as tourists
	Emphasis on both the functional and the landscaping aspect
	Should be a high-performing system
Functional aspect	Conserve the local fauna, such as bird sanctuaries
	Provide destinations for all age groups within communities
	Provide spaces for open community discussions and thinking
	Use open spaces for community gatherings such as for lunch and eating spaces
	Open spaces to be host for community events, festivals and carnivals
	Support recreational activities, providing community benefit
	Maintain, restore and expand the urban forest
High-performing open space	Renovation of highly utilized open spaces
	Activation of underutilized signature open spaces
	Emphasis on public and signature art of the city
	Maintain and repair open spaces to the highest level of quality
	Create awareness amongst residents
	Ensure public safety and security in the public spaces

Balance of access	Balance of public, communal and private open space. Special zones for senior citizens
	Connection between public open spaces and communal open spaces
	No resident should be denied the basic accessibility to 1 tree per person and 9 sq m of open area per person
	Spaces should be readily accessible to those with limited accessibility
Spaces for city needs	Each parcel of open space to have a clearly defined purpose
	Develop new recreational programmes and service-level goals for the recreational spaces
	Development of civic-serving open spaces
	Development of open spaces for tourist and leisure activities
	Preserve natural historic, scenic and recreational features of the city
Biodiversity	Implementation of environmentally sustainable design principles in developing space
	Coordinated protection of existing spaces
	Protect, preserve and restore native and sensitive habitats, species and natural resources
	Create awareness regarding local biodiversity and natural habitats
Community 'heart'	Inclusion of facilities, plazas and commercial and civic components that provide a 'heart' for communities and development
Transport links	Encourage alternative modes of transportation to and from open spaces
	Strong emphasis on connections and walkability
	Linking of recreational trail to biking and hiking trail systems

Conclusion

The green or tree cover of cities and their open spaces are necessary for a city's well-being. They determine the well-being—mental and physical—of the residents and thus are important factors to consider when planning and developing a city. The component encompasses in it factors of environment (biodiversity and natural habitat, conservation), infrastructure (roads, boulevards, real estate), and green architecture (open spaces, rainwater harvesting, zero run-off).

NOW YOU KNOW:

- Open spaces provide areas for social engagement, peace, recreation, relief and social and environmental health
- Open space includes recreation parks, sports grounds, natural areas, landscaped greenways, plazas, or other land used for community activity
- There are three types of open spaces—public, communal and private open spaces
- Open spaces reduce stress, enhance psychological well-being, provide spiritual reflections and increase physical activity
- Environmental benefits include maintenance of the ecosystem, climate change mitigation, natural drainage, and natural water reservoir replenishment
- Economic benefits of open spaces in urban areas include enhanced productivity, increased housing value, reduced health costs, increased household spending and enhanced tourism value
- Forest cover in Indian cities ranges from 416 for every 100 people in Gandhinagar to less than 20 in Bangalore, Jaipur and Ahmedabad
- For increasing the open spaces in India, measures are required from policy makers, the administration and through citizen participation.

10

Governance Models: How to Administer the New Cities and Make Them Innovate

This chapter outlines the administrative and municipal structure and their functions in Indian cities. It provides information on the financial and regulatory structure of municipal corporations. Further, the chapter describes the various measures taken by Indian municipal corporations to improve the infrastructural components of cities. The chapter finally recommends a system for urban governance in the smart cities.

Administrative and Local Governance in an Indian City

The Census of India 2011 defines an urban area as a place with a local governance body like municipality, corporation, cantonment board or notified town area committee. Criteria for other places include a minimum population of 5,000, non-agricultural male working population to be more than 75 per cent and a population density of a minimum 400 persons per sq m. Thus urban areas are mostly cities or towns.

An Indian city comes under six layers of administrative levels of governance. The foremost is the Government of India, followed by states, divisions, districts, municipal corporations and wards. The towns and the urban agglomerations are parts of districts and municipal corporations. Some of the states are divided into regions which are non-official administration divisions—mainly geographical or historical, and the boundaries of the divisions don't coincide with those of the regions.

The cities are further segregated into metropolitan cities or tier-1 cities, corporation or tier-2 cities and municipalities or tier-3 and tier-4 cities. These are governed by municipal corporations, municipal councils and town councils. The sizes of the municipalities vary—they could be as large as a district or small as a tehsil.

Municipal governance was incorporated in India by the resolution of the 1919 Government of India Act under the powers of a democratically elected government. The Government of India Act of 1935 brought the local governance of the cities and the towns under the purview of the state government with specific powers allotted to them.

The purpose of municipal governance in a city is to create a local governance framework promoting responsiveness and accountability, policy guidance and strengthening of the legal, fiscal, economic and service delivery functions of the municipalities. It also fosters citizen participation in the local governance through the administrative bodies.

The Urban Local Bodies or ULB in India were established in 1991 and fall under four categories—municipal corporation, municipalities or municipal council, town area committee and notified area committee. The first two are fully representative bodies and the latter two were designated as elected bodies. The last category was abolished with the 74th Amendment Act in 1992. The municipal areas are declared according to factors as specified by the state governments, taking into consideration the population, population density, revenue generated, employment and economic importance of the area.

Current Structure of Municipal Governance in a City

The municipal governance of a city is a three-layered local governance system, with the municipal corporation occupying the topmost places in the hierarchy, followed by councilors, a municipal commissioner and a mayor. The municipal corporations govern the wards which have their own heads.

Municipal Corporation: For an urban centre with a population greater than 300,000 people, there is a municipal corporation which governs the entire city. It is an institution set up under a special statute by the state's legislature. It has the greatest autonomy among all forms of local government.

Councillors: These are members of the municipal corporation, who have been elected on the basis of universal adult suffrage, and who will hold office for a period of five years. The councillors together are called the municipal council and exercise deliberative and executive functions of the municipal corporation.

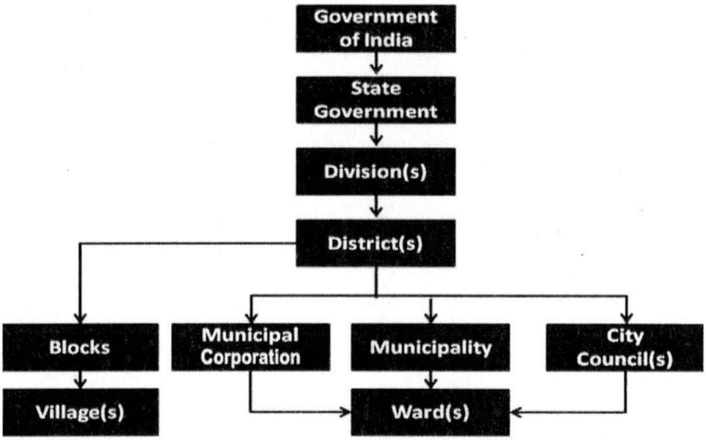

Figure 1: Administrative structure of India

Municipal Commissioner and Mayor: An Indian Administrative Service officer, the municipal commissioner has the executive powers of the municipal corporations and all local governance. The mayor and deputy mayor are political executives elected for a period of one year by the members of the municipal corporation. The mayor is the political head of the corporation and the one who presides over the corporation meetings.

Wards: These are the subdivisions or districts of a city divided according to their population, and are represented by elected representatives from each ward. Individual wards within a corporation for large cities like Mumbai and Delhi have their own administrative committees known as ward committees.

Notified Areas: It is a land area earmarked for future development. Notified areas have a notified area committee whose chairman and members are nominated by the state government. It functions like a municipality. As the notified areas have a population below 20,000, they are not part of urban cities and are considered under Panchayati Raj Institutions or PRIs.[i]

Town Area Committee: It is constituted for the municipal governance of smaller towns. It has members partly elected and partly nominated by state governments. It performs discretionary functions like street lighting, drainage, roads, conservancy, etc.

Townships: PSUs and some private companies like Tata and Birla have been setting up township housing colonies for their staff and workers. Currently, only PSUs are allowed to set up townships which are mainly outside the cities.

Cantonment Board: It was set up for facilitating the provision of civilian facilities to military officials and their families. It is centrally

---

[i] The Panchayati Raj system is a three-tier system in a state, with elected bodies at the village, taluk and district levels.

administered by the Defence Ministry and consists of elected and nominated members. The commanding officer of the station is the president of the cantonment board. The cantonment areas can be set within the city or outside the city boundaries.

Other than the municipal bodies, there are few other departments like the pollution control board, housing boards, water supply and sewage boards, etc., statutory bodies set up under an act of the state government. These bodies are experts in their respective fields and are staffed by specialists. Additionally there are the development authorities for planning and controlling the development within their urban areas. The members and the chairman for the same are appointed and controlled by the state governments.

The Delhi municipal corporation is an exception to the rule, being set up by the state government, owing to Delhi's status as the National Capital Territory. There, the power to set up a municipal corporation is with the Central government. The Delhi municipal corporation is further divided into North Delhi Municipal Corporation, South Delhi Municipal Corporation and the East Delhi Municipal Corporation for better administration.

Functions of Municipal Corporations

The functions of a municipal corporation are divided into obligatory and discretionary functions. Water and electricity supply, road transport, construction and maintenance, management of public streets are some of the obligatory functions of municipal corporations. Functions like construction of public places for recreation (park, garden, museum, theatres, and stadiums), tree plantation and city beautification, public housing, relief to the destitute and disabled fall under the discretionary functions of the corporations. Some of the functions included under the power of municipal corporations after the 74th amendment are protection of the weaker sections of society, promotion of urban amenities and facilities, promotion of cultural and aesthetic aspects, burial grounds, vital statistics and records of the city (population, population density, IMR, MMR, death rate, birth rate), and public amenities.

The functions of municipal corporations are listed in detail in Table 1.

Table 1: Functions of municipal corporations or ULBs in cities

Urban planning	Formulation, implementation, and revision of master plans as well as city development plans
	Monitoring, evaluation and reporting to town planning
Regulation of urban planning	Devise benchmarks and indicators for measuring progress of government projects
	Monitor the infrastructure development in the city
Regulation of land usage	Details of building construction and completion certificate
	Details of approved industries and commercial complexes
Planning of economic and social development	Assess the status of economic and social development in the city
	Capacity building for development in the city
	Integration of the city's infrastructure, economic planning and development schemes with the social and economic well-being of the residents
Roads and bridges	Maintenance and construction of roads
	Plantation of trees and beautification of the boulevards
Water supply	Construction and maintenance of water treatment plants
Public health, sanitation and solid waste management	Management of public health facilities
	Epidemic control
	Public toilets
Slum improvement and upgradation	Water and electricity supply
	Health facilities
Urban poverty alleviation	Low cost housing
Fire services	City fire brigade operations and maintenance

Case Study: Municipal Governance Model in Shanghai

Shanghai, situated on the east coast of China, has emerged as one of the fastest developing cities in the world. It is now the largest city in China with over 24 million inhabitants. It is known as one of the prime financial epicentres for the global economy.

Shanghai, which literally means 'on sea', developed as a small harbour village during the Song Dynasty (960-1279 AD). Over many centuries, it slowly developed into a harbour town—though frequently affected by war and conflicts. Its true economic potential began to be realized only in modern times and mostly post 1991, when it began economic reforms.

Shanghai has a dual party government system like all other governing institutions in the mainland of the People's Republic of China (PRC). In the last few decades, the city has produced many of the country's senior leaders.

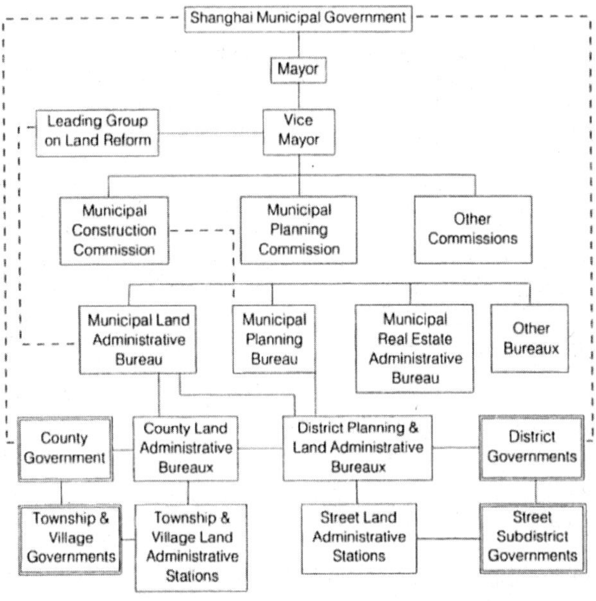

Figure 2: Administrative structure in Shanghai

The mayor of the Shanghai Municipal People's Government is the highest ranking executive official in Shanghai. Since Shanghai is among the four direct-controlled municipalities of China, the mayor occupies the same level in the order of precedence as a provincial governor. However, in the city's dual party government system, the mayor has less power than the Communist Party of China's Shanghai municipal committee secretary, colloquially termed the 'Shanghai CPC party chief'.

Shanghai is administratively equal to a province and is divided into 17 county-level divisions: 16 districts and one county. Even though every district has its own urban core, the real city centre is between Bund to the east, Nanjing Road to the north, Old City Temple and Huaihai Road to the south. Prominent central business areas include Lujiazui on the east bank of the Huangpu River, and the Bund and Hongqiao areas on the west bank of the Huangpu River.

Governance for Smart Cities

Measures to Improve Governance and Transparency

The conventional cities in India in terms of governance are marred by issues dealing with transparency and corruption. For these to be kept out of smart cities, appropriate measures need to be taken. E-governance and RTI are great steps towards this vision. Some of the measures which will make the governance structure simple and effective are discussed below:

Complete Master Planning at the Beginning

Most urban development in India has happened either with complete private sector control or at least with a large participation from private developers. While this is a promising way to bring private investment and saving into the realm of urban development, the problem has been the lack of centralized and, more importantly, fixed plans.

In many Indian cities, the infrastructure was put under great stress when unplanned conversion happened from low to high density or from residential to commercial. The roads, power lines, sewage facility, etc. were not designed for higher densities of population in these places—or to accommodate the newly migrating population and its needed amenities. The painstaking work of widening roads, digging lines and upgrading wires is done in an already populated zone.

Smart cities need to look and plan for the future. A single, 25-year vision of the future master plan has to be created, which will govern the development of the city. Besides this, we advocate a Five Year Plan, an action plan for immediate developmental activities, and a one-year mission plan for creating benchmarks for judging the progress towards the action plan.

Plan	*Frequency and validity*	*Key features*
Master Plan	25 years	Long term, well-defined land usage and land development plan—drawn on a timeline and digitized.
Action Plan	5 years	Five-year plan for development at local levels—using prevailing technology, cost models and challenges. Should fit into the vision laid in the master plan.
Mission Plan	1 year	Yearly plan for development along the Action Plan. Will contain the fine prints of financial models, timelines for individual projects and the necessary procedural issues (such as diversions, etc.).

There is another benefit of fine-tuned plans. One major product of arbitrary land usage and density conversion is corruption. Urban planning is notorious for such kick-backs, and by having a publicly known twenty-five year vision of the city, such avenues for discretion and hence corruption can be eliminated. Moreover, with discretion out, there will be competition in prices and hence a flattening in real estate will happen, leading to affordable quality space availability in urban India.

Digitization of All Records

How often do we hear news of an urban planning disaster—the same road or land is dug up twice and thrice in a single year! First to lay water pipes, then to lay electrical wires and then to mend communication cables which were accidentally cut while laying wires, just because those laying the wires did not have information on the presence of fragile communication cables along the road. In an era when we have almost as many mobile phone connections as literate people, how does such a communication gap happen in an expensive process of urban development?

Smart cities need to be 100 per cent digitized in their planning—which means the entire layout, over the ground and under the ground, should be digitally available and updated in real time with changes. To enable this, the municipal body of the smart city should have a digital governance cell which can be the owner of this digital data and responsible for updating it with any changes in the landscape. Any activity which changes the city's features should be mandatorily reported to this cell.

Such a real-time up-to-date town plan should be available online and on mobile-based applications.

E-governance to Simplify Transactions and Reduce Corruption

E-governance is the implementation of technology in governance for effective delivery of government services. It uses ICT for back-end integration of technology with the manual systems to make the process simple, effective and transparent. India has a National e-Governance Plan (NeGP) for improving the delivery of government services to citizens and businesses with the vision of 'making all government services accessible to the common man in his locality, through common service delivery outlets and ensure efficiency, transparency and reliability of such services at affordable costs to realize the basic needs of the common man.'[1]

Integration of ICT with governance would make the processes centralized and result in their decentralized implementation. It would have a citizen-centric orientation and will help in inter-operability of the various e-governance applications and optimal utilization of the ICT infrastructure and resources. Simple and transparent processes evolving from the integration of ICT would result in greater transparency of the system and will help in the reduction of corruption.

Access to Information

Public information should be readily accessible to the citizens and enterprises to further develop applications and processes. Currently, not all government and public data is in the public domain and it requires an RTI or Right to Information application to be filed for exploring individual cases. In the case of sensitive government information, the information may be withheld from the public, but for most of the other cases it should be made accessible.

In smart cities, access to information from cloud sources could help companies and government design processes and applications which make lives more comfortable and services easily available. One could use the combined application of public data on diseases and public health institutions and dispensaries for providing emergency services to citizens. The urban information system could also provide information on services like administrative boundaries, land parcel details, roads, electricity, water supply, sewerage / waste water disposal, storm water drainage, natural drains, solid waste management, civic amenities, and direction of flow of rainwater.[2] Many such examples of use of information are available from developed countries.

Decentralization of Local Bodies

Local governance helps the strengthening of local accountability of the members of the local bodies. It helps in capturing the gaps and constraints in local policy implementation and in creating platforms to evolve civil society. Their assessment and the formulations of indicators help to capture the specific needs of the smaller groups of society like working women, the destitute and the disabled.[3] The indicators would help local governance in including them in the administrative processes, thus decentralizing the power vested in the municipal bodies.

Adequate Staffing and Operational Strength for Local Bodies

Local bodies should have adequate staff and the necessary capacity for investing, recommending and taking action upon the issues and challenges faced by them. Low staffing affects the financial resource base, making it shrink to manage the minimum level of services and amenities. The quality of municipal service delivery and the building up of an environment conducive to effective governance depends to a large extent on the quantity and quality of human resources available in municipality bodies. In most of the local bodies, norms for staffing and posts are not prescribed and need to be standardized rationally across states for them to perform their functions efficiently.

Effectiveness of the Vigilance Department

The vigilance department should have the necessary freedom to pursue investigations against corrupt officers and politicians. Along with that, it should have the necessary staff to investigate the vigilance cases registered with it. For effective completion of departmental enquiries, the governments need to set time limits and monitor compliance closely.

Citizen Facilitation Centres

These are centres for citizens to file complaints related to the functions under the jurisdiction of the municipality like solid waste management, drainage, storm water drains, roads and traffic, factories, licence issues, water supply, pest control, buildings, encroachments, etc. These centres can also look after the following functions:

- Fee collection for birth and death certificates
- Preparation and distribution of birth and death certificates
- Registration of birth and death information provided by hospitals
- Fee collection for water tankers, tap connection, etc. and generating receipts
- Fee collection of licence fees, generating receipts and distribution of licences
- Fee collection from citizens/contractors for all types of work and projects of town planning, advertisement department, fire brigade, etc. and generating receipts
- Distribution of RTI forms
- Entry on computer, manual register
- Distribution of contractors' completion work
- Distribution of cheques collected from the cashier department
- Implementation of e-tendering application.

Public-Private Partnership or Privatization

Municipalities can also delegate some of their functions to PPP players for better, optimal and cost-effective management and implementation. This is the preferred mode of management in road, water and electricity management, fee collection and development of housing and hospitality centres. SPARC's projects on the city master plan information system, the preparation of urban area base map using high resolution satellite imagery, and the urban water body conservation plan in Bhubaneshwar and

Cuttack are some examples of employment of private players in municipal functions.[4]

Accountability and Auditing

Measures need to be implemented to strengthen accountability and audit in local government by the formation of local authority audit committees. The committee's report would be included in the local body—municipality's annual reports. The local government auditor would make a recommendation based on its findings and would report it to the municipality and the CAG. The audit would also include reports on the local body's performance in fulfilling national, regional and local mandates. This would involve external evaluation expertise, political and administrative experience, and an independent chair.

Urban Innovation Centres

Cities contribute to humanity by innovations which they create. Smart cities hence need to emerge as centres of thinking, research and innovation. They need to plan and create such centres of advanced thinking and incubation of innovation. These Urban Innovation Centres need to be based within the academic institutions in the city—such as colleges and research facilities.

An Urban Innovation Fund needs to be earmarked by the governing body to fund some of these innovations, as enterprises and large corporations should be incentivized to nurture and mentor such independent innovators which may span services, education, IT, agriculture and other manufacturing avenues.

Case Study: Harvard's iLab—Building an Eco-system to Foster Innovation

Harvard University is among the top universities in the world and is situated in Massachusetts. Established in 1636, Harvard is America's oldest institution of higher learning. Harvard has the largest financial endowment of any academic institution in the world, standing at $32.3 billion as of June 2013. It boasts of many notable alumni, including eight US Presidents, 62 living billionaires and 150 Nobel laureates.[5]

In 2011, the university launched the Harvard Innovation Lab (i-lab), which serves as a resource for students from across Harvard and other nearby institutions who are interested in entrepreneurship and innovation. The programme offered by the i-lab is designed to help students grow their entrepreneurial and innovative ventures at any stage of development, and covers almost every disciplinary area.

The i-lab fosters collaboration among Harvard students, faculty, entrepreneurs, and members of the nearby areas of Allston and Greater Boston communities. Community members are invited to attend many of the regular events hosted at the i-lab, to stop at the InnoBreak Café (a small café offering coffee and snacks), and utilize the community lobby open workspace to stimulate discussions.

The i-lab differs from other entrepreneurship centres in its size, model, and governance.

First, it accepts any student or team from any Harvard school with any idea, fostering cross-disciplinary, and cross-university collaboration. It also allows inter-institution teams, with members beyond the Harvard community participating, as long as they have one Harvard member in them. The i-lab resources support student ventures spanning social and cultural entrepreneurship, health and sciences, technology, and consumer fields.

Second, it is student-centred and faculty-enabled, with programming supplied by schools across Harvard, to help students take their ideas as far as they can go.

Third, the i-lab serves as a new model for university collaboration as it is co-governed by each of the Deans of Harvard and the Provost of the university—hence truly inter-disciplinary.

The i-lab combines foundational learning provided by Harvard faculty who teach innovation and entrepreneurship, with resources for students to apply to their ideas and help them grow. Programming at the i-lab is based on the pedagogy which follows a four-part approach:

- Foundational learning for innovation
- Expert resources (workshops and one-on-one appointments with lawyers and entrepreneurs)
- Experiential learning experiences (challenges, winter break trips, and start-up weekends)
- Venture incubation programme (incubation, mentoring, private workshops, community building events)
- Looking ahead.

The i-lab has 30,000 sq ft of space, with more than 250 workstations, 24 conference rooms, most with projection capability, a workshop/prototyping room, a next-generation classroom, video conference suite, treadmill desk, and stocked kitchen.[6]

NOW YOU KNOW:

- Urban areas are places with a local governance body like municipality, corporation, cantonment board or notified town area committee
- Cities are governed by municipal corporations, municipal councils and town councils
- The municipal urban governance system's main function is to create a local governance framework promoting responsiveness and accountability, policy guidance and strengthening of the legal, fiscal, economic and service delivery functions of the municipalities
- Urban municipal governance is a three-layered local

governance system with the municipal corporation consisting of councillors, a municipal commissioner and a mayor

- A city constitutes of wards, notified areas, town area committees, townships and cantonment boards
- The functions of a municipal corporation include
  - » Urban planning
  - » Regulation of urban planning
  - » Regulation of land usage
  - » Planning of economic and social development
  - » Roads and bridges
  - » Water supply
  - » Public health, sanitation and solid waste management
  - » Slum improvement and upgradation
  - » Urban poverty alleviation
  - » Fire services
- Municipalities have two categories of revenues—non-tax and tax revenues
- Municipal bodies are regulated by the state governments and follow the dictums of the incumbent government
- JNNURM is a project for development of urban infrastructure and governance.

11

Money Talks: The Costs of Building a City

In the earlier chapters, we explored the facilities in the existing cities and the ones required for newer, smarter cities. In this chapter, we will explore the various costs involved in planning, developing, constructing and maintaining such projects for a new city.

The Story of the Delhi Metro

The Delhi Metro is the world's 13th largest metro system with a total length of 193.2 km, serving 140 stations. It currently runs between Delhi, Gurgaon, Noida, and Ghaziabad in the National Capital Region of India and is in its third phase of construction. This will connect Faridabad with the Delhi NCR through the metro.[1] It is operated by the Delhi Metro Rail Corporation Ltd, which is a partnership between the Government of India and the Government of Delhi. The Delhi Metro project has been a cost-effective solution for successfully decongesting Delhi roads and is a prime example of successful project management. DMRC now provides consultancy to other cities in India to develop and build their metro rail projects.

The Delhi Metro has been planned in four phases, to be completed by 2021, connecting the satellite towns of Delhi and has cost close to $3 billion[2] till 2014, since its inception in 1984.[3] It is a world-class example of an infrastructural solution which is eco-friendly and sustainable for the future.

The funding for the first two phases of the Delhi Metro project had been raised partly through equity capital from the Government of India and the Government of Delhi and 60 per cent through long-term debt from the Japan Bank for International Cooperation. The rest was recovered through operations and property development and grant-in aids to the tune of $310 million from various agencies. By 2014, Delhi Metro had paid back the loan for Phase I and the interest for Phase II to the Japan International Cooperation Agency.

GIFT City

GIFT City, the ambitious smart city project of the Government of Gujarat, has 30 building blocks, 125 buildings, three landmark buildings, three schools, four hotels and a 200-bed hospital. The total real estate development of these office, commercial and residential spaces is estimated to be carried out at a cost of Rs 34,774 crore, to be financed by private developers.[4] This is almost 50 per cent of the entire financing required for developing the city.

The GIFT City is being promoted by the Gujarat Urban Development Company Limited (GUDCL) and Infrastructure Leasing and Financial Services Ltd (IL&FS). GUDCL is the 'designated agency of the Government of Gujarat to facilitate urban development by assisting the state government and other agencies in the formulation of policy, institutional capacity building, project implementation; and to assist in raising funds from multilateral agencies for various projects to facilitate sustainable development of urban areas, both new and existing, in order to achieve high living standards and growth of economic activities'.[5]

For development of the city, Gujarat International Finance Tec-City Company Ltd (GIFTCL) was set up as a joint venture between the Gujarat Urban Development Company Limited (GUDC) and Infrastructure Leasing & Financial Services Limited (IL&FS), with each entity holding 50 per cent of the shares in GIFTCL.

Table 1: GIFT City financials[6]

Source of Fund	*Rs (crore)*	*Phase 1*
GIFT Unit Fund	12,426	661
Strategic Investors	5,555	–
Debt	17,514	1,157
Developers	34,774	–
Total	70,270	1,818

The first phase of the development of the city started in 2012. The infrastructure cost for the first phase would be funded partly by debts from banks—Syndicate Bank, Bank of India, Bank of Baroda, Punjab & Sindh Bank and Corporation Bank—to the tune of Rs 1,157 crore. The rest Rs 661 crore would be funded by equity and internal accruals. The first phase of the investment is to be utilized for developing the public infrastructure of the city, including its road network, district cooling system, automated solid waste management system, sewerage treatment plant as well as power distribution system.

Costs of Building a City

From inception to maturity as a full-fledged habitat, a city goes through different phases of development over the years. Cities in their current states have been mostly results of decades and centuries of development and changes in the city culture and infrastructure. The cities of New York, Tokyo, Beijing, Delhi, Mumbai, London, Rome, etc. have been in existence for hundreds of years, and have evolved to reach their current stages of urbanization and development. The cities of Navi Mumbai, Chandigarh, Gandhinagar and Noida are around 30-40 years old, founded or planned in the 1970-80s and are still developing.

In the current day, ruled by technological advances in all fields, the time required to build a city has come down drastically, while costs have sky-rocketed. In the earlier chapters, we explored the facilities in the existing cities and the ones required for newer smarter cities. In this chapter, we will explore the various costs involved in planning, developing, constructing and maintaining such projects for a new city.

Transport

Highways and Expressways

These are the most essential components for connectivity of the smart city to other cities. These may involve connecting it to neighbouring cities which are at a distance of 20-30 km, like Delhi-NCR and the cities of Faridabad, Ghaziabad and Gurgaon; or a distance of 100 km like that between Mumbai and Pune. The roads would be multi-lane, all-weather roads capable of taking the load of private, public and commercial (or industrial) traffic. These roads might be access-controlled or partially controlled for traffic and might or might not collect tolls. In 2010, the cost of building such expressways was around Rs 200 million per km[7] according to the NHAI, and this rose to around Rs 500-600 million per km in 2013.[8] A 100 km expressway thus means a projected investment of about Rs 60,000 million, out of which a part is funded by public-private partnerships, a part by loans and a part from the government's revenues from taxes. The expected costs further rise by 10-12 per cent when the project is delayed.[9]

Estimated costs for building a 100 km expressway in 2013 are detailed in Table 2.

Table 2: Cost components for building a 100 km expressway in India[10]

Component	*Quantity*	*Rs (crore)*	*Unit (Rs)*
Land requirement	1,000 hectare	228.8	
Excavation cost (murum, tunnels, roads)	200 lakh cu metres	500	250 per cu metre
Cement	7 lakh metric tonnes	350	5,000 per tonne
Steel	28,200 metric tonnes	146.64	52,000 per tonne
Diesel	700 lakh litres	427	61 per litre
Water	300 crore litres	5.4	18 per 1,000 litres
Electricity	53 lakh units	1.59	3 per unit
Explosives	3,000 metric tonnes	4.5	15,000 per tonne
Machineries		350	

Mass Rapid Transit System

In India the highest speed of premier trains like Rajdhani and Shatabdi, majorly used for inter-city connectivity, is currently around 130 kmph. Increasing their speed to 160-200 kmph would reduce the transit time by 15-20 per cent without much increase in the cost of the project.[11] This requires the upgrading of tracks, rolling stock, locomotives and signalling but might not be very viable for intra-city traffic de-congestion. Building high-speed rail facilities with speeds greater than 200 kmph would cost Rs 700-1,000 million per km against the regular cost of Rs 60-70 million per km.[12] These projects might help in building smart or satellite cities around the existing cities. They may also reduce the traffic load in the main city as well as the connecting time between the two cities. Delhi-Jaipur and Mumbai-Pune double-decker train services are a few good examples of how high-speed railways can be used for connecting two cities.

High-speed metro or tram or rapid transit systems are solutions which might help in decongesting the city traffic. The problem with the high-speed metro system is that it is costlier to build than a railway system. It requires acquisition of large stretches of public land, elevated corridors or underpasses and underground tunnels, etc. In comparison to metro and monorails, the Bus Rapid Transit System is slower but requires less legality, and would have a significantly smaller project cost for development.

Table 3: Cost components for building a BRTS lane in an existing roadway system in a city

Cost Component	*Cost (Rs)*	*Units*	*Hypothetical Project*
New BRT lane in existing roadway	67,063,120	per km	5,935,086,083[a]
Station development	13,189,082	per station	329,727,058[b]
On-board information and articulated bus*	111,282,866	per vehicle	2,782,071,647[c]
Traffic signal priority	7,913,448	per intersection	395,672,422[d]
ITS, safety, security system	14,837,712	per vehicle	370,942,789
Capital Cost			9,813,500,000

* It refers to a bus design which consists of two sections linked by a pivoting joint

Costs are based on following assumptions

a. Length of BRT corridor = 88km

b. Number of BRT stations = 25

c. Number of BRT buses = 25

d. Number of intersections = 50

The Delhi Metro cost a whopping Rs 200 crore and Rs 600 crore per km on elevated and underground lines respectively.[13] In contrast, the Mumbai monorail project which was inaugurated in 2014 is expected to cost only Rs 123 crore per km spent over three to four years.[11] For creating the mass rapid transit system using metro or monorails or buses and trams, it is imperative that the factors be compared and analysed properly to come to the final solution.

Table 4: Cost components, Delhi Metro Phase 1[14]
(Cost in million Rs at 2004 prices)

Cost Components	*Foreign Exchange*	*Local Cost*	*Total*
Civil works	0	31,327	31,327
Electrical works	0	6,970	6,970
Signalling and telecommunication	2,574	1,930	4,504
Rolling stock	4,596	6,403	10,999
Land	0	3,339	3,339
General establishment and consultancy charges	322	4,779	5,101
Contingencies	230	1,593	1,823

Airports

Airports are another important aspect of city infrastructure, crucial for inter-city connectivity. Developing a good network of airports in most of the cities of a country is important for good connectivity and development of low-cost air traffic in future.

The proposed new international airport in Navi Mumbai is estimated to cost nearly $2 billion (Rs 1.245 billion) and would handle traffic exceeding 100 million by 2030.[i] The airport is to be built on the outskirts of the financial capital to cater to the growing air traffic in the Mumbai region. It is expected to be operational by 2017. The airport is planned to be developed by the City and Industrial Development Corporation of Maharashtra Ltd (CIDCO) in two phases, with the pre-development cost being Rs 27 billion[15] and the two phases costing Rs 95 billion together.[16]

[i] http://www.ndtv.com/article/cities/india-issues-global-tender-for-building-navi-mumbai-airport-479708

The upgradation of the Netaji Subash Chandra Bose International Airport in Kolkata is another example of the time taken in Indian cities for converting older airports to newer technologies and renovating the existing infrastructure. The project, started in 2007, took four years to complete, costing Rs 1,942.51 crore.[ii] The upgradation resulted in the shifting of the international terminal from the existing location to the newly built integrated terminal, whereas the domestic terminal continued in its earlier location. The annual capacity of the terminal spread over 180,000 sq m area is 20 million passengers.

Development cost percentages for different components of an airport are listed in Figure 1. Of these, access cost to the airport and airport capacity development cost can be reduced by using innovation and optimal use of resources. If the city is well connected to the airport through bus or metro systems, the required capacity of the airport can be reduced even at peak hours. Also, designing the airport to sustain future usage will reduce costs of reconstruction and retro fittings.

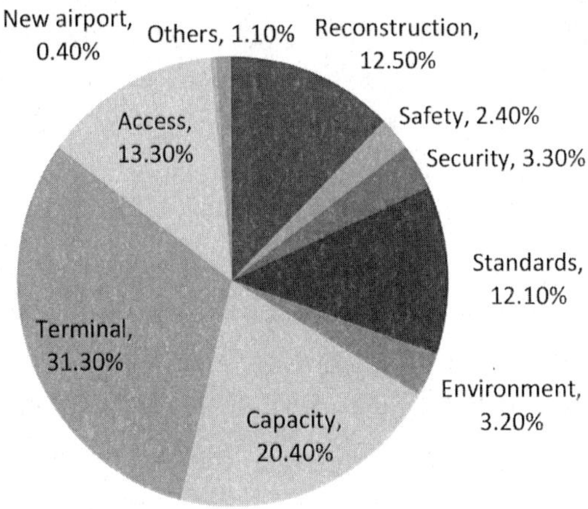

Figure 1: Cost components for airport development

[ii] Source: AAI

The costs involved in developing transport means like roadways, lanes, metro routes, stations, airport terminals, etc. are huge. Making the structure compliant with the current standards and the future demands requires correct assessment of the population and its demands. By having a city in which the population and the traffic situation assessment is fully controlled, the uncertainties involved in the construction of the roadways, metro and airports can be reduced. Reduction in uncertainties and ambiguity in traffic situations and capacity management will give the authorities a better hold on the development requirement of the transport amenities of a city. Hence, suitable enhancements can be done at the initial stages to reduce reconstruction and maintenance costs.

Civic Amenities

A major chunk of the money spent on a city's development is spent on civic amenities like electricity (power distribution), waste management, sewage system, sewerage and drainage system, gas system, ICT and public parking. Traditionally, these basic amenities of civic life have been provided by municipal bodies. Decentralization of these tasks at the local levels is the best way to manage these amenities so that there is no gap between the demand and the supply.

The installed capacities of the amenities should be in compliance with the demands of the city and its population. Smart cities would be designed for a particular population size and would have the amenities designed and developed accordingly. Knowing the population and its demands ahead of time would help the authorities take up any reconstruction, enhancements or retrofitting to meet the prevailing standards. For example, for a city planned for 25,000 people with a per capita consumption of 1,000 kwh per annum, the electricity department would be able to calculate the domestic consumption of the population. Similarly the calculations can be done for water requirements, sewerage augmentation, waste management, gas systems, parking requirements, etc.

Table 5: Civic amenities' estimated cost per capita

Component	*Per Capita Cost*	*Notes*
Sewerage augmentation	Rs 1,620	
Conventional treatment	Rs 162	
Septic tank with soak pit	Rs 4,050	
Twin pit without superstructure	Rs 378 (15 users) to Rs 648 (5 users)	
Household connection of treated water	Rs 9,000[17]	Based on 2005 prices
Non-household water connection	Rs 3,600	Based on 2005 prices

Recreation centres

Core infrastructure requirements for a city would also include the development of areas for recreation. This might include movie theatres, gaming arenas, stores, dramatic theatres, community halls and destinations for culture, entertainment and shopping. Smart cities would have a global village and global knowledge village which would be the centres of attraction for tourists and locals alike, for celebrating culture, art, theatre, commerce and cuisine from around the world. Such villages would have art galleries, retail shops, entrepreneurship and innovation shops and complexes, and serve as ideal places for training centres, professional centres and HR companies.

Creation of such centres for culture and knowledge would require bringing together the best of the architecture and real estate development. The smart city would have land space allocated for the development of such multipurpose cultural and knowledge centres. The development of such centres would require either full government sponsorship or Public-Private Partnerships.

Financing

Any real estate development project can be financed through equity, debt or government funds. Traditionally, it has been government bodies that have looked into the development requirements for a city. It was done through the formation of municipal societies and other development associations which had a government fund sanctioned for the project. Navi Mumbai was developed after forming City and Industrial Development Corporation (CIDCO), which was controlled by a board of directors appointed by the state government. It was mainly formed as a management organization, with technical and non-technical staff, including officers, engineers and subordinate staff. Its operations were funded by state government grants and through operational revenues (taxes and user charges) collected from Navi Mumbai till the Navi Mumbai Municipal Corporation, which took over the operations, was formed.

In the NCR (National Capital Region) of Delhi, there is the DDA or Delhi Development Authority which looks after the major development projects within the city state and their financing. Lately, they have been seeking private developers or Public-Private Partnership players for development of new sub-cities in the capital city.[iii] Similarly MMRDA or Mumbai Metropolitan Region Development Authority is looking for partnerships in rolling out transportation systems. The Delhi Metro is a shining example of breaking the public sector government funding pathway by raising 70 per cent debt and 30 per cent equity from various sources.

Financing Methods

A business or development project can finance its capital costs and operations either through equity or debt. Equity financing is the cash paid by the backers of the project like the government or a private development firm. Based on the amount invested by each party, they may receive a share in the development project or company, proportional to their investment. Debt financing, in contrast, is

---

[iii] http://indiatoday.intoday.in/story/delhi-to-get-five-new-sub-cities-with-half-a-million-houses-to-be-built-in-next-7-years/1/259936.html

capital borrowed from a lender—bank, private financing institution or government, at a fixed rate of interest and with a predetermined maturity date. The principal is paid in full by the maturity date or there maybe periodic repayments as part of the loan arrangement. Debt can be in the form of a loan or bonds.

Local governments have two major sources of funding—revenues through taxes and user charges, and through intergovernmental transfers or grants. The local governments provide a mix of public and private goods for which charges are levied accordingly. For public goods, taxes are levied on the residents, and for private goods the charges are levied on the users. Another model is that of intergovernmental transfers, usually from the central or state government to the local government to maintain the minimum standards of public services. JNNURM grants for upgradation of urban infrastructure by the states and the municipalities fall under specific purpose transfers. Under JNNURM, the local bodies are also allowed to provision loans from financial institutions.

Table 6: Financing pattern for JNNURM

Urban Infrastructure Funding Pattern	*Centre Grant*	*State Grant*	*Loan from Financial Institutions*
Cities with more than 4 million population	35	15	50
Cities with more than 1 million population	50	20	30
Cities in north-eastern states and Jammu & Kashmir	90	10	-
Other cities	80	10	10
Setting up destination plants	80	10	10

Local governments seldom have large cash surpluses to pay for the cost of big capital projects—be it development or real estate. The financing can be done either through the government resources, i.e., the local government's revenues from its operations, by accumulating savings in their current account budget (pay-as-you-go financing[iv]) or by tapping credit markets (pay-as-you-use financing[v]). The decision of going for one of the three options lies in the cost benefit analysis. Another important consideration is whether the burden of the debt should be taken by just the current taxpayers with the future generations paying for it or vice versa.

Borrowing or taking loans from financial institutions is the preferred way of financing big infrastructure projects of local governments, as it helps in easing the large and undesirable fluctuations in local taxes during the period of the project. These loans can be contracted by the municipalities only after being permitted by the state governments to do so, with mostly the state government guaranteeing the local borrowings. Thus, the local borrowings become a state liability and hence the 'states are reluctant to guarantee municipal bonds because their fiscal responsibility legislation requires them to limit their committed liabilities to half a per cent of the Gross State Domestic Product (GSDP) and their fiscal deficit at 3 per cent of GSDP'.[vi] Most states have issued guidelines for local borrowing such as: borrowing should be for less than 30 years; the interest rates should not exceed interest rates on government securities; and there should be sufficient provisioning for debt servicing.

In 1996, Credit Rating Information Services Ltd (CRISIL) began rating the municipal corporations which allowed them to issue municipal bonds in the capital market. Ahmedabad Municipal

---

[iv] A 'pay-as-you-go' basis from current revenues encourages government to 'live within its income' by letting it pay the expenses from its current earnings.

[v] A 'pay-as-you-use' financing lets the government fund from its future earning of revenue from its developments and services used by future generations. Hence many argue that public projects providing services over many years should be paid for by people according to their use or benefit.

[vi] *Urban Governance and Finance in India*, M. Govinda Rao and Richard M. Bird.

Corporation was the first municipality to issue bonds worth Rs 1 billion with a credit rating of A+. Since then, many credit rating agencies have been rating the municipal corporations, allowing them to issue tax-free municipal bonds. The critical requirement for issuance of municipal corporation bonds is that the debt-service coverage ratio is to be maintained at a minimum of 1.25 throughout the borrowing period. Despite this, there has not been much activity in the municipal bond market due to over-collaterization.

In addition to the regular taxation, the local bodies can charge one-time development fees, based on the land area being developed, to the property developers in the area covered by the municipal bodies. The objective is to finance the development project by taxing the party most likely to be benefited from the increased property value as a result of the new infrastructure. The property developers, in turn, charge development fees to property owners or residents, thus recovering their expenses.

Public-Private Partnership is another way by which the public sector can ask the private sector to contribute funds for specified services or developments in return for certain rights or future incomes. There are many services such as water supply, sewerage, solid waste management, recreational facilities, rainwater harvesting, and urban transportation where public-private partnerships have been tried by different local governments with considerable success. This way, the public sector does not have to spend big money upfront for development activities, and there is also increased efficiency due to better service delivery. The level of the private party's contribution can vary from services to monetary contributions.

12

Seven Steps: Modelling a Smart City

In the previous chapters, we have discussed various dimensions of an ideal city. We addressed various dimensions such as energy, infrastructure, aesthetics, open spaces, environment, education, healthcare and aspects of happiness and well-being of the citizens in a sustainable manner. This chapter will now bring these aspects together and integrate them into the process of actual town planning which is needed for building 21st century smart habitations.

Let us now evolve a smart city from scratch and set forth the numbers to give it a holistic perspective.

Step 1: Top-level Division into KDA and SDA

We will organize the city along two critically important zones—the Key Development Area (we will refer to this as KDA) and the Satellite Development Area (or SDA).

KDA essentially is the core of the economic activity within the smart city, and represents most of the employment opportunities and social amenities. SDA is the much larger surrounding area, equally important, as it supports the habitation in the KDA. KDA acts as the key market for the SDA and the planning of these two zones needs to factor in the balancing of the needs and competencies of the two zones. In a nutshell, between the KDA and SDA, we advocate a closed loop market—that is, as far as possible they consume each other's services and production. Of course, there will always be a large fraction of products which need to be imported into the smart city (and also surplus exports).

At this point it is also important to conduct a baseline survey of the various human development indices and economic states of the KDA and SDA, which will be useful for goal setting and monitoring.

Step 2: Setting the Dimensions

We will model a mid-sized smart city along these dimensions, considering a population of about 1,000,000 citizens, divided across the KDA and SDA zones in the ratio of 30:70 respectively. An optimal 15 km x 15 km smart city would budget about 2,500 acres for the KDA, with a dense population, and 53,000 acres for the SDA—with a much lower density.

Table 1: Some key features

	KDA	*SDA*
Population	300,000	700,000
Area	2,500 acres	53,000 acres
Population Density	29,600 per sq km	3,250 per sq km
Principle Activities	Key economic and social centre with quality human development features, including healthcare and higher level education	Supports and thrives on KDA's economic growth and shares the key social infrastructure available in the KDA.

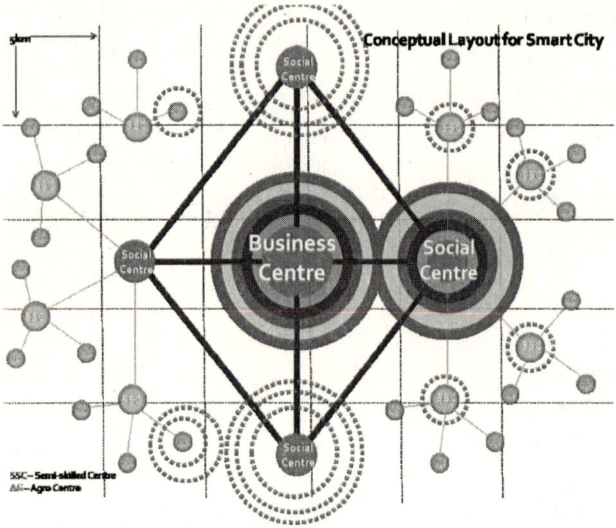

Figure 1: Conceptual layout of a smart city

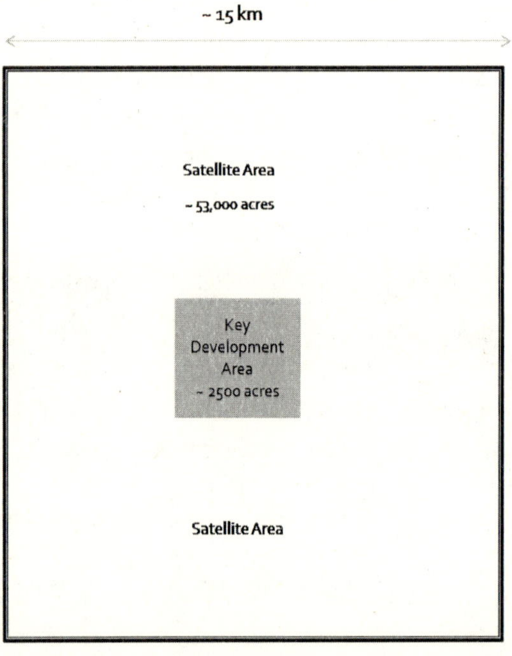

Figure 2: SDA and KDA for a smart city

Now, in case of greenfield development of a smart city, that is, development of a city from scratch, earmarking such distinct KDA and SDA would be simpler and would need administrative enforcements. However, in case of any brownfield development, where the smart city is being developed out of an existing city or urban habitation, this would be a relatively difficult task. In such events, instead of aggregating the KDA as a single unit in the centre, it can be split into multiple zones of high socio-economic activities, which together roughly add up to a similar area. The division can also be based on the availability and existing layout of roads and other means of transport and resources.

Step 3: Identifying Key Economic and Social Activities

The next step of designing a smart city would be to identify a core competency to pursue. We recommend a single competency focus—it could be manufacturing such as FMCG, consumer durables, automobiles, pharmaceuticals, etc. A smart city could also be modelled along a service area such as BPO, finance and banking, tourism, healthcare, education, etc.

The question is—how to identify the key economic and social activities which a smart city needs to pursue? The smart cities would be designed using a four-pronged approach to meet next generation demands of smart urban habitation. The 4Cs of the four-pronged solution are shown in Figure 3—the critical components being Community, Culture, Construction and Climate.

1. Community focus is through:
    - Employment creation
    - Education avenues, including skill development
    - Healthcare access, including advanced healthcare
    - Identifying the key skills of the community and economic development around them

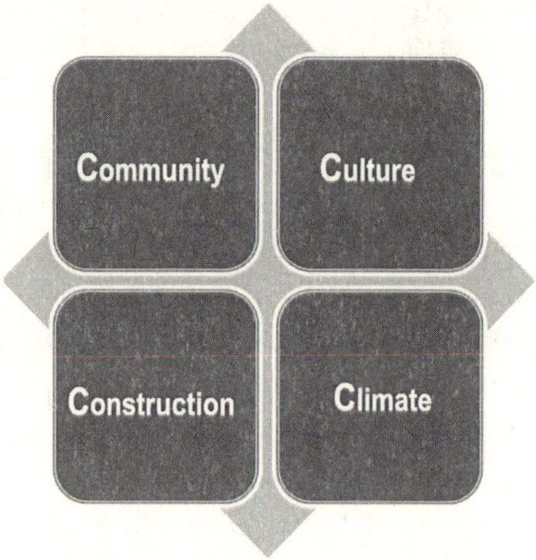

Figure 3: 4C model for identifying the core activities of a smart city

- Balanced working class—ensuring livability for all classes
- Community recreation and ownership of assets
- Community knowledge centres
- Community awareness and preparedness on handling calamities and emergencies

2. Culture is a key aspect for creating resilient and sustainable habitations.

   It implies that:

   - Local fabric needs to be preserved and nurtured, along with respect and tolerance for a cosmopolitan habitation
   - Avenues for cultural exchange and learning
   - Avenues for learning—including music, dance and literature
   - Security, especially of at-risk segments of the society

3. Smart infrastructure is necessary to support development and habitation.

   It implies that:

   - Quality infrastructure—material and construction
   - Town planning and placement of key infrastructure

- Futuristic planning—design for economic expansion
- Market-focused infrastructure creation
- Greener and smarter buildings
- Infrastructure design and maintenance
- Amenities and utilities layout
- Resilience against all forms of natural disasters

4. Climate change and pollution is a major challenge which needs to be addressed.

   Key issues include:
   - Determining the overall carbon foot print of the habitation and strategies for reducing it
   - Waste management
   - Recycling and reuse technologies
   - Water purification and recycling
   - Bio-gas technologies
   - Creating green industry corridors and eco-jobs and eco-entrepreneurship.

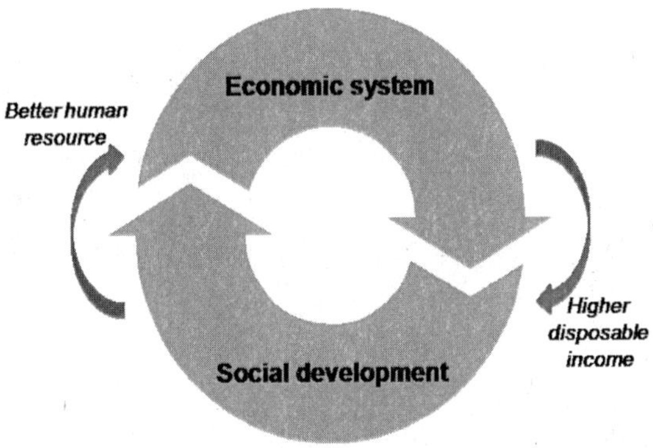

Figure 4: Economic development and social development

For the sake of our model, let us assume a service-centric city which would need to generate about 320,000 jobs, out of which we envision that 160,000 would be in the organized sector. Of these organized sector jobs, roughly about 110,000 will come within the KDA, pertaining to the core competence identified or its direct subsidiaries.

We will model our current smart city as a commercial and hi-tech base with high concentration of white-collar jobs (assuming about two-thirds of the employment being from the white-collar sector). Of course, models with different composition of white and blue collar jobs can be evolved. The dimensions and size of our current smart city model is comparable roughly to any mid-sized city such as Udaipur.

The KDA will be the centre of economic activity around services and manufacturing, which we envisage will be more than 75 per cent of the economic wealth of the smart city. This would include the core economic activity identified for the smart city.

Using the concept of Smart ICT and Supply Chain, we will target to meet the basic demand of perishables, such as fruits and vegetables, of the KDA by sourcing them from the SDA—thereby creating an ICT-driven, low-storage demand-supply chain. We envisage this to happen using ICT applications, such as mobile app-based ordering tools which would connect the demand from KDA directly with the supply from SDA.

Table 2: Employment in a smart city

Total number of jobs to be created	300,000
Total organized sector jobs needed	201,000
% of organized sector jobs in KDA	67%
Total white-collar jobs to be created in KDA (75%)	101,000
Total blue-collar jobs to be created in KDA (25%)	33,000

Assuming a requirement of 75 sq ft of industrial space for white-collar workers and 300 sq ft for blue-collar workers, the net industrial area needed to be developed is about 17 million sq ft.

For housing the 300,000 people within the KDA—and assuming 1,000 sq ft homes for families with about five members each—about 60 million sq ft of residential area would be needed to be developed.

Assuming that about 50 sq ft of commercial and social

infrastructure would be needed per person, another 15 million sq ft of commercial area would need to be developed—distributed across shopping spaces, social assets, entertainment, etc.

Finally, as a thumb rule, in a healthy smart city, 150 sq ft of open space would be needed for every citizen—translating to the development of 45 million sq ft of open places—largely parks, foundation, pavements, roads, etc.

Let us summarize this as a table.

Table 3: Space allocation in a smart city

Type	*Area per person (sq ft per person)*	*Total area to be developed (million sq ft)*
Residential	200	60
Commercial	50	15
Industrial	58	17
Open space	150	45
Total area available in KDA		109
Floor Space Index Residential, Commercial and Industrial		1.4

Step 4: Linking KDA and SDA

We envision KDA and SDA to be seamlessly connected economic systems. SDA is essentially the support system for KDA for its basic needs—food, low-skilled workforce, supply chain for its economic engine, recycling, recreation, economy housing and hospitality, green cover, etc.

SDA is an agglomerated rural/sub-urban economic system and we envisage it to be designed around the existing proven models of PURA (Providing Urban Amenities in Rural Areas) or RURBAN (Rural-Urban).

Let us discuss the PURA model for SDA development in detail.

WHAT IS PURA?

PURA stands for Providing Urban Amenities in Rural Areas. It is a unique cluster-based rural development system which was proposed by the 11th President of India, Dr A.P.J. Abdul Kalam, and Srijan Pal Singh in their book *Target 3 Billion*. PURA essentially envisages a group of up to 50 villages, and hence about 50,000 people being considered as a single economic entity around a core competency which could be vertically integrated and augmented with technological and enterprise infusion. PURA then concerns four levels of connectivity—namely—physical, electronic, knowledge and economic.

Physical connectivity essentially refers to the necessary 'hardware infrastructure' needed for PURA implementation. It encompasses roads with the necessary transportation interventions, physical spaces and buildings, as well as the electrical connections on which all development shall ride.

Electronic connectivity is the necessary ICT infrastructure needed for ensuring connectivity with the rest of the world. This is enabled using modern communication tools—including internet, WiFi, WiMax, telecom coverage and land mapping.

Knowledge connectivity is the third layer, which is critical for the creation, dissemination and access to the targeted knowledge products in the PURA complex. These may include competency-specific training and skill development, healthcare and education amenities, targeted societal up-skilling and other such knowledge-centred productivity enhancement. In some cases, this may be the main wealth creation source as well.

The last layer in PURA is economic connectivity. It is perhaps the spindle around which all other planning for connectivity is supposed to be spun. It is based on the identified core competency of the PURA area—and is supposed to be the principal wealth creator for the benefitting population. Economic connectivity is essentially those products and services which shall be the hallmark of the PURA. In case of smart habitations, we envision this to be a function of the demand created within the KDA.

According to our current model under consideration, we estimate a potential to create about 12,000 jobs as a result of the economic connectivity within each PURA complex in the SDA. Out of these, about 40 per cent would be organized sector jobs.

In our current model we will plan for the following parameters for the SDA.

Table 4: SDA parameters

Population under SDA	700,000
Number of PURA complexes	14
Number of villages/rural units	700
Average population per PURA complex	50,000
Jobs per PURA complex	12,000 (about 5,000 of which would be in the organized sector)

SDA would lend self-sustenance to the entire model of the smart city in terms of food, supplies and also energy.

Step 5: Building Material and Design

We have already discussed the importance of better building material for construction, which may include nano-materials for reducing the cost of construction as also for reducing the environmental impact.

KDA needs to have vertically growing buildings, at an average of eight storeys for each building—comprising about 700 such buildings of different dimensions spread across residential, commercial and industrial zones.

We propose cities which require no vehicular movement for routine activities like going to office or school, or shopping and visiting friends, within the KDA. To enable this, buildings need to be connected at the first floor level—creating a network above the roads and the ground, which can be motorized, or built as a cycling track. For all visits of less than three kilometres, citizens should be able to use this sky walkway—reducing the congestion on roads. This will also reduce the need for roads—hence providing zones for open spaces. It will reduce too the need for expensive mass transit systems such as metro rails—as people would be able to sky-walk to their destinations. Conventional mass transit, such as buses, need to be solar (or even hydrogen) powered—to reduce emissions.

These open spaces will need to be built as centres of cultural exchange, open air lunch and dinner places and avenues for events and discussions.

SDA will be a far flatter structure, and as envisioned under PURA, it will consist of circular road networks—which will link into the KDA, providing seamless access to people and material between SDA and KDA.

Of course, we realize that some of these thoughts are futuristic—but we also believe that cities should be built with ideas which are timeless—and they need to encourage innovations of today which will become realities of tomorrow.

Step 6: Building Sustainability, Governance and Resilience

Humans consume 31 per cent of all the primary production on earth—which is the solar energy converted to food by plants through photosynthesis. This is the only source of food available to all species—directly or indirectly. On the other hand, humans are less than 0.5 per cent of the total biomass present on this planet. Clearly, we are over consuming way beyond our share on the planet.

As shown in the earlier chapters, the mushrooming of megacities and large cities has only worsened the burden on the planet. A typical urban lifestyle which mandates long trips for work and home, air-conditioning facilities and dense packing of amenities within a small area adds to the energy intensity of the civilizations within them.

We believe it is time 21st century smart habitations are designed-to-sustainability. Smart planning means exploring ways to reduce the net carbon footprint per capita for the settlement and for reducing the cost and quantity of material and energy which goes into the construction and operation of a building. Smart cities need to be energy and water independent—that is, a large portion of their energy requirement should come from renewable and naturally abundant sources such as solar power and rainwater harvesting.

We had earlier envisioned that smart cities would flatten the housing and real estate market in the nation by creating millions of square feet of new space which would be well within the reach of the new urban middle class—at around Rs 3,000 per sq ft at current price levels in 2015.

Rooftop Solar Power: One of the most promising initiatives aimed at creating energy independence in towns and cities is through the installation of rooftop solar power, which can be in conjunction with the even more radical building-side solar power. Each building in a smart habitation is a potential power station which can be used to offset significant energy demands from the grid, especially during day time.

For the model we have evolved, taking an average of eight floors in every building, we have a net available rooftop area of over 13 million sq ft within the KDA itself. We estimate, besides this, there would be about 39 million sq ft of available rooftop area in the SDA—making it a rooftop space of over 52 million sq ft in the entire smart city.

Table 5: Rooftop solar power in a smart city

Total rooftop area in the KDA	13 million sq ft
Rooftop area in SDA (% of core)	300%
Total rooftop area overall	52 million sq ft
Cost of developing one sq ft of solar rooftop	Rs 100
Power generated per sq ft of installed solar rooftop	3 watts
% of rooftop utilized for solar power	50%
Total rooftop for solar power	38 million sq ft
Total power installed (KW)	65,537 KW
Total power installed (MW)	65 MW
Average number of scaled hours for solar power per day	8.22 hours/day
Average energy produced per person from rooftop solar power (for 1 million people in SDA and KDA)	0.54 KWh/day
Average per family per month	81 KWh/month
Estimated cost of setting up rooftop solar power in KDA and SDA	Rs 2.5 billion
Energy needed per person (Delhi as a benchmark)	3 KWh per day
% savings in energy due to the installation of rooftop solar power	19%

Let us assume that 50 per cent of this available space is actually used for solar power generation. Under the present circumstances and the technology available, this is equal to almost a 65 MW power plant (though it would operate only during the day) and generate about 80 units (Kilo Watt hours) of energy per family per month, about one-quarter of the average power consumption of a citizen in Delhi.

Building resilience (or protection against disasters) would require careful structural design—especially in areas which are prone to earthquakes, tsunamis and floods. It would be a convergence of structural engineering, material science and architecture which lend resilience to our model smart city. Each building would be rated in terms of how safe it would be in situations of disasters—and this information would be used to benchmark prices. The smart city municipality shall maintain and update such records.

This municipality shall be at the core of governance in the smart city. The model we are proposing shall be, to the extent possible, a 'cash-less' city—with available payment gateways at all commercial installations. This will not only ease the comfort level of the citizens but also provide checks on tax evasions, corruption and bribery and reduce street robberies and thefts—which happen due to availability of cash with the citizens. The municipality would be a democratic body which will have benchmarked against a five-year development plan—which must fit the overall vision and town plan of the city.

Step 7: Financial Modelling

Now that we have set forth all the aspects of our modern smart city, the next step is to evaluate the financial implication of creating such a space. Let us re-visit some numbers and add some value of construction to them.

A)

Area for development of KDA	= 2,500 acres
Basic development cost per acre of KDA (includes roads, electrical lines, sewage, etc.)	= Rs 3,000,000
Total cost of basic development of KDA	= Rs 7.5 billion (**Rs 750 crore**)

B)

Now, let us look at the cost of building development according to the zone.

Type	*Total area to be developed (million sq ft)*	*Cost of development per sq ft (at sale value)*	*Total value (investment needed from final consumer in Rs billion)*
Residential	60	2,500	180
Commercial	15	3,000	45
Industrial	17	1,000	17.6

Type	*Total area to be developed (million sq ft)*	*Cost of development per sq ft (at sale value)*	*Total value (investment needed from final consumer in Rs billion)*
Open space	45	50	1.5
Total investment needed for development			244.1 Or approx. **Rs 24,410 crore**

C)

Similarly, the SDA will have to be developed along the lines of PURA model—each PURA cluster covering about 50 villages. The investment needed for each PURA is about Rs 130 crore (Rs 1.3 billion) and an additional Rs 10 crore (Rs 100 million) for each PURA towards connecting it to the main KDA via road or other network. Hence,

Number of PURA in SDA = 14
Development cost for each PURA = Rs 1,400,000
Total cost of development of SDA (14 PURAs) = Rs 27.1 billion (**Rs 2,710 crore**)

Hence, the total investment needed for the model smart city would be 750 + 24,410 + 2,710

= Rs 27,860 crore (Rs 278.6 billion)

We can add another Rs 2.5 billion to this for the cost of rooftop solar power, taking the total cost to

= **Rs 28,110 crore** (**Rs 281.1 billion**)

Now, let us address what the financial model for such a city will be.

Ideally, the component B should come from saving and credit raised by the individual buyers—hence, about 87 per cent of the total investment will come from bank loans raised by individuals buyers or through their saving (which also means that the flattening of price of real estate is an important step, as more and more buyers need to be attracted to the model city).

The remaining 13 per cent, or about Rs 37.1 billion (Rs 3,710 crore) needs to be provided as investment capital, either by the developer or in a Public-Private Partnership mode with the government. Of course, this will happen over a period of about five years—hence, a yearly funding of about Rs 750 crore needs to be earmarked for this project.

Now, let us look at the model smart city from the perspective of an individual buyer of a house. Assuming a five-member family, owning a 1,000 sq ft house in the KDA, with two earning members—the investment needed would be 1,200 x 2,500 = Rs 3 million or 30 lakh. Assuming 50 per cent of this amount is usually raised through loans, for a period of 20 years (at 10.4 per cent interest) the monthly installment would be roughly Rs 14,500 (or about Rs 174,000 per year). In an average middle class home, with two earning members, this would be about 20 per cent of the annual income[i] in the first year, which is a manageable amount. Hence, our model smart city will be financed via the enterprise and energy of the urban middle class—largely youth.

Scaling the Model—A Policy Implication

Now, let us imagine what the scalability of such a model would be. Can ten smart cities be realized in the five years? Or can there be many more? Let us answer these questions.

First of all, for every smart city, about Rs 750 crore (7.5 billion) needs to be pumped in, most likely in the PPP mode. For ten smart

---

[i] Average income per capita in Delhi was Rs 201,000 per annum in 2012-13, about Rs 1 million per family.

cities in the next five years, that is about Rs 7,500 crore per year of funding, about 3.2 per cent of the defence budget of India in 2014-15, or about 0.4 per cent of the total budgetary spending in 2014-15, which is a relatively small number. Of course, some part of it will come from private developers; we will assume about a quarter of this.

Hence, for the next five years, if we plan to spend 1 per cent of the total budgetary spending on the initial development of smart cities, with 20 per cent of spending coming from private developers, the total number of smart cities which can be developed within this time would be about 100.

Now, assume within these 100 smart cities, post basic development, the investment for residential, industrial, commercial and surrounding village development (SDA) needed would be about Rs 27,000 crore (Rs 270 billion) for each city. Assuming this investment period to be ten years, the needed investment would be about Rs 2,700 crore (Rs 27 billion) per city per year, for ten years. Hence, for all 100 cities, the net investment needed from household and mobilization from savings would come to about Rs 270,000 crore (Rs 2,700 billion). This is about 2 per cent of the GDP for each of the ten years. This is definitely a possible number—given that real estate is anyway a favoured financial investment in the nation.

The catchment population of every such smart city would be 1 million people, hence a total population of 100 million people, which is about 9 per cent of the national population. If one looks at current household gold reserves, they stand at Rs 7,000,000 crore (Rs 70,000 billion). Proportionately, with certain adjustments, the gold value held at the household level for the beneficiary population in a single smart city would be about Rs 8,000 crore (Rs 80 billion). Hence, almost a quarter of the total investment mobilization needed for creating a smart city can be generated from the gold assets held by the beneficiary population itself. It is time to consider a gold-backed financial credit tool for developing smart cities.

Finally, does such an investment in a smart city make sense for the nation? Assume an initial average income of Rs 100,000 per person per annum in the smart city. It is most likely that with a planned economic engine, good access to market and KDA-SDA economy, there would be an augmentation of 25 per cent in the average annual per capita income in smart cities, over and above the existing national trend.

That translates into an additional income of Rs 2,500 crore (Rs 25 billion) per smart city per year and Rs 250,000 crore (Rs 2,500 billion) for the 100 such cities that we have proposed. This translates into additional GDP growth of about 3 per cent for the nation.

Additionally, about 300,000 jobs per smart city will be created—hence additional quality employment for about 3 crore people (30 million) across all 100 smart cities. Many of these jobs will be for women and for disadvantaged segments—who can safely and comfortably work in the planned cities.

Notes

Chapter 1: The Global Demographic Shift: When Did Who Start Living Where?

1. http://www.history.com/this-day-in-history/new-amsterdam-becomes-new-york
2. http://www.citylab.com/commute/2011/12/evolution-traffic-fatalities-new-york/741/
3. http://wgordon.web.wesleyan.edu/papers/imperialism.htm
4. http://src-hokudai-ac.jp/publictn/acta/17/pdf/itani.pdf
5. http://www.metmuseum.org/toah/ht/?period=10&region=eaj
6. *The Emergence of Civilization: From Hunting and Gathering to Agriculture* by Charles Keith Maisels.
7. *Handbook to Life in Ancient Rome* by Lesley Adkins and Roy A. Adkins.
8. worldhistorysite.com/population.html
9. ibid
10. www.demographia.com/db-worldua.pdf
11. http://www.ons.gov.uk/ons/guide-method/census/2011/census-history/200-years-of-the-census/1801-1901/index.html
12. ibid
13. ibid
14. http://www.geohive.com/earth/his_history1.aspx
15. ibid
16. ibid
17. ibid
18. ibid
19. http://worldhistorysite.com/population.html

20. ibid
21. http://www.ggdc.net/maddison/other_books/appendix_B.pdf
22. Webber, 1899
23. http://worldhistorysite.com/population.html
24. http://worldhistorysite.com/population.html
25. http://worldhistorysite.com/population.html
26. http://worldhistorysite.com/population.html
27. www.geohive.com/earth/his_history1.aspx
28. ibid
29. Estimates from various sources
30. http://www.geohive.com/earth/his_history3.aspx
31. ibid
32. ibid, 2050 world population estimates
33. http://www.geohive.com/earth/his_proj_continent.aspx
34. World Population Prospects: The 2012 Revision, http://esa.un.org/wpp/
35. Population, total, http://data.worldbank.org/indicator/SP.POP.TOTL
36. Population density (people per sq. km of land area), http://data.worldbank.org/indicator/EN.POP.DNST
37. Urban Population Percentage, http://data.worldbank.org/indicator/SP.URB.TOTL.IN.ZS
38. GDP per capita, PPP (current international $), http://data.worldbank.org/indicator/NY.GDP.PCAP.PP.CD

Chapter 2: Troubles of Agglomeration: Old Order Challenges and Density Pressures on Resources

1. Urban India Unleashed, McKinsey
2. http://web.worldbank.org/WBSITE/EXTERNAL/TOPICS/EXTURBANDEVELOPMENT/EXTURBANPOVERTY/0,,contentMDK:20227679~menuPK:473804~pagePK:148956~piPK:216618~theSitePK:341325,00.html
3. http://www.newgeography.com/content/002808-world-urban-areas-population-and-density-a-2012-update
4. ibid
5. http://www.ftconferences.com/userfiles/file/Urbanization

percent20in percent20Megacities percent20v2 percent2016-10-54.pdf ?PHPSESSID=aeaf378a38e29732ed15931d964887f3

6. http://zeenews.india.com/bbv/economic-disparity-in-india_878713.html
7. NBER Working Paper, Urban Inequality
8. Key Indicators for Urban Poor in INDIA from NFHS-3 and NFHS-2, UNHRC
9. http://ibnlive.in.com/news/10-railway-commuter-in-mumbai-die-per-day/64635-3.html
10. http://en.wikipedia.org/wiki/Mumbai_Suburban_Railway#Fatalities
11. *Cities and Development* by Jo Beall and Sean Fox.
12. ncrb.gov.in/adsi2013/ADSI-2013.pdf
13. Image source: http://www.gettyimages.in/detail/photo/dharavi-mumbai-high-res-stock-photography/130964259
14. Census 2011, India—Household Data
15. http://www.thehindu.com/todays-paper/tp-national/tp-newdelhi/65-million-people-live-in-slums-in-india-says-census-data/article5188234.ece
16. ncrb.nic.in/CD-CII2012/Statistics2012.pdf
17. Ottensmann,1977
18. Gordon and Richardson, 1977
19. 'Measuring Urban Sprawl: A Case Study of Hyderabad' by K. Madhavi Lata, Dr V. Krishna Prasad, Dr K.V.S. Badarinath and Dr V. Raghavaswamy.
20. Multiple sources and Data.gov.in
21. http://www.thehindu.com/news/cities/Delhi/sanitation-hygiene-services-almost-nil-in-india/article3695716.ece
22. http://infochangeindia.org/environment/news/poor-sanitation-pulls-india-s-gdp-down-by-64.html
23. Rural and Urban Water Supply and Sanitation, pariskara.kar.nic.in
24. *Water Management in India* by P. C. Bansil.
25. http://timesofindia.indiatimes.com/city/bangalore/Contaminated-water-proves-a-quiet-killer/articleshow/29268087.cms
26. http://www.forbes.com/sites/judeclemente/2014/07/22/urbanization-reducing-poverty-and-helping-the-environment/

Chapter 3: Measuring Tapes: The Metrics for 21st Century Cities

1. http://www.giswatch.org/sites/default/files/gisw2010thematicthecarbonfootprint_en.pdf
2. http://www.siemens.com/entry/cc/features/greencityindex_international/all/en/pdf/gci_report_summary.pdf
3. IBI Group, Smart Education
4. EPA Report, Equitable, Healthy, and Sustainable Communities
5. CIDOB, Beyond Smart Cities: It's Time for Urban Sustainable Development
6. http://hdr.undp.org/en/humandev
7. *The Quality of Life* by Martha Nussbaum and Amartya Sen.
8. 'The Interconnected City: Improving the Quality of Life of Citizens', Thales Group.

Chapter 5: Power Equations: Smart Energy for New Habitation

1. www.unep.ch/etb/ebulletin/pdf/Cities percent20and percent20building percent20brief.pdf
2. http://www.statesmansyearbook.com/sybarchives?entry=sybarchives_yg1880-1889
3. http://www.echelon.com/assets/blt90a1f2966b4dcfc1/Lighting-City-of-Oslo-Street-lighting-case-study.pdf
4. http://epa.gov/climatechange/ghgemissions/sources/agriculture.html
5. Smart Energy Consumption and the Smart Grid, Siemens white paper
6. Central Electrical Authority, Government of India, Installed Capacity>>August
7. www.esci.umn.edu/courses/1001/1001_paola/.../1001_13_Energy.ppt
8. 'Solar Energy Perspectives: Executive Summary' (PDF).International Energy Agency. 2011
9. EU data
10. http://ethanolrfa.org/pages/World-Fuel-Ethanol-Production

11. ibid
12. http://cleantechsandiego.org/san-diegos-thriving-algae-biotechnology-industry-continues-to-fuel-regions-economy/
13. http://www.electricityforum.com/news/jun09/Sugarcanebagasseamajorbiomasssource.html
14. *Target 3 Billion* by A.P.J. Abdul Kalam and Srijan Pal Singh.
15. Department of Energy, USA (energy.gov)>Services>Technology Development>Smart Grid
16. http://perspectives.mvdirona.com/2014/02/15/EnergyEfficiencyOfCloudComputing.aspx
17. 'Smart and Green Cities', Seeram Ramakrishna (NUS, Singapore) and Daniela La Rosa (University of Catania, Italy).

Chapter 6: Connected Homes: IT-enabled Living and Working

1. https://igbc.in/igbc/html_pdfs/aboutGBC/IGBC%20Annual%20Review_2013-14.pdf
2. ibid
3. ibid
4. USGBC Press Release, 1 May 2014, U.S. Green Building Council Releases Ranking of Top 10 Countries for LEED Outside the U.S.
5. CII
6. ITC Green Centre, Gurgaon
7. House Rating Schemes—From Energy to comfort Base, Maria Kordjamshidi
8. http://www.rediff.com/money/2006/jan/14wipro.htm
9. ITC Green Centre—Blueprint for protecting the future.
10. ibid
11. ibid
12. ibid
13. http://www.ce.tuiasi.ro/~bipcons/Archive/266.pdf
14. http://www.nanowerk.com/nanotechnology/reports/reportpdf/report162.pdf
15. Nano Materials in Construction, http://www.reinste.com/pdf/nanotechnology%20in%20construction.pdf

Chapter 7: The Dynamic City: Infrastructure for the Smart City

1. Town Planning System of Indus Valley Civilization (Harappan Civilization)
2. Census Data for 2011, Government of India
3. Asian Development Bank, 2007
4. ibid
5. World Bank 2010
6. ibid
7. TERI 2001
8. competitionnotes.com/wp-content/.../01/ENVIRONMENT-ENGG.-I.doc
9. Census 2011, Government of India
10. Diarrhoea: Why Children Are Still Dying and What Can Be Done
11. www.ncbi.nlm.nih.gov/pubmed/20620115
12. http://www.unicef.org/health/files/Final_Diarrhoea_Report_October_2009_final.pdf
13. http://www.telegraph.co.uk/news/worldnews/asia/india/8859987/Half-of-Indias-cities-have-no-piped-water-or-sewer-systems.html
14. ibid
15. www.communityledtotalsanitation.org/country/india
16. http://www.smartdrain.com/
17. www.ibef.org/download/roads-august-2013.pdf
18. ibid
19. Outcome Budget, Ministry of Road Transport and Highways, Government of India
20. www.ibef.org/download/roads-august-2013.pdf
21. www.irsfm.com/SAFEWALKING.php
22. ibid
23. http://blog.digital.telefonica.com/2014/05/21/big-data-smart-cities/
24. http://www.libelium.com/smart_roads_wsn_smart_infrastructures/
25. Statistical Summary, Indian Railways, 2011-12
26. http://www.nationsencyclopedia.com/WorldStats/CIA-World-Factbook-Roadways.html
27. www.ijsrp.org/research-paper-0613/ijsrp-p1834.pdf

28. Government of India, Budget speech 2014
29. Delhi Metro: Excellence in Management, UNDP
30. http://www.indiainfrastructure.com/confpdf/conf-airport-development2014.pdf
31. http://www.indiaairportsummit.com/
32. indianpowersector.com/home/about/
33. http://siteresources.worldbank.org/EXTFINANCIALSECTOR/Resources/282884-1303327122200/272bhatia_Gulati.pdf
34. Power Line Communications for Smart Grid Applications by Lars Torsten Berger, Andreas Schwager and J. Joaquín Escudero-Garzás
35. Effect of System Load Factor on Transmission & Distribution Losses
36. Transmission and Distribution Losses, TERI
37. http://electrical-engineering-portal.com/total-losses-in-power-distribution-and-transmission-lines-2
38. ICT concepts for optimization of mobility in smart cities

Chapter 8: Social Paradigm: New Models for Building Infrastructure

1. Census India
2. *Efficiency of Social Sector Expenditure in India* by Brijesh C. Purohit
3. www.ashanet.org/projects-new/documents/933/Isha_Vidhya_report.doc
4. http://siteresources.worldbank.org/EDUCATION/Resources/278200-1121703274255/1439264-1193249163062/India_CountrySummary.pdf
5. www.aises.nic.in/surveyoutputs
6. UNICEF, http://www.unicef.org/india/children_2356.htm
7. *The Hindu*, '42 per cent of Indian children are underweight'
8. http://www.unicef.org/india/children_2355.htm
9. https://www.cia.gov/library/publications/the-world-factbook/geos/in.html
10. Data.worldbank.org
11. http://planningcommission.nic.in/news/press_pov1903.pdf
12. Labour Bureau, Government of India, 2012

13. Global Employment Trends 2014
14. Employment -Unemployment Situation In Million Plus Cities of India
15. Literacy-march-boomerangs-on-Kerala-Experts, *Times of India*
16. *Social Equity and the Urban Environment* by Jim Falk.
17. http://www.dnaindia.com/india/report-no-entry-for-dalits-in-gujarat-temple-1798612
18. Directive Principles of State Policy

Chapter 9: Green Cover: Ensuring Ecological Friendliness in the New Cities

1. http://www.newindianexpress.com/cities/bangalore/66-Percent-Green-Cover-Lost-in-40-Years-Study/2014/05/09/article2214383.ece
2. http://www.teriuniversity.ac.in/mct/pdf/assignment/Rama-Shankar-Sinha.pdf
3. 'Infrastructure for Information Technology Industry in Bangalore City' by M.N. Shobha, Krishne Gowda and B. Mahendra.
4. *Health, Well-Being and Open Space* by Nina Morris.
5. Australian Bureau of Statistics (ABS).Children's participation in organised sport and leisure activities.
6. http://www.arborenvironmentalalliance.com/carbon-tree-facts.asp
7. http://www.biodiversity.ru/coastlearn/bio-eng/boxes/maint.html
8. http://www.greeninfrastructurenw.co.uk/climatechange/doc.php?docID=95
9. 'Urban Greenery Status of Some Indian Cities: A Short Communication' by Pradeep Chaudhary, Kenjum Bagra and Bilas Singh.
10. Best Practice Open Space in Higher Density Developments Project
11. Ministry of Environment and Forestry, Government of India
12. Census 2001, Government of India

Chapter 10: Governance Models: How to Administer the New Cities and Make Them Innovate

1. http://india.gov.in/e-governance/national-e-governance-plan
2. http://www.sparcindia.com/UrbanAreas.aspx

3. http://www.gaportal.org/areas-of-governance/local-governance-and-decentralization
4. http://www.sparcindia.com/UrbanAreas.aspx
5. Taken from the Harvard University Website http://www.harvard.edu/
6. https://i-lab.harvard.edu/about and personal visit of one of authors to the iLab

Chapter 11: Money Talks: The Costs of Building a City

1. http://pib.nic.in/newsite/erelease.aspx?relid=74442
2. pmi.org.in/manageindia/volume3/issue04/cover.story.html
3. 'Social Cost-Benefit Analysis of Delhi Metro' by M.N. Murty, Kishore Kumar Dhavala, Meenakshi Ghosh and Rashmi Singh.
4. GIFT city financials, http://giftgujarat.in/documents/GIFT-Corporate-Presentation-Website-November-10112014.pdf
5. http://giftgujarat.in/faq.aspx
6. ibid
7. http://businesstoday.intoday.in/story/highways-to-prosperity/1/5111.html
8. http://www.thehindubusinessline.com/industry-and-economy/logistics/is-india-ready-to-drive-on-the-expressway/article4917434.ece
9. http://businesstoday.intoday.in/story/highways-to-prosperity/1/5111.html
10. http://www.larsentoubro.com/lntcorporate/pmiv/pdf/FinancialViabilityofProject%E2%80%93CasestudyonMumbai%E2%80%93PuneExpressHighway.pdf
11. http://www.thehindubusinessline.com/opinion/the-highspeed-trains-are-coming/article5922851.ece
12. http://www.trafficinfratech.com/high-speed-rail-in-india/
13. http://www.businessworld.in/news/economy/india/metro-vs-monorail-the-big-debate/1019978/page-1.html
14. RITES
15. http://www.business-standard.com/article/economy-policy/phase-1-of-navi-mumbai-airport-to-be-completed-by-2018-114020500216_1.html

16. http://timesofindia.indiatimes.com/city/mumbai/Navi-Mumbai-airport-project-cost-escalates-by-Rs-400-crore/articleshow/40617815.cms
17. http://www.unwater.org/downloads/mdg_global_costing.pdf, 2005 costs

Index

Acknowledgements

In writing this book, our thoughts and ideas have evolved through two decades of business experience and interactions with various stakeholders, including IT companies, manufacturing firms, bureaucrats, environmentalists, social and spiritual leaders, bankers and investors, employees, educationists, healthcare institutes, the tourism industry and a general population aspiring to raise the quality of life of their families and to establish enterprises. A large portion of the thoughts expressed in this book are essentially extensions of the contemplations, anxieties, dreams, perils, ambitions, hopes and challenges of all these citizens revolving around the fundamental need of the entire human society—to live peacefully and with prosperity.

We thank all these stakeholders, friends, acquaintances, some even strangers, and the young community for openly sharing their views and thoughts. These took the shape of a coherent theory and examples in this book. We sincerely hope that our book has captured their ingenious thoughts.

We would like to express our special gratitude to His Excellency Dr A.P.J. Abdul Kalam, whose inspirational idea of PURA has been a source of personal motivation to both of us and has also been the cornerstone of the model we have evolved for 21st century urban habitations in this book. We were also inspired by the teachings of His Holiness Sri Sri Ravi Shankar about 'Vasudhaiva Kutumbakam'. The idea that the world is one family is the spindle around which we tried to weave the culture of an ideal smart city.

We would like to acknowledge the works of various champions of urban innovation whose ideas we drew upon in this book. We would like to thank Ms Meenakshi Deogam and Ms Meenal Ajmera, who helped us gather all the ideas we put forth. Their research and inputs were instrumental in bringing out this book. We would also like to thank Mr Saurav, Mr Jayraj Pandya, Mr Abhisek Tulsiyan and Mr Jaydip Samani, who gave specific inputs for different chapters. We thank Ms Sandhya Sridhar for helping us with the editing and improving the quality of the content.

Our heartfelt gratitude to Ms Rangapriya Goutam, Ms Aparna Goutam and Mr Ranga Nagaraju from the MARG family for helping us tirelessly in putting this book together.

Finally, we would like to sincerely acknowledge the contribution of Mr Krishan Chopra, Publisher and Editor-in-Chief of HarperCollins, along with his colleagues Mr Siddhesh Inamdar and Art Director Ms Bonita Vaz-Shimray for their support in bringing out this book in record time.